AUGUST LIVSHITZ

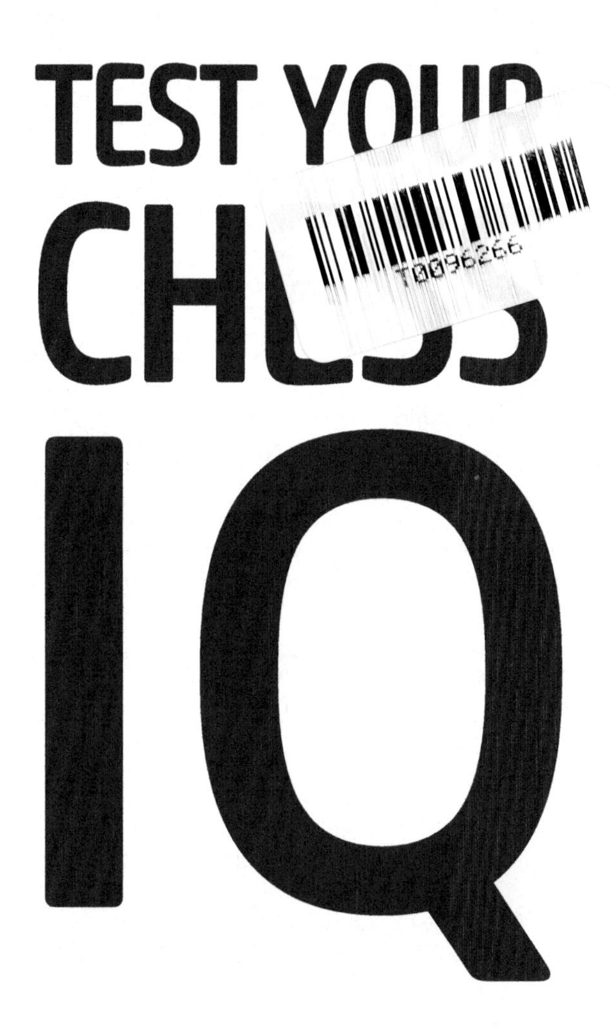


## First Challenge

EVERYMAN CHESS
www.everymanchess.com

First published in 1981 by Pergammon Press
This edition Published by Gloucester Publishers Ltd (formerly Cadogan Chess) in 1988

Copyright © 1981 August Livshitz
English Translation Copyright © 1988 Ken Neat

All rights reserved. No part of the contents of this book may be reproduced, stored in a retrieval system or transmitted in any form or by any means, electronic, electrostatic, magnetic tape, photocopying, recording or otherwise, without prior permission of the publisher.

**British Library Cataloguing-in-Publication Data**
A catalogue record for this book is available from the British Library.

ISBN: 978-1-857744-139-0

Distributed in North America by National Book Network,
15200 NBN Way, Blue Ridge Summit, PA 17214. Ph: 717.794.3800

Distributed in Europe by Central Books Ltd.,
50 Freshwater Road, Chadwell Heath, London, RM8 1RX Ph: 44(0)845 458 9911

All other sales enquiries should be directed to Everyman Chess:
Email: info@everymanchess.com; Website www.Everymanchess.com

Everyman is the registered trademark of Random House Inc. and is used in this work under license from Random House Inc.

**EVERYMAN CHESS SERIES**
Chief Advisor: Byron Jacobs
Cover Design: Horacio Monteverde
Printed and bound in the UK by TJ International Ltd, Padstow, Cornwall.

# Contents

# Editor's Note

A SUPERB trainer from the Soviet Chess School, August Livshitz has produced a classic handbook to help the aspiring player develop his or her combinational skills. The different tactical themes have been carefully selected and arranged to build and consolidate themes learnt, and will prove excellent study material either for home study or a group in a school or chess club.

For the serious student it is imperative to pay careful attention to the following introduction by the author, as this holds the key to approaching the tests in a systematic way and achieving the maximum possible improvement from the course.

When studying the diagrams, please note that 'W' ('B') beside a diagram number indicates that it is White (Black) to move, while '=' indicates that the player to move is aiming for a draw rather than a win.

This book is the first of a three-volume graduated series, and the companion volumes, **Test Your Chess IQ: Master Challenge** and **Test Your Chess IQ: Grandmaster Challenge**, are also available from Cadogan.

# Introduction

"Combination is the soul of chess."
Alexander Alekhine

ANYONE beginning a systematic study of chess is invariably faced by the question: with what should I start? One of the greatest of chess teachers, the Czech grandmaster Richard Reti, wrote: 'First you should learn to make combinations, before attempting to play positionally.' This principle has been confirmed throughout the history of chess, and we seriously advise every chess player to firmly adopt it.

The combinations given in this book are the fruits of the efforts not only of outstanding masters, but also of little-known players, and even of players who are quite unknown. It cannot be disputed that systematic work on the solving of the given combinations will raise your chess strength significantly, and allow you to determine for yourself the class of player to which you belong. One of the greatest players of all time, the former World Champion Jose Raul Capablanca, defined the importance of an acquaintance with combinations as follows: 'The majority of chess players are interested primarily in combinations and direct attacks on the king; such an interest is to be whole-heartedly encouraged, since it develops the imagination, which is so necessary for a chess player. And only later, when a player achieves considerable strength, do questions associated with the positional aspect of play begin to interest him.'

## *Combinational themes*

In order to consolidate the acquisition of skill, the tests in this book have been arranged according to definite combinational themes. Most of these themes are self-explanatory ('double attack', 'discovered check', 'utilization of open files', etc.), but others may be unfamiliar (e.g. 'diversion', 'decoy', 'interference'). Attempts at solving these tests will soon familiarize the reader with the meaning of these various themes, but for anyone who requires prior knowledge on the subject of combinational themes, we can recommend pp. 10–50 of Neishtadt's *Catastrophe in the Opening* (Pergamon Press, 1980).

It may sometimes seem that the motif or theme of the combination is not exactly the one indicated. Don't be in a hurry to follow your first inclination, and assign the combination to a different theme. It should be pointed out that one frequently comes across combinations in which various ideas are combined. These are closely related one to another, and the theme is defined depending on the final goal. To explain this, let us take the following example:

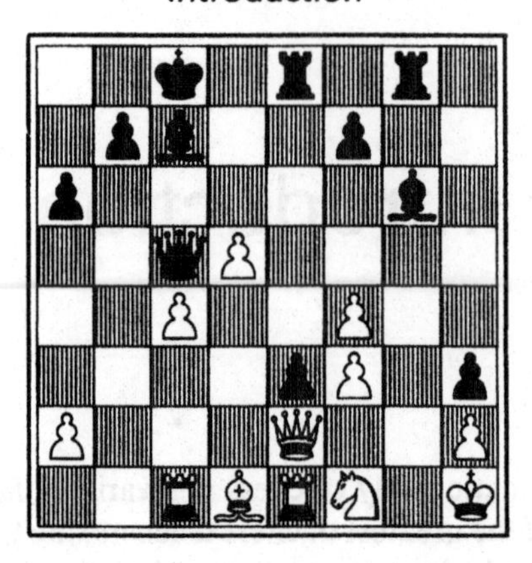

This position is taken from the game **Bakulin–Bronstein**, played at Kiev in 1965. It is Black to move. The unfortunate position of the white king (the motif of the combination) allows the following combination to be carried out:

1 . . . **Bd3!!** The very first move pursues two aims: the vacating of the 'g' file, and the diverting of the white queen. **2 Q×d3** The only reply, otherwise the knight is lost. **2 . . . Rg1+!!** The king is decoyed to g1. **3 K×g1 e2+** Discovered check. **4 Ne3** 4 Kh1 is met by 4 . . . Qf2, when mate is inevitable. **4 . . . R×e3 5 Qf5+ Re6+!** Again discovered check. **6 Kh1 Qf2!** White resigned, since on 7 Qg4 there follows 7 . . . Q×e1+ 8 Qg1 Q×g1+ 9 K×g1 e1=Q mate. One combination, but how many combinational themes!

## *Typical mistakes and how to avoid them*

In order to relate a player's success in solving these tests to his 'chess IQ', some sample tests were sent to a number of players, covering a wide range of ability. The solutions submitted also revealed various errors of a general nature:

1. The correct idea is found, but an incorrect order of moves employed, making the combination less effective, or even totally unsound.
2. The solution found is insufficiently incisive. If one side has a crushing position, you can normally expect there to be a crushing solution!
3. Occasionally, moves are suggested which are physically impossible! This normally occurs due to difficulty in envisaging the position several moves ahead, a skill which can only come with practice.
4. The most common error is an underestimation of the opponent's resources. Try to take account of all the opponent's possible defences!

## *Getting the most out of this book*

By solving a series of positions all displaying the same theme, a player will gradually acquire a 'feel' for when such a combination is possible. Until such a skill is acquired, it is advisable to make an evaluation of each position, before endeavouring to find the combination. In the solving of each position, we therefore recommend that, instead of rushing in and examining the first sacrifice which comes to mind, you should ask yourself the following questions, which should enable maximum benefit to be gained from the book:

1. What is the material situation? (If I am a rook down, I will have to find something pretty drastic, such as mate or the win of the opposing queen!)
2. Are there any (permanent) strategic factors in my favour? Do I control the centre, do I have a superiority of forces around the opponent's king, is his king exposed, does he have any weak pawns or squares, etc.
3. Are there any (temporary) tactical factors that I can exploit? Is the opponent's back rank weak, are any of his pieces undefended, are there any geometrical relationships between the pieces, etc.
4. Having determined the advantageous features of my position, can I find a sequence of moves which will exploit them, using the stated theme as a guide?

## *Tackling the tests*

All the examples in this book are given in the form of tests, in each of which there are eight positions to be solved. A correct solution to a position scores 5 points, so in each test there are 40 points to be gained. The solver should remember that a game of chess does not continue indefinitely, and that the solving of each test must be limited by time. In each specific test we indicate approximately the time which is allowed. If you confine yourself to this time, well and good. If on the solution of the test you spend more than the indicated time, then from the total sum of points gained you should subtract penalty points at the rate of 1 point for every extra 5 minutes. If, on the other hand, you solve the test more quickly, then for each 5 minutes saved add 1 point to your score. If you are unable to solve all the positions, then subtract 5 points from your total for each unsolved example.

The tests are intended for players of club strength, corresponding approximately to third to fourth categories in the USSR (about 160–120 on the BCF scale, or 1900–1550 on the ELO scale). How should you set about solving the tests on your own? Apart from a chess set, you will need pen and paper to write with. Set up the first position, and WITHOUT MOVING THE PIECES, attempt to solve it using the procedure outlined above. On finding the solution to the first position, write it out in full. On no account should you check your answers after each individual position. If you have solved all the positions correctly, and within the allotted time, you score the indicated number of points. It is not a tragedy if the number of points you score at first is low. You will see for yourself that, after you have tackled four or five tests, the number of points you score will constantly increase.

Your solutions to a test should be checked only when you have finished solving all the positions in the given test. We deliberately repeat and draw your attention to this point. The time spent checking should not be included in the time allotted to the solving of the test. If you experience difficulty in trying to solve a position, do not be in a hurry to look up the answer. Remember that, by solving a position yourself, you have already made a step forward.

## *Your chess IQ*

The question as to how often you should do these tests will no doubt have occurred to you. It is desirable that you should solve one or two tests a week. The total number of points that you can score is 2240, plus the bonus points for using less time.

As was mentioned earlier, a set of sample tests was sent out to a wide range of volunteers, and on the basis of their solutions we can suggest the following table for assessing your 'chess IQ', which we give in terms of a BCF or ELO rating:

| Percentage score | Actual score | BCF rating | ELO rating |
| --- | --- | --- | --- |
| 100 | 2240 | 200 | 2200 |
| 90 | 2015 | 175 | 2000 |
| 80 | 1790 | 150 | 1800 |
| 70 | 1570 | 125 | 1600 |
| 60 | 1345 | 100 | 1400 |
| 50 | 1120 | 75 | 1200 |

It is no tragedy if you score less than 1100 points, so don't be discouraged. Clearly, you still have to work at it. You will discover your deficiencies, and it follows that you will have the opportunity to eradicate them. And it is only by trying that you achieve anything.

## *The progress chart*

At the back of the book we give a chart on which you can record your scores. To give an example of the scoring procedure in a particular test, suppose that in one position you fail completely to find the solution—deduct 5 points. In another position you find the correct initial move, but fail to consider the best defence—deduct 3 points. (The matter of exactly how many points to deduct for an incomplete solution we leave up to your judgement and honesty.) You solve all the other six positions correctly, but take a total time of 53 minutes, compared with the recommended time of 45 minutes. Your basic score is therefore $40-8=32$, the excess time is 10 minutes (to the nearest 5 minutes), which means a penalty of 2 points, leaving a net score of 30 points.

There is also a space in which to record your comments on a particular test. (Perhaps on the degree of difficulty of the test or a particular position, or—heaven forbid!—a mistake in the author's solution.)

Good luck!

# Tests
# 1–56

## Test 1 Positions 1–8

Theme—'Double attack', time for thought—45 minutes.

1 W

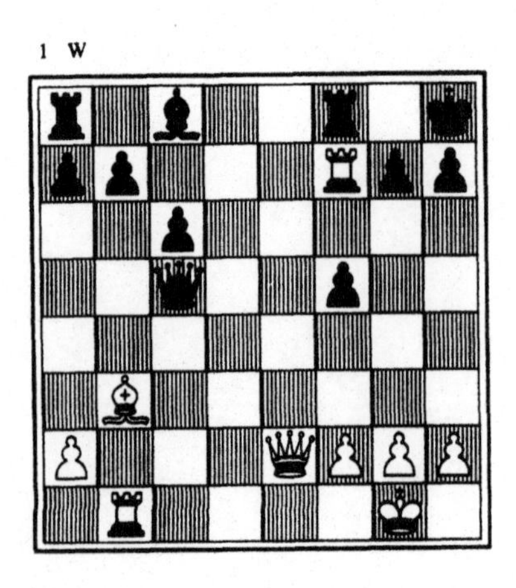

2 W

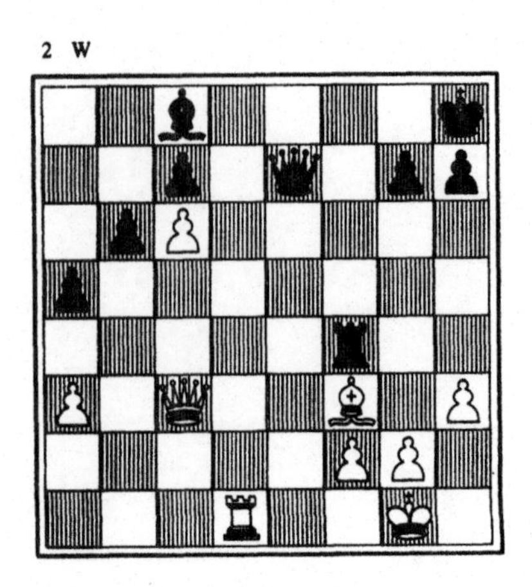

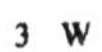
3 W

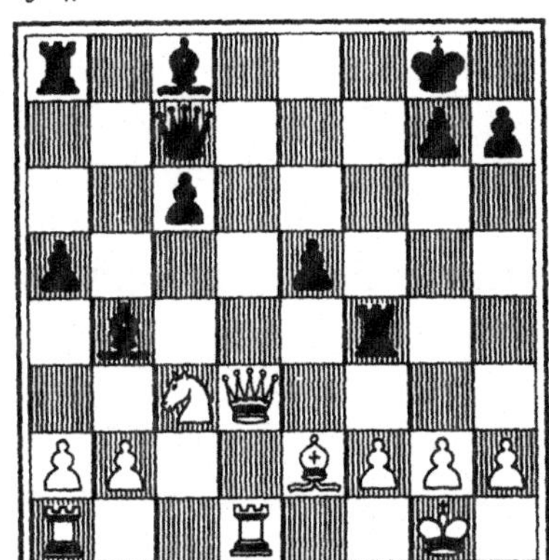

4 B

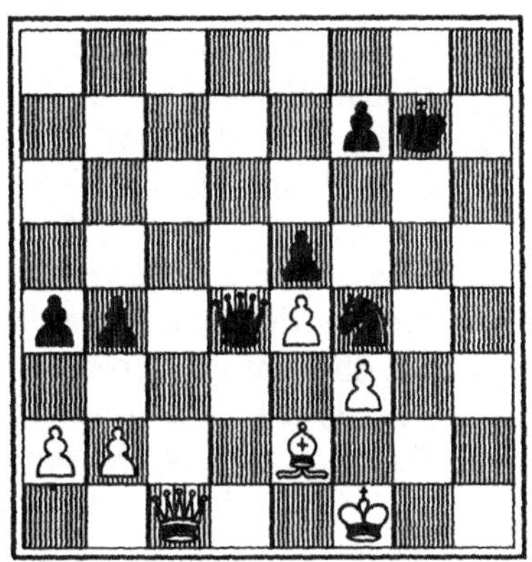

5 B

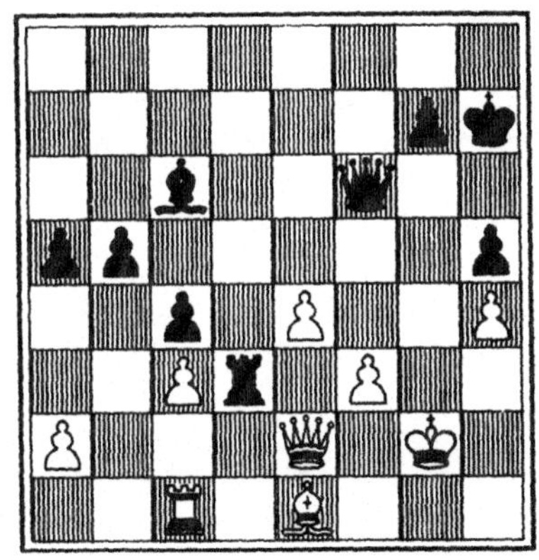

6 B

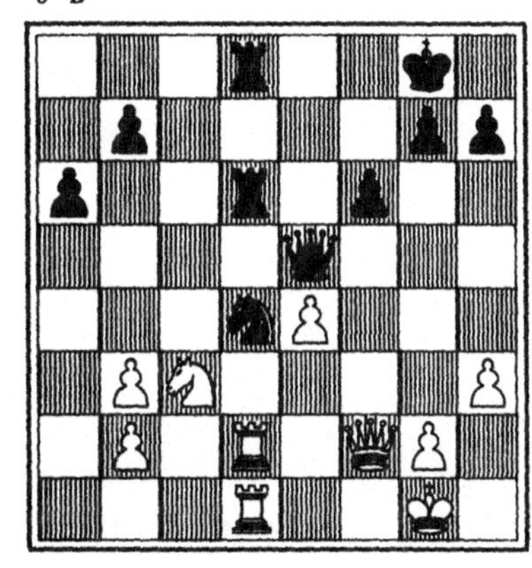

7 B

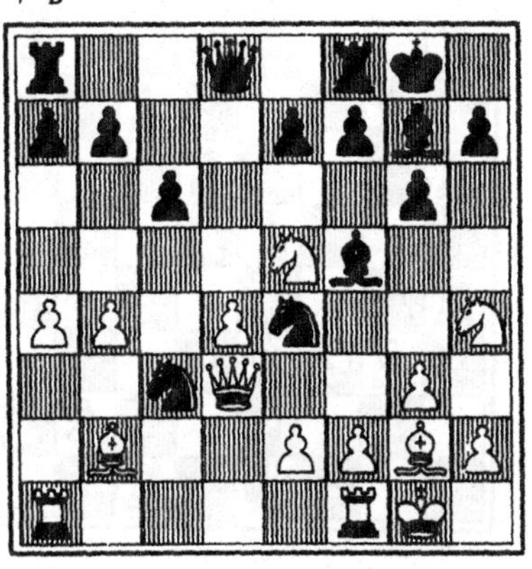

8 W

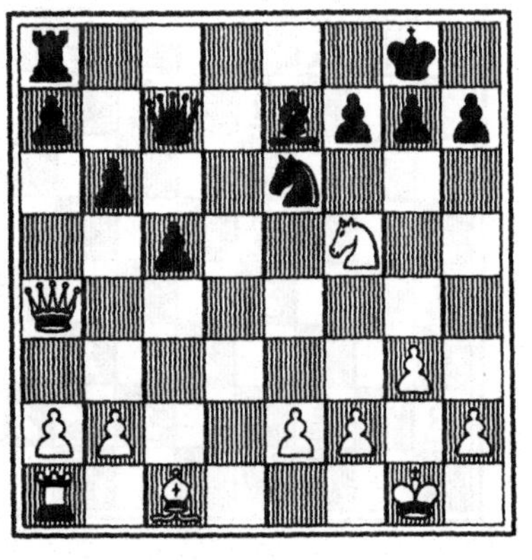

## Solutions to Test 1

1. Böök–Saila, Stockholm, 1946.
   1 Qe5!! Resigns.
2. Szabó–Bán, Budapest, 1947.
   1 Qe5!! Qf8 2 Q×f4! Resigns.
3. Domuls–Lutskan, USSR, 1976.
   1 Nd5! c×d5 2 Q×d5+ Kh8 3 Q×a8 and wins. White missed this opportunity in the game, which ended in a draw.
4. Tolush–Simagin, Moscow, 1952.
   1 . . . Qg1+! 2 K×g1 N×e2+ White resigns.
5. Gligoric–Smyslov, Amsterdam, 1971.
   1 . . . Qf4!! White resigns (any move by the rook is answered by *2 . . . R×f3! 3 Q×f3 B×e4*).
6. Dehlplank–Pardon, Corr., 1976.
   1 . . . Nf3+! White resigns (since if *2 g×f3*, then *2 . . . Qg5+* and *3 . . . R×d2*).
7. Bassler–Scheichel, Groningen, 1972.
   1 . . . N×g3! White resigns (*2 N×f5 Nc×e2+!*, or *2 Q×g3 N×e2+*).
8. Krogius–Martyushov, Tula, 1949.
   1 Qc6!! Resigns (*1 . . . Q×c6 2 N×e7+* and *3 N×c6*).

## Test 2 Positions 9–16

This test is more difficult than the previous one, and so the time allotted is greater—50 minutes.

9 B

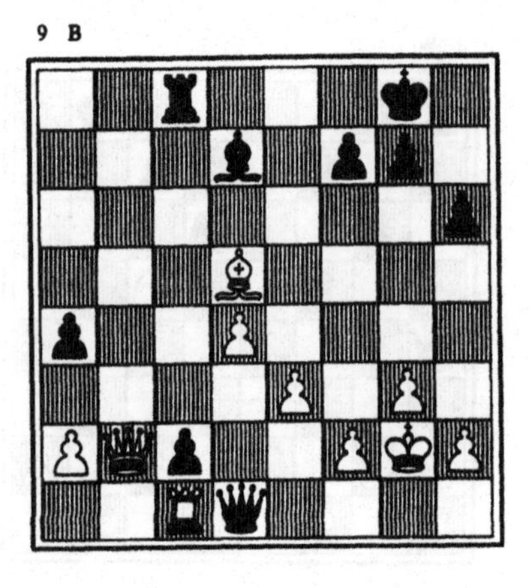

10 W

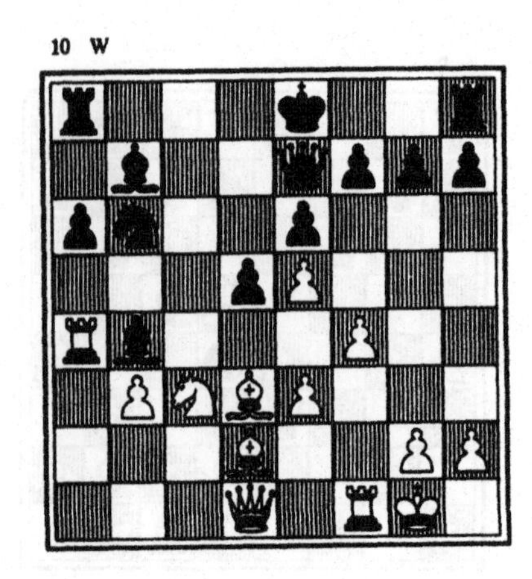

11 W

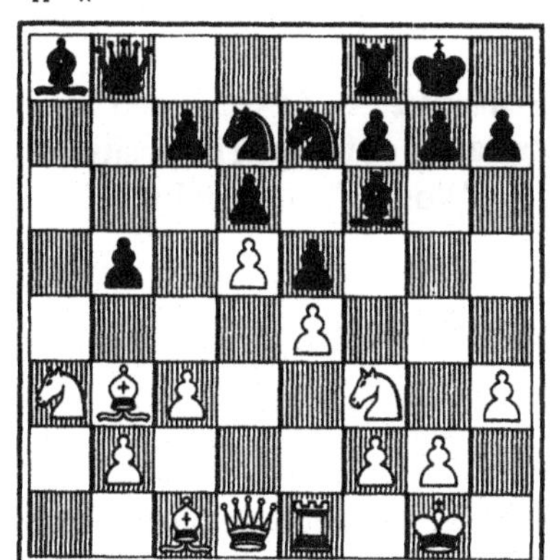

12 B

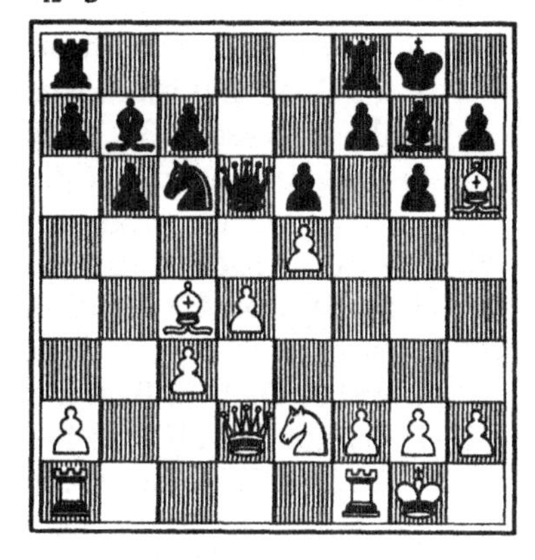

13 B

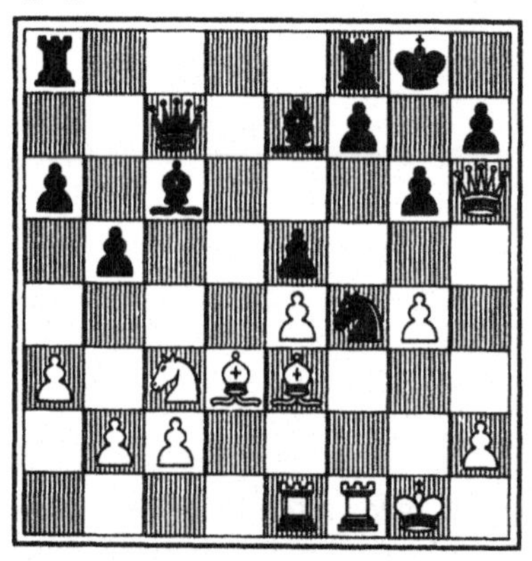

14 W

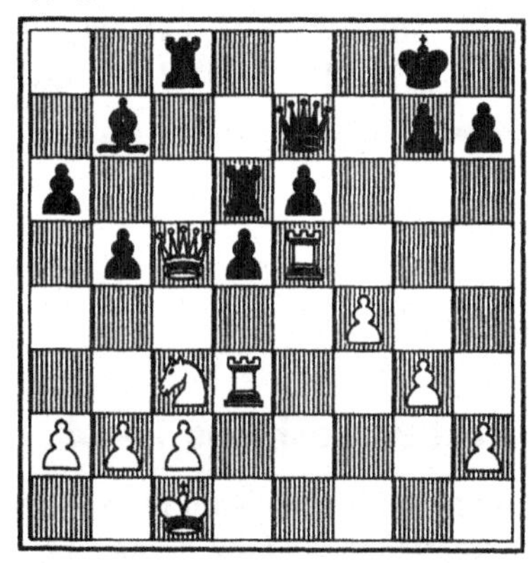

15 W

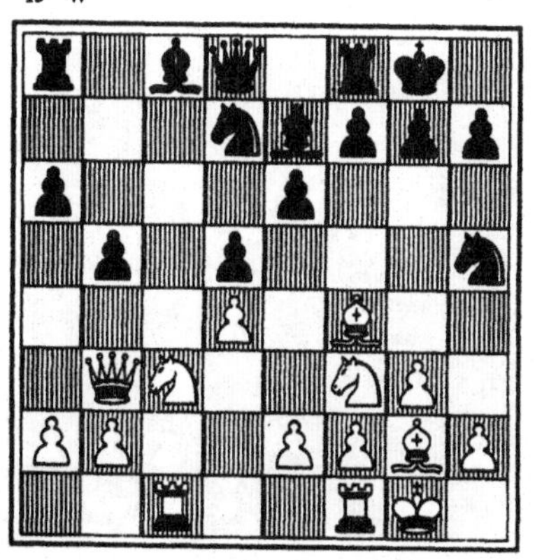

16 W

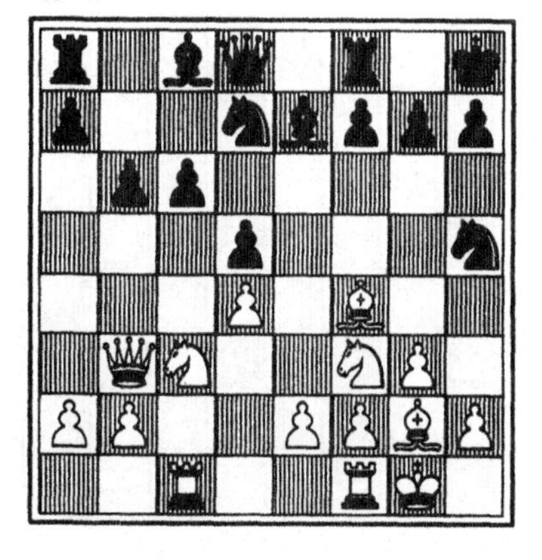

## Solutions to Test 2

9. Epen–Roislag, Amersfoort, 1946 (variation).
1 . . . Qh5!, and Black wins, in view of the two threats of 2 . . . Q×d5+ and 2 . . . Bh3+ followed by 3 . . . Qd1+, against which White has no defence. The position in the diagram was adjudicated, the adjudicator being Ex-World Champion Euwe. The result of the adjudication was . . . a draw.
10. Kolarov–Khadzhipetrov, Sofia, 1955.
1 R×b4! Q×b4 2 Na4!, and White won two pieces for a rook.
11. Boleslavsky–Smyslov, Moscow, 1950.
1 N×b5! Q×b5 2 Ba4, and White won a pawn.
12. Debarnot–Rogoff, Las Palmas, 1976.
1 . . . N×e5! 2 d×e5 Qc6!, and Black regains his piece, remaining a pawn up.
13. Paoli–Andersson, U., Dortmund, 1973.
1 . . . Bg5! 2 B×f4 (or *2 Q×g5 Nh3+*) 2 . . . B×h6 White resigns.
14. Mattison–Wright, Bromley, 1945.
1 N×d5!! Qd7 2 Ne7+!! Resigns.
15. Boleslavsky–Bisguier, Helsinki, 1952.
1 N×d5!! e×d5 2 Bc7 Qe8 3 Q×d5 Resigns.
16. Sokolsky–Nei, Odessa, 1960.
1 N×d5!! c×d5 2 Bc7 Qe8 3 Q×d5 Resigns.

### Test 3 Positions 17–24

This is not much more complicated than Test 2, but you have already gained some experience, and the theme is familiar, so the time you should spend is 40 minutes. If you manage everything, 40 points are yours, but if not, then for each position not solved deduct 5 points.

17 W

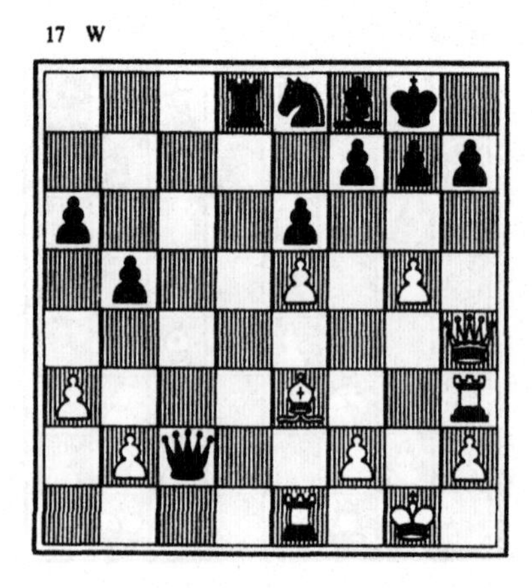

18 B

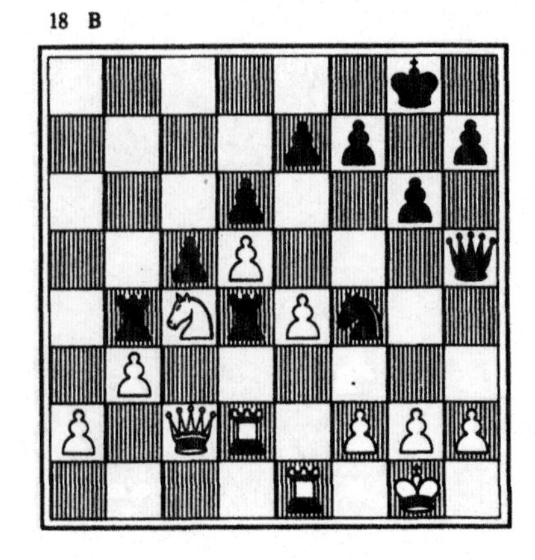

19 W

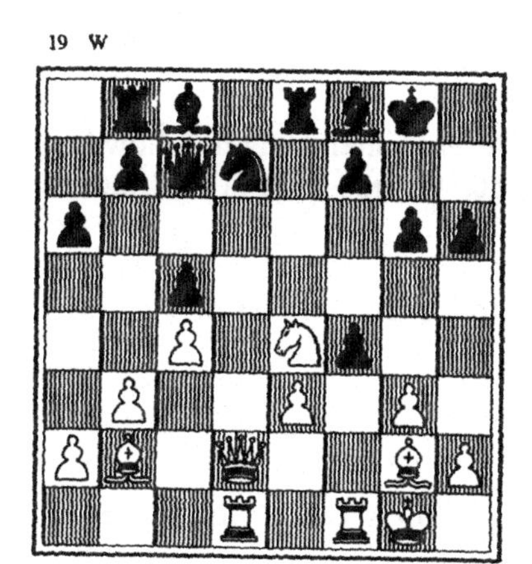

20 W

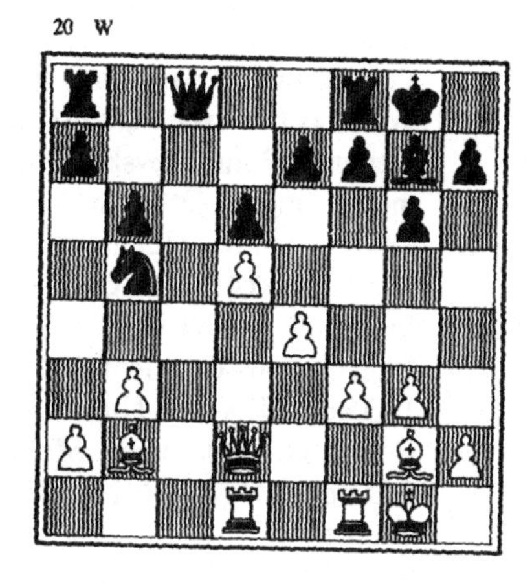

21 B

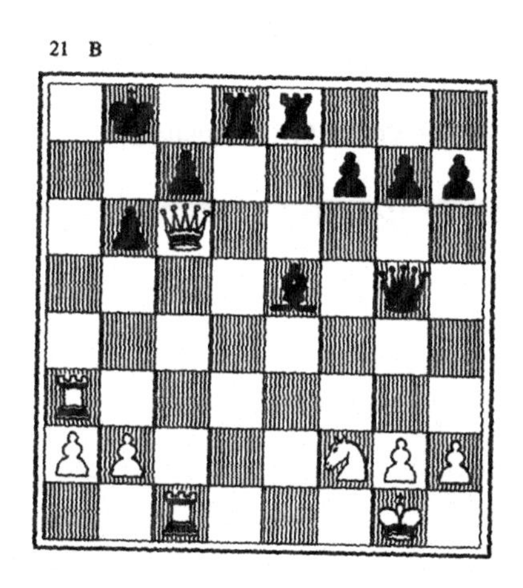

22 W

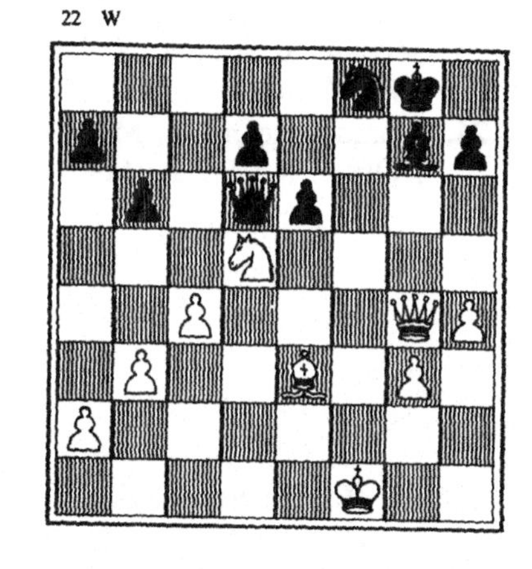

23 W

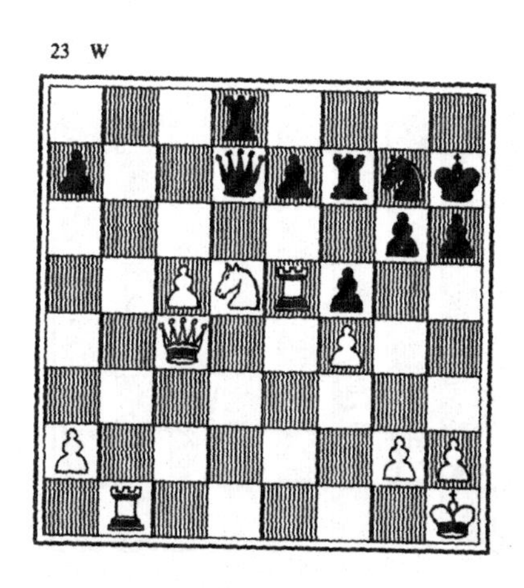

24 W

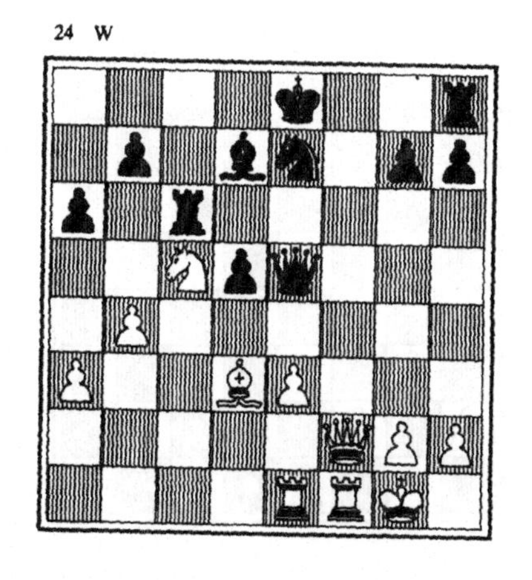

## Solutions to Test 3

17. Polugayevsky–Antoshin, Leningrad, 1956.
White is the exchange up, and is bound to win. But it is interesting to follow how elegantly Polugayevsky concludes the game . . . 1 g6!! Q×g6+ 2 Rg3 Qd3 (the only move, since *3 Q×d8* was threatened) 3 Bg5! Resigns.
18. Lovass–Titkos, Hungary, 1971.
1 . . . Rb×c4!! 2 b×c4 R×d2 3 Q×d2 Qg5! White resigns (on *4 f3* or *4 g3* there follows *4 . . . Nh3+*).
19. Chernyakov–Belyuchik, Lodz, 1953.
1 Q×d7!! B×d7 2 Nf6+ Kh8 3 N×e8+ Resigns.
20. Botvinnik–Golombek, Moscow, 1956.
1 B×g7 K×g7 2 Rc1! Qd7 3 a4 Resigns (on *3 . . . Nc7 4 Qc3+* Black loses his knight).
21. Sznapik–Gaprindashvili, Sandomierz, 1976.
1 . . . Q×c1+! 2 Q×c1 B×b2! and Black wins, since if 3 Q×b2, then 3 . . . Re1 mate.
22. Duckstein–Johanson, Moscow, 1956.
1 Nf6+! Kf7 2 Q×g7+!! K×g7 3 Ne8+ Resigns.
23. Serra–Paidusis, Varna, 1962.
1 R×e7!! Qc6 (if *1 . . . R×e7*, then *2 Nf6+*) 2 R×f7 R×d5 3 Qc3! Resigns.
24. Momo–MacGovan, Moscow, 1956.
1 Qf8+! R×f8 2 R×f8+ K×f8 3 N×d7+ Ke8 4 N×e5 Resigns.

## Test 4 Positions 25–32

The last one on this theme. It is considerably more complicated than the previous tests. Time for solution—50 minutes.

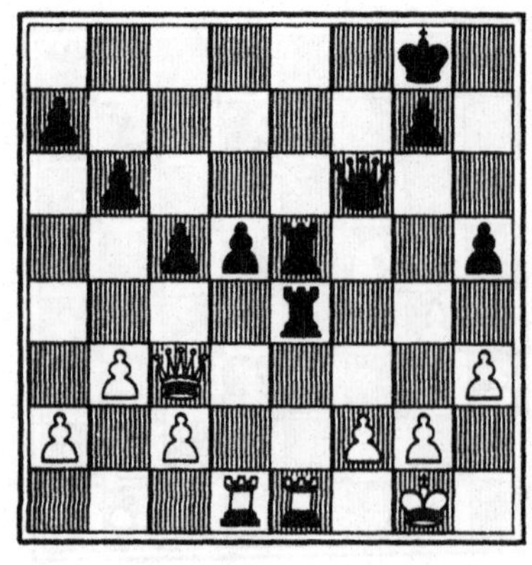

26 W

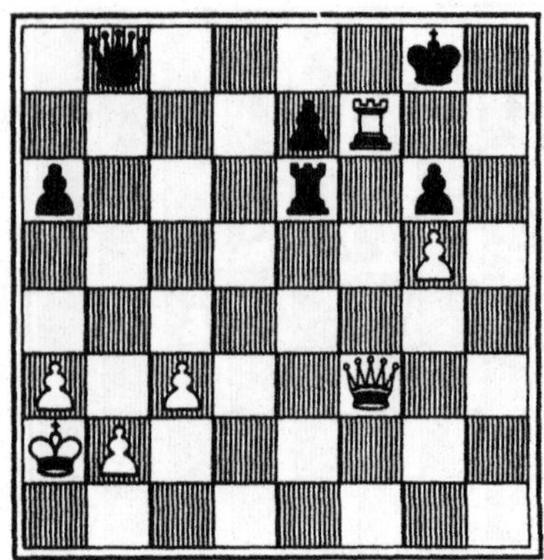

27 B

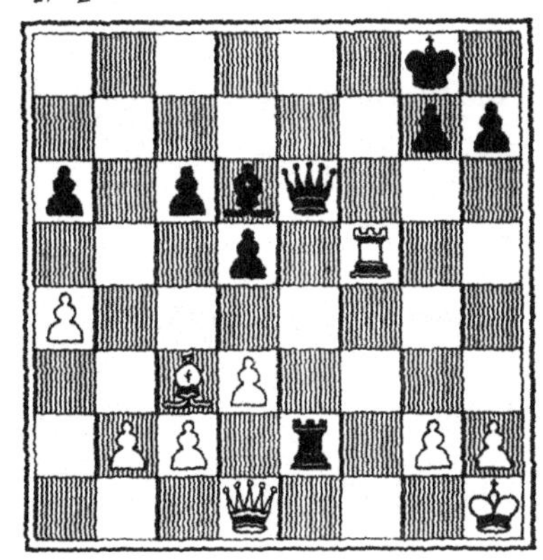

28 W

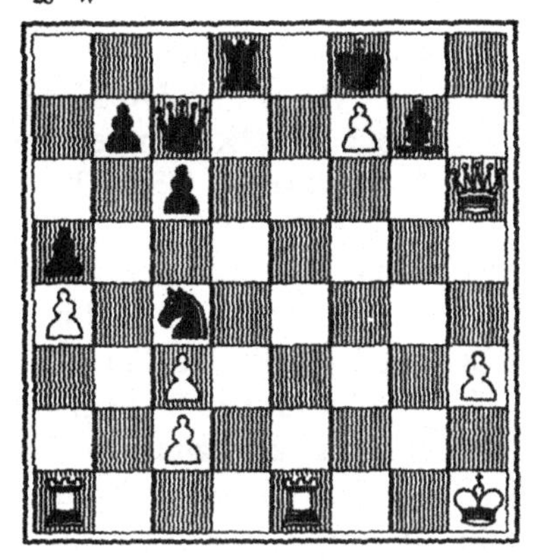

29 W

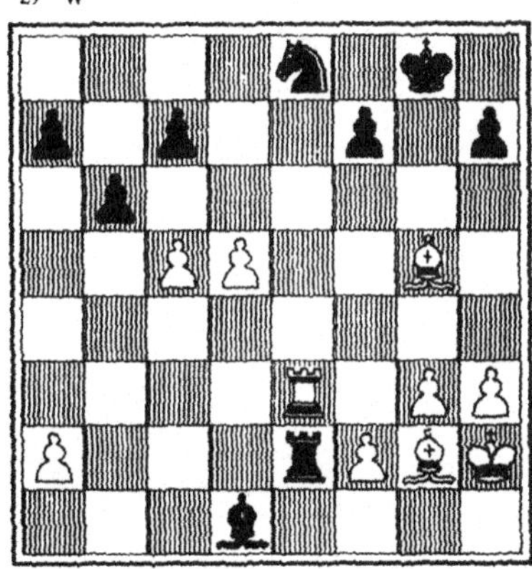

30 W

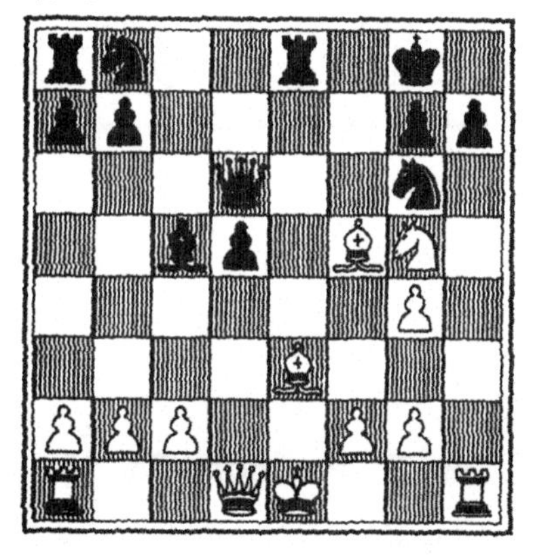

31 W

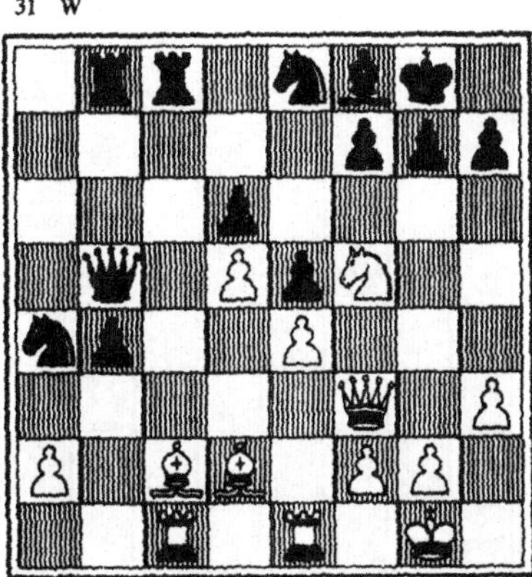

32 W

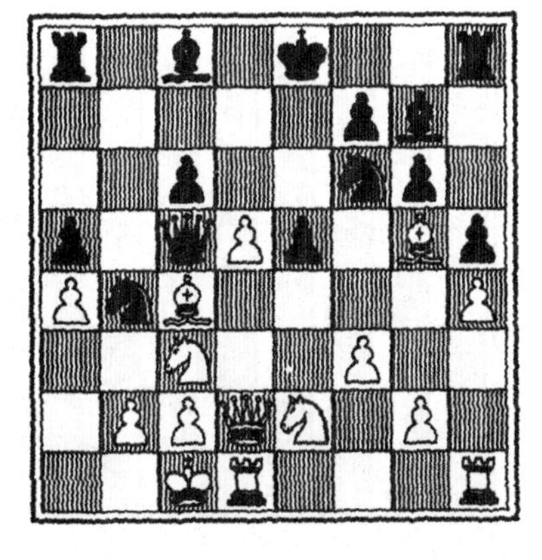

## Solutions to Test 4

25. Bagirov–Kholmov, Baku, 1961.
1 . . . R×e1+! 2 R×e1 Re2!! White resigns (against the two threats of *3 . . . Q×f2+* and *3 . . . Q×c3* there is no defence).
26. Byrne–Tarjan, USA Ch., 1975.
1 Qh3! Resigns (*1 . . . K×f7 2 Qh7+, 3 Qh8+* and *4 Q×b8*).
27. Geller–Tseshkovsky, Moscow, 1974.
1 . . . d4 2 Ba5 (*2 Bd2* is met by *2 . . . R×d2*) 2 . . . Re5! White resigns.
28. Popov–Buljovcic, Sombor, 1966.
1 Re8+! R×e8 2 Q×g7+! K×g7 3 f×e8=N+!! Resigns.
29. Boleslavsky–Taimanov, Moscow, 1952.
1 d6! c×d6 2 c×d6 N×d6 (on *2 . . . R×e3* there follows *3 d7!*) 3 Rd3 Resigns.
30. Strautinsch–Gunderman, Corr., 1970.
1 B×g6 h×g6 2 Rh8+! K×h8 3 Nf7+ Resigns.
31. Balashov–Bronstein, 43rd USSR Ch., 1975.
1 B×a4 Q×a4 2 R×c8 R×c8 3 Nh6+! g×h6 (or *3 . . . Kh8 4 Q×f7 Nf6 5 Qg8+ N×g8 6 Nf7* mate) 4 Qg4+ Kh8 5 Q×c8 Resigns.
32. Rantanen–Cardoso, Skopje, 1972.
1 B×f6 B×f6 2 Ne4 Qe7 (*2 . . . Q×c4 3 Nd6+*) 3 d6! Qd8 4 d7+! Kf8 (if *4 . . . B×d7*, then *5 Q×d7+ Q×d7 6 N×f6+*) 5 N×f6 Resigns.

## Test 5 Positions 33–40

Time for thought 40 minutes. Since the theme, 'Discovered attack', is new, the test is relatively simple. For the correct solution of all positions, add 40 points to your score. Deduct 5 points for each position not solved.

33 B

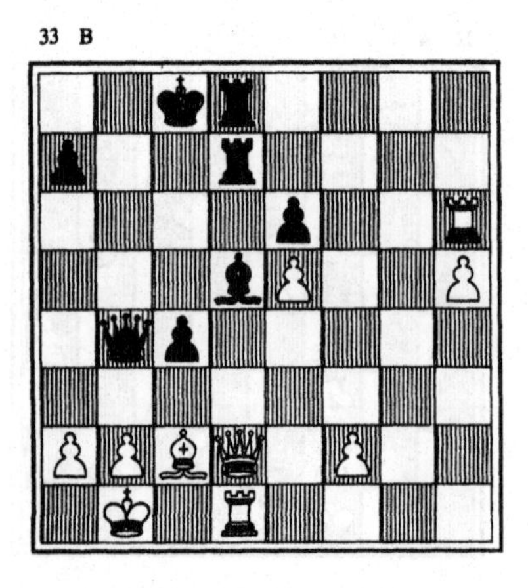

34 W

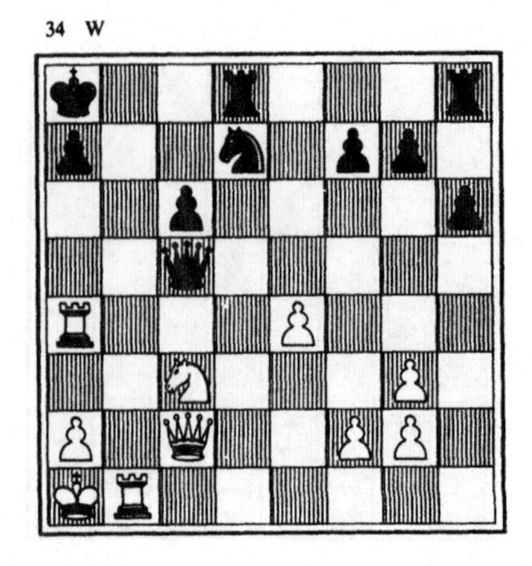

35 W

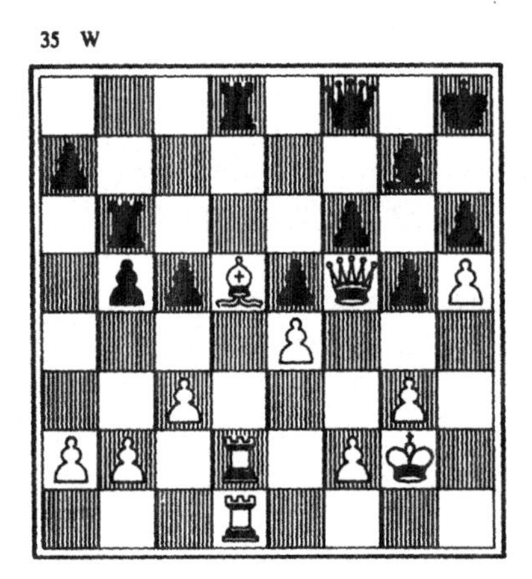

36 B

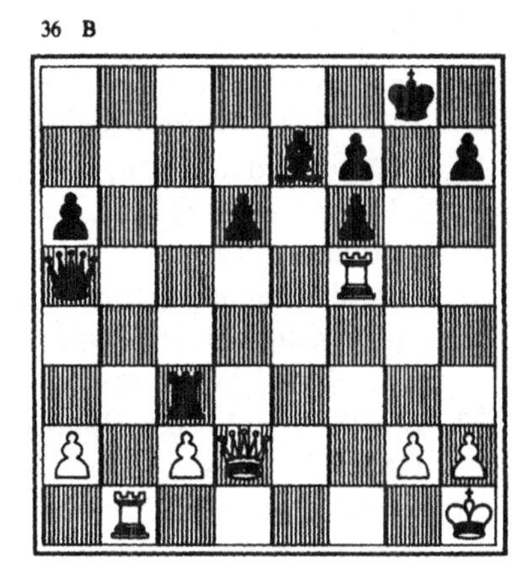

37 W

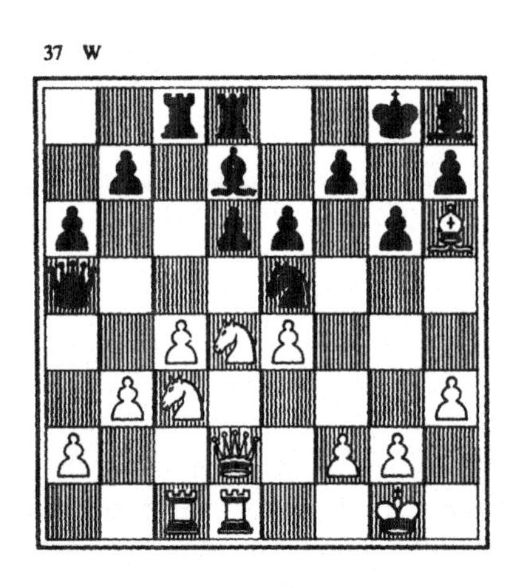

38 W

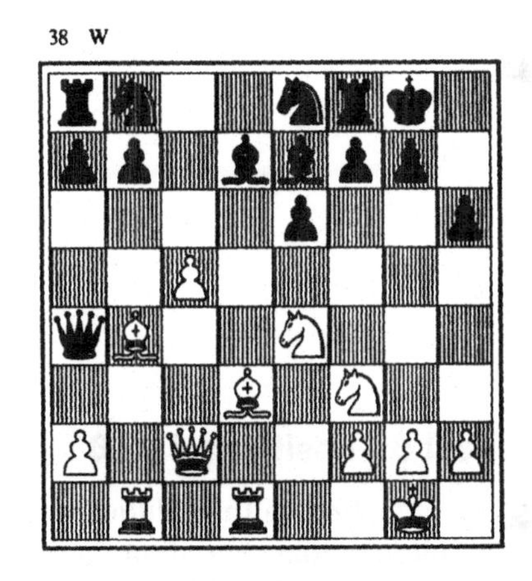

39 W

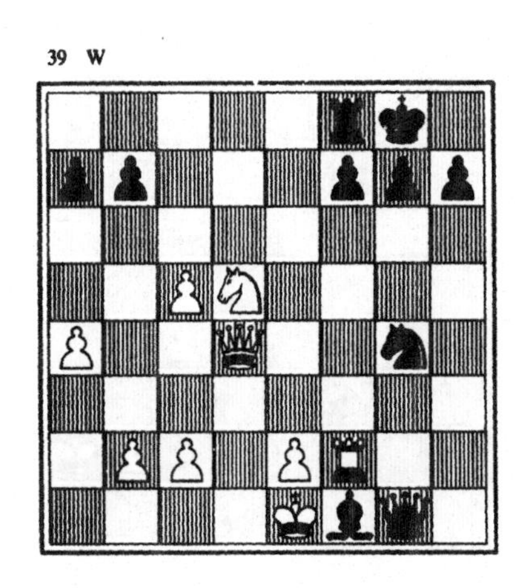

40 B

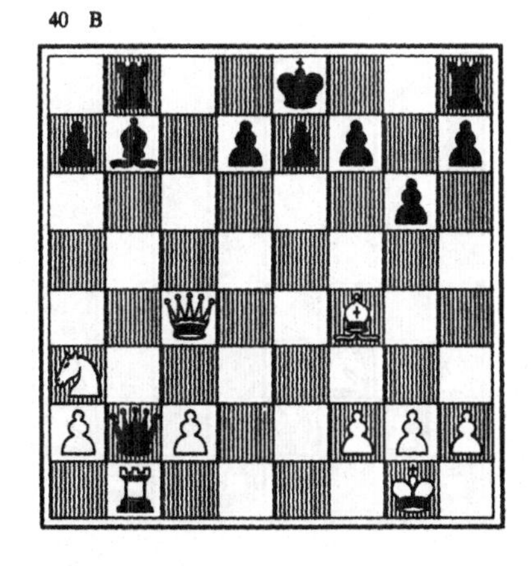

## Solutions to Test 5

33. Petrusha–Yushkevich, Minsk, 1967.
    1 . . . Be4!! White resigns.
34. Böök–Halfdanarsson, Beverwijk, 1962.
    1 Nd5!! Resigns (*1 . . . c×d5 2 R×a7+!!*, or *1 . . . Q×c2 2 Nc7* mate).
35. Trifunovic–Aaron, Beverwijk, 1962.
    1 Bg8! Resigns (against *2 Qh7* mate or *2 R×d8* there is no defence).
36. Maric–Gligoric, Belgrade, 1962.
    1 . . . Rb3!! White resigns.
37. Bonch-Osmolovsky–Ragozin, Lvov, 1951.
    1 Nd5! Resigns.
38. Nilsen–Laustsen, Denmark, 1959.
    1 c6! Q×c2 2 B×c2 N×c6 3 B×e7 N×e7 4 R×d7, and White won.
39. Bryntse–Eriksen, Corr., 1950.
    1 Ne7+! Kh8 2 R×f7!! Resigns.
40. Johansson–Messing, Berlin, 1973.
    1 . . . Q×b1+!! 2 N×b1 Ba6!! White resigns.

## Test 6 Positions 41–48

Pay attention to the solutions when checking your answers. In a number of positions, besides the main variation there are also subsidiary variations, and if your solutions are incomplete, or if a subsidiary variation is omitted, for each instance reduce your score by 2–3 points. Fifty minutes are allotted to this test.

41 B

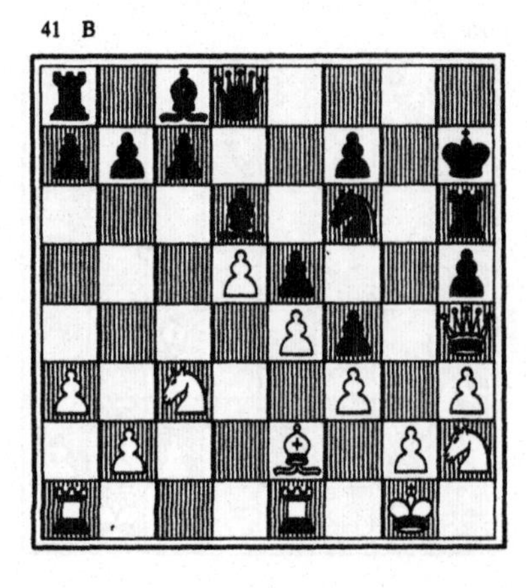

42 W

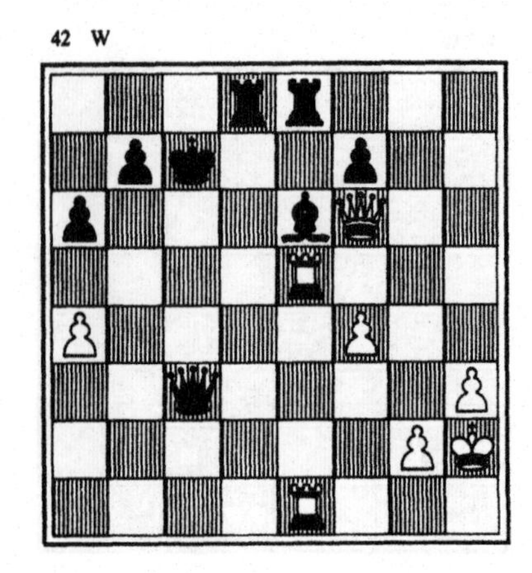

43 W

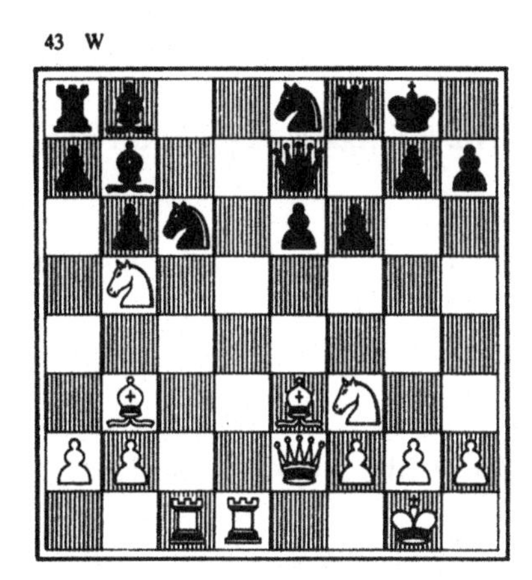

44 W

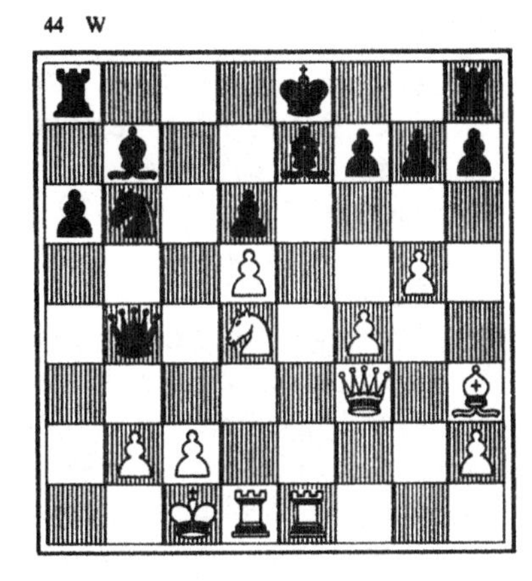

45 W

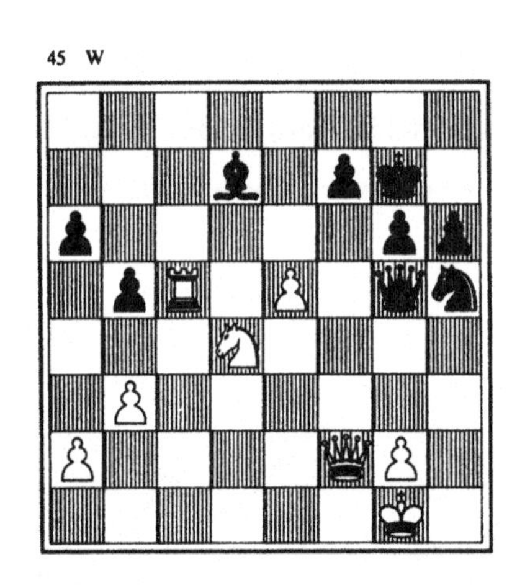

46 W

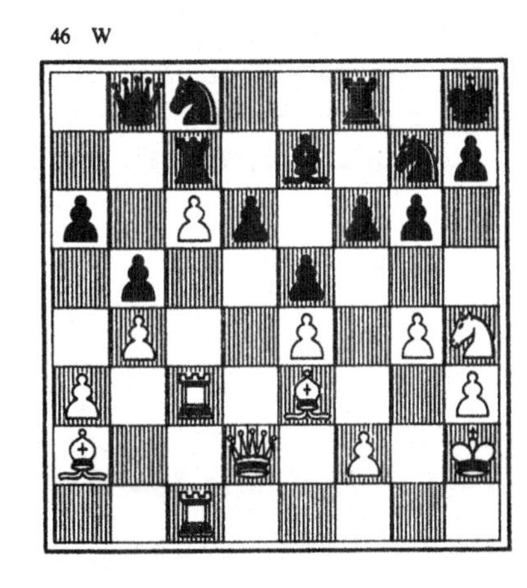

47 W

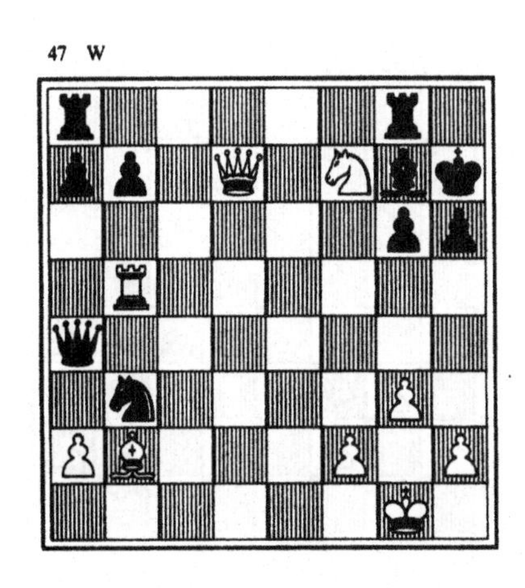

48 W

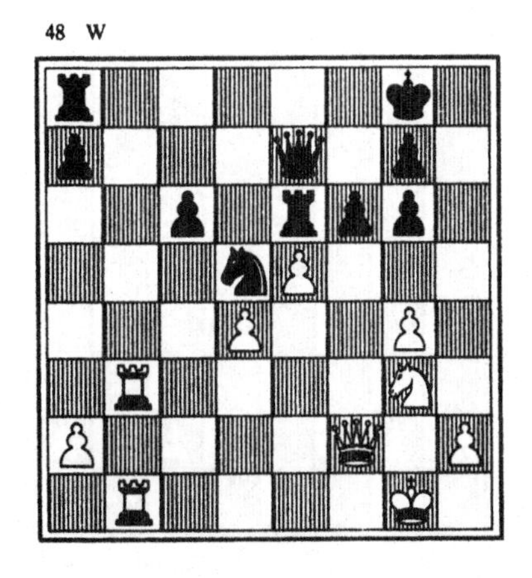

## Solutions to Test 6

41. Zalesnu–Engers, Corr., 1972–3.
1 . . . Bc5+! White resigns (*2 Kh1 Ng4!! 3 Q×d8 Nf2+ 4 Kg1 N×e4+ 5 Kh1 Ng3* mate, or *2 Kf1 Ng4!! 3 Q×d8 N×h2* mate).
42. Richter–Winz, Berlin, 1957.
1 R×e6!! Resigns (*1 . . . Q×f6 2 Rc1+* and *3 R×f6*, or *1 . . . Q×e1 2 R×e1 R×e1 3 Qc3+*).
43. Kiffmeyer–Sandmeyer, West Germany, 1970.
1 Bc5! b×c5 2 B×e6+ Kh8 3 Rd7 Resigns.
44. Kuindzhi–Jansa, Lvov, 1960.
1 R×e7+! K×e7 2 Qe4+ Kd8 3 Nc6+ B×c6 4 Q×b4 Bb5 5 Q×d6+ Resigns.
45. Strautinsch–Muller, Corr., 1971–3.
1 e6!! Q×c5 2 Nf5+ Q×f5 3 Q×f5 Resigns (on *3 . . . g×f5* there follows *4 e×d7*).
46. Deschauer–Meyer, Corr., 1952–3.
1 N×g6+!! h×g6 2 Ba7! Q×a7 3 Qh6 mate.
47. Parr–Wheatcroft, London Ch., 1938.
1 Rh5!! Q×d7 (on *1 . . . Qa5* there follows *2 R×h6+! B×h6 3 Ng5* mate) 2 Ng5+ Kh8 3 R×h6 mate.
48. Bagirov–Zilbershtain, Rostov, 1971.
1 Rb8+! R×b8 2 R×b8+ Kh7 (or *2 . . . Kf7 3 Ne4!*) 3 Nf5!! Resigns (*3 . . . g×f5* is answered by *4 Qh4+* and *5 Qh5* mate).

## Test 7 Positions 49–56

Theme—'Discovered Check'. A relatively simple test. Taking into account your previous experience and the two previous tests, you should easily cope with it. Time for this test is 40 minutes.

49 W

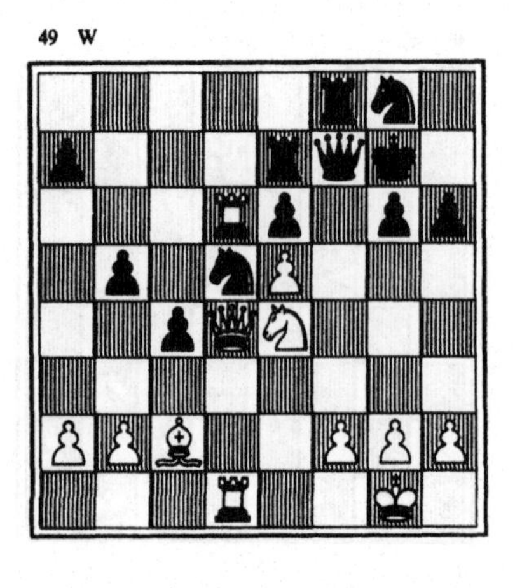

50 B

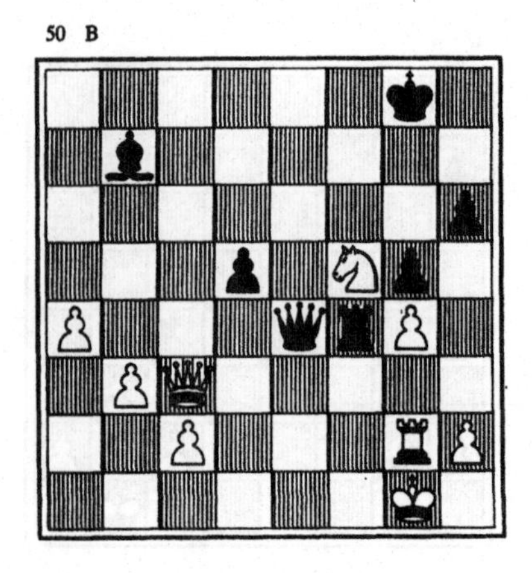

51 W

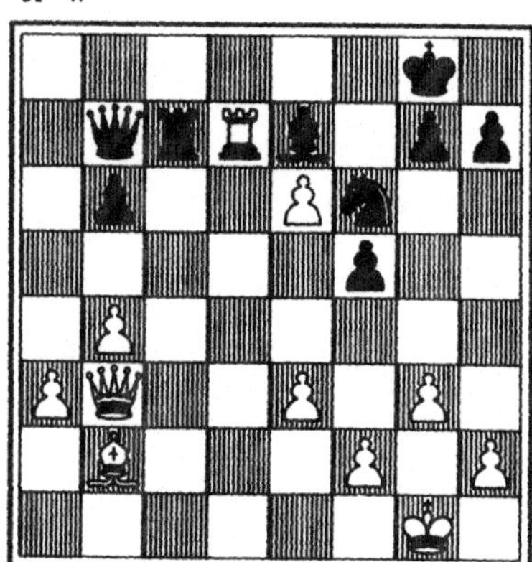

52 B

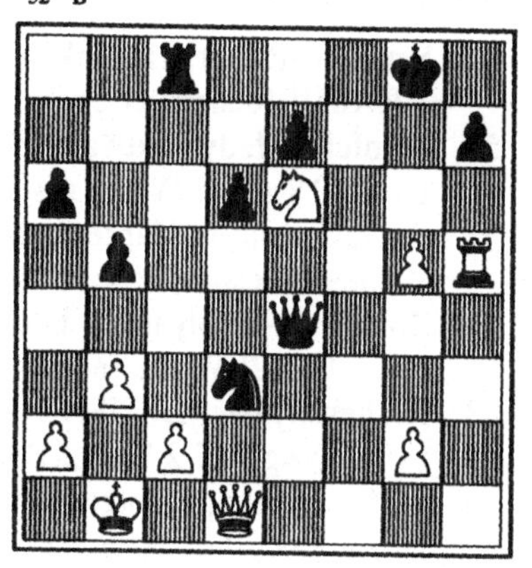

53 B

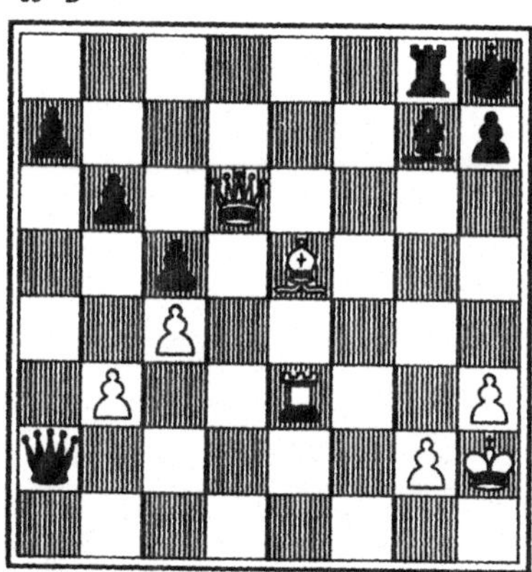

54 B

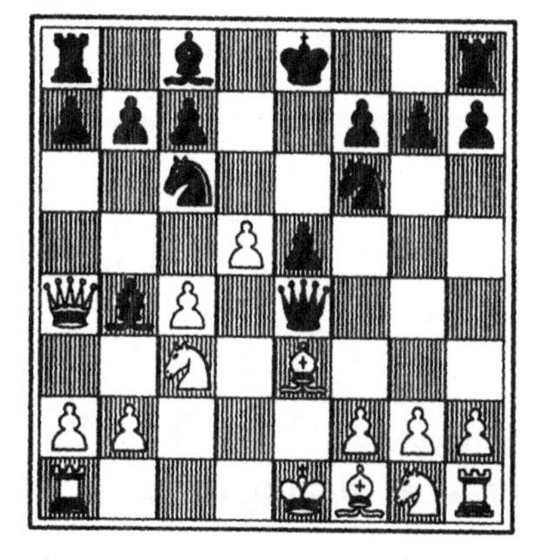

55 B

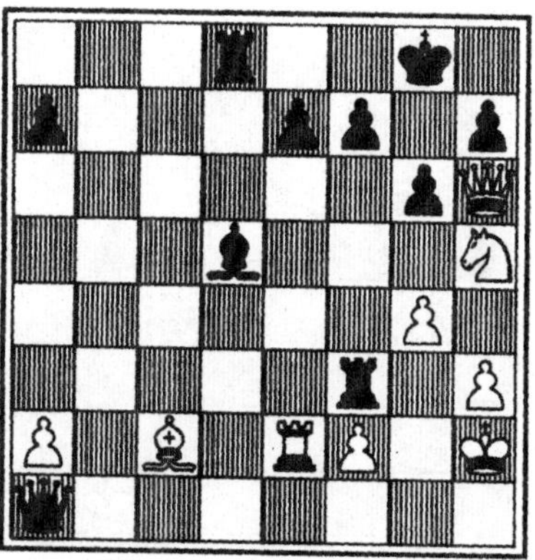

56 B

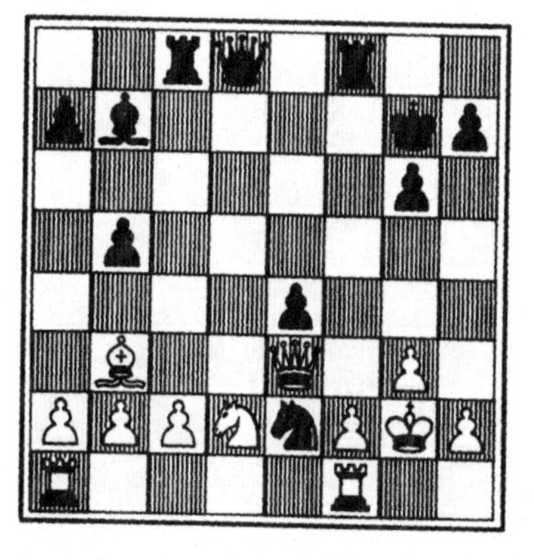

## Solutions to Test 7

49. Smyslov–Rabar, Helsinki, 1952.
 1 R×d5!! Resigns (*1 . . . e×d5 2 e6+*).
50. Grinfeld–Medyanikova, Tbilisi, 1973–4.
 1 . . . Q×g2+!! White resigns (after *2 K×g2 d4+* Black wins).
51. Kochiev–Maric, Kapfenberg, 1976.
 1 Rd8+! Resigns.
52. Zolotarev–Steblyanko, USSR, 1976.
 1 . . . R×c2! White resigns (*2 Q×c2 Qe1+*, or *2 K×c2 Nf2+*).
53. Reshevsky–Byrne, USA, 1973.
 1 . . . Q×g2+!! 2 K×g2 B×e5+ White resigns.
54. Lochov–Bishop, Corr., 1946.
 1 . . . N×d5!! 2 c×d5 B×c3+ White resigns.
55. Kristev–Tringov, Skopje, 1961.
 1 . . . Qh1+!! White resigns (on *2 K×h1* there follows *2 . . . R×h3+3 Kg1 Rh1* mate).
56. Olsson–Dahl, Västerås, 1959.
 1 . . . Q×d2!! 2 Q×d2 e3+ White resigns.

## Test 8 Positions 57–64

A continuation of the previous theme. The examples are slightly more difficult, but nevertheless not exceptionally so. For this test the time for solution is 45 minutes.

57 B

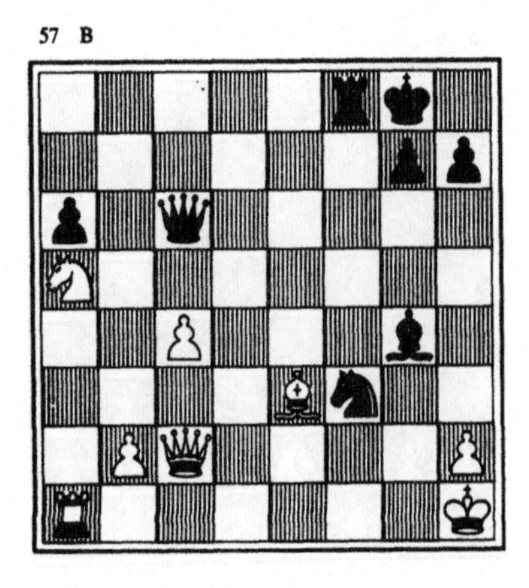

58 W

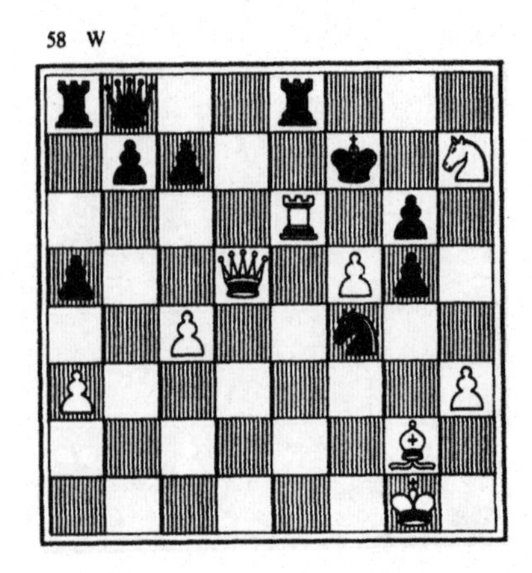

59 W

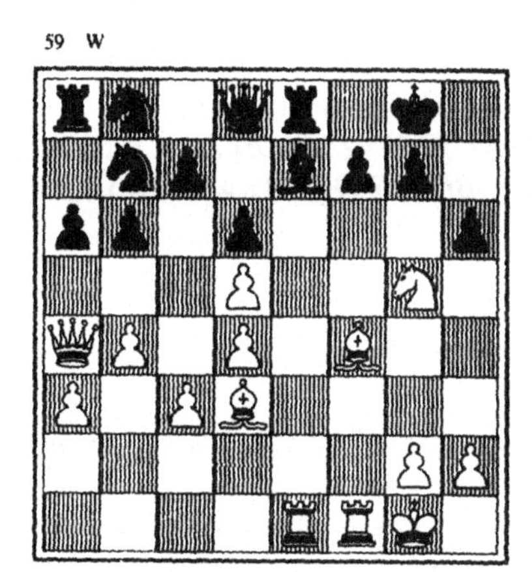

60 B

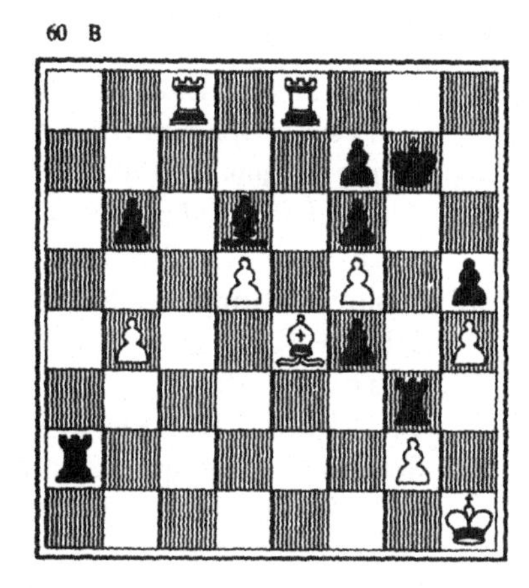

61 B

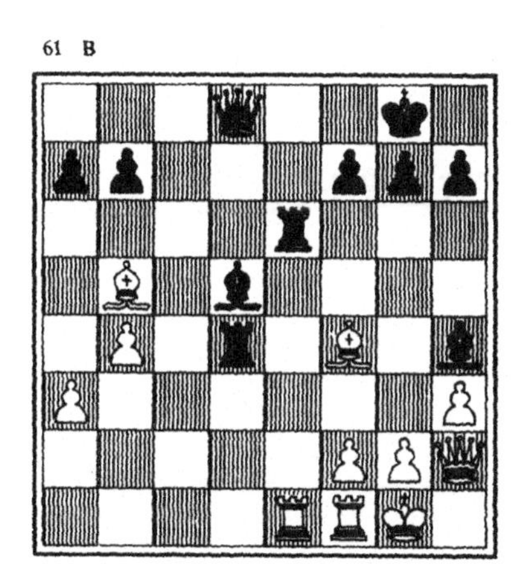

62 B

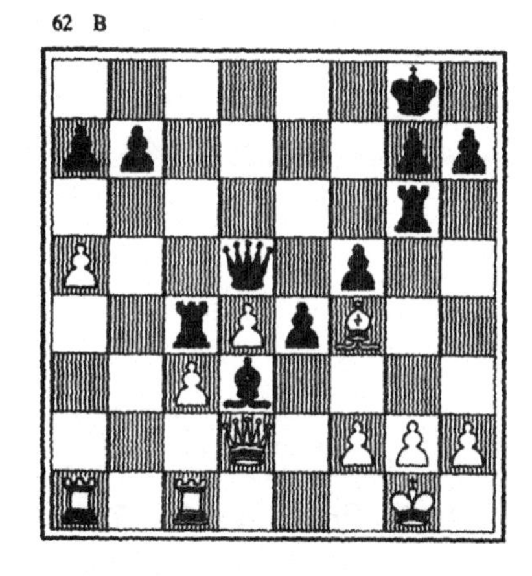

63 B

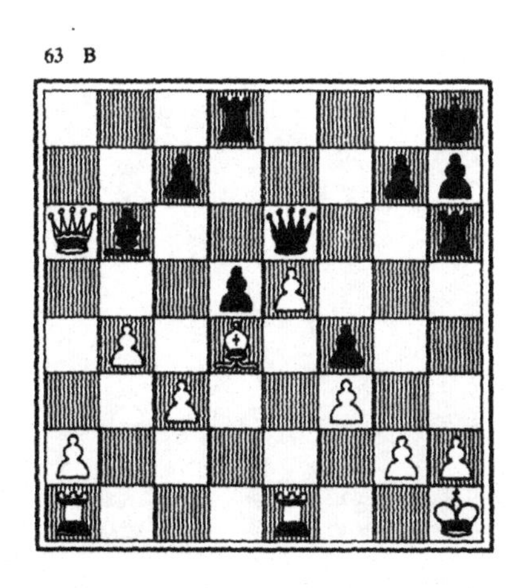

64 B

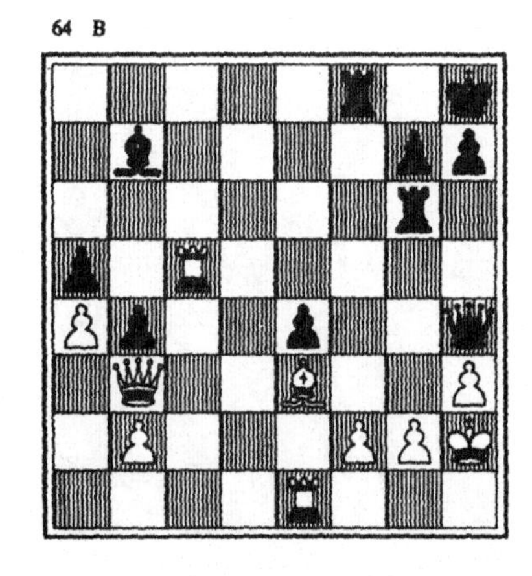

## Solutions to Test 8

57. N. N.–Evans, London, 1946. (From a simultaneous display with clocks.)
 1 . . . Ne1+!! 2 Kg1 (or *2 N×c6 Rf1+ 3 Bg1 Bf3+ 4 Qg2 B×g2* mate) 2 . . . Qh1+!! White resigns (if *3 K×h1*, then *3 . . . Rf1+ 4 Bg1 Bf3+ 5 Qg2 B×g2* mate).
58. MacKelvie–Challis, Hastings, 1951.
 1 Re7++!! K×e7 2 f6 mate.
59. Kislov–Viktorov, USSR, 1971.
 1 Bh7+ Kf8 2 Ne6+! f×e6 3 B×d6 mate.
60. Ivanov, N.–Belenky, Leningrad, 1974 (variation).
 1 . . . Ra1+ 2 Kh2 Rh3+! 3 g×h3 (*3 K×h3 Rh1* mate) 3 . . . f3+ 4 Re5 B×e5 mate.
61. Serebrisky–Solmanis, Kaunas, 1946.
 1 . . . B×f2+!! 2 K×f2 Qb6!! (*2 . . . Qh4+* is a mistake on account of *3 Kg1 R×e1 4 Bg5!!*) 3 R×e6 R×f4++ White resigns (on *4 Kg3* comes *4 . . . f×e6 5 R×f4 g5*; no better for White was *3 Be3 Rd2+*).
62. Troianescu–Pogáts, Bucharest, 1951.
 1 . . . R×g2+!! 2 Kh1 (on *2 K×g2* there follows *2 . . . e3+*) 2 . . . e3! 3 Q×e3 R×f2+ White resigns.
63. Chekhover–Lutikov, Leningrad, 1951.
 1 . . . R×h2+! 2 K×h2 Qh6+ 3 Kg1 B×d4+ White resigns.
64. Schmid, L.–Rossolimo, Heidelberg, 1949.
 1 . . . R×g2+!! 2 K×g2 R×f2+! 3 B×f2 e3+! White resigns.

## Test 9 Positions 65–72

The theme in this and the two following tests is 'The pin', one of the most commonly occurring. Time for this test—40 minutes.

65 W

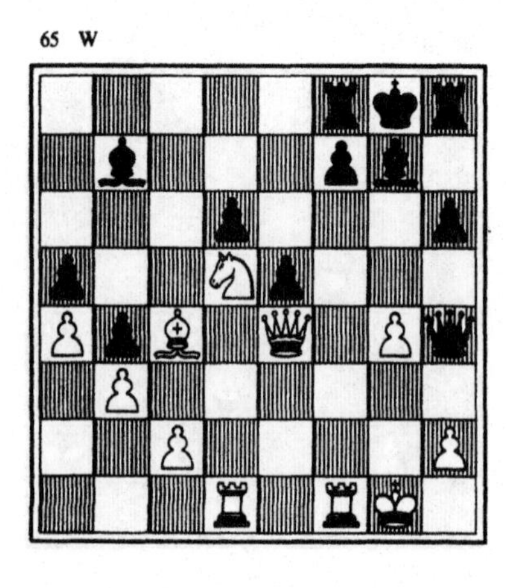

66 W

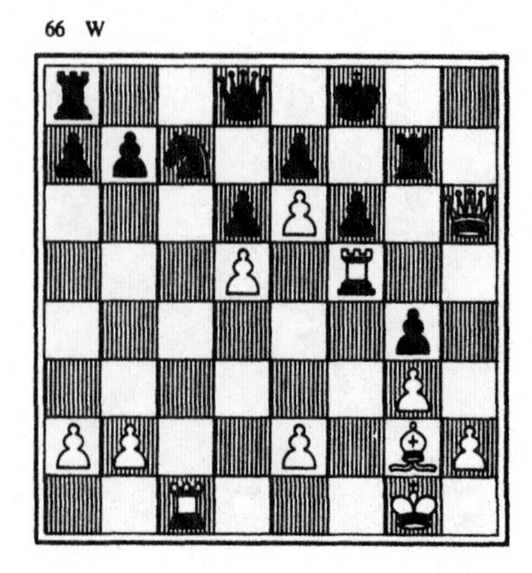

67 W

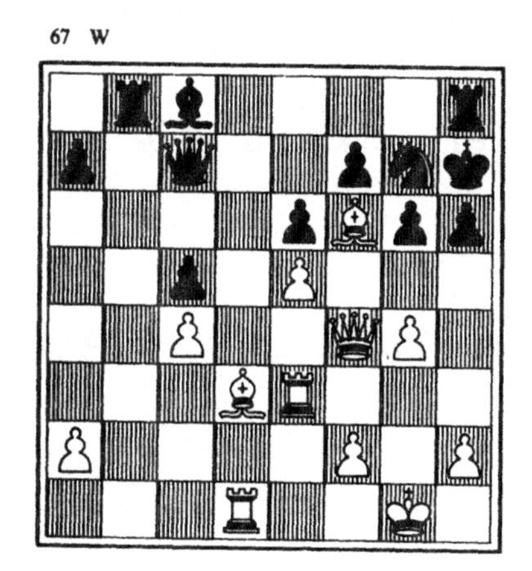

68 W

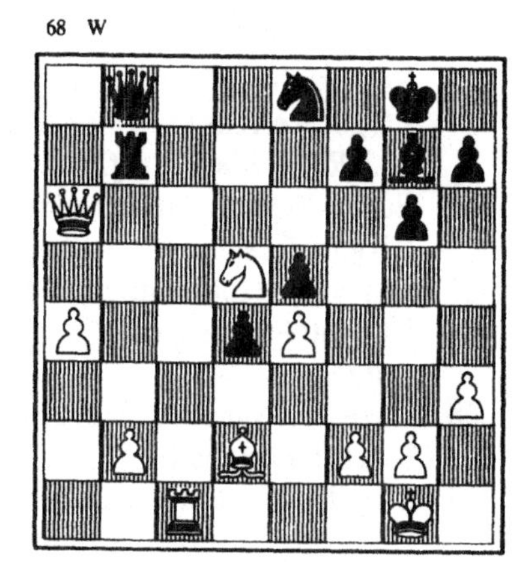

69 W

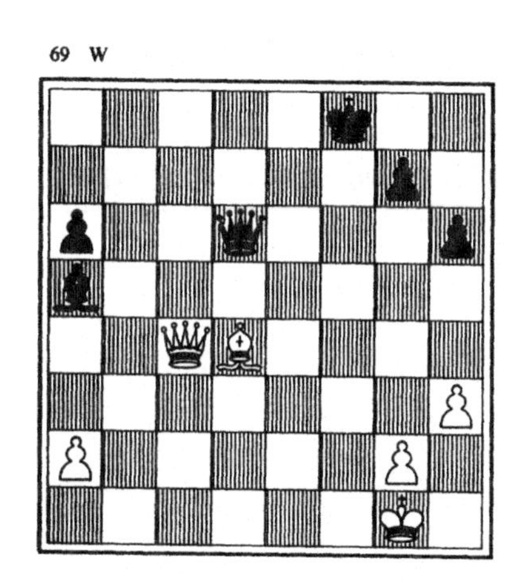

70 W

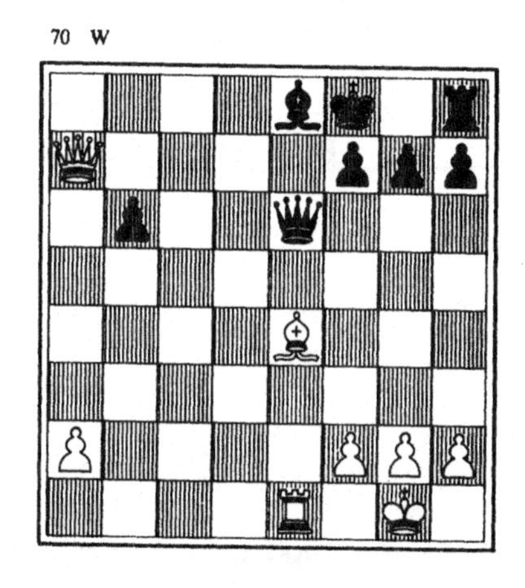

71 W

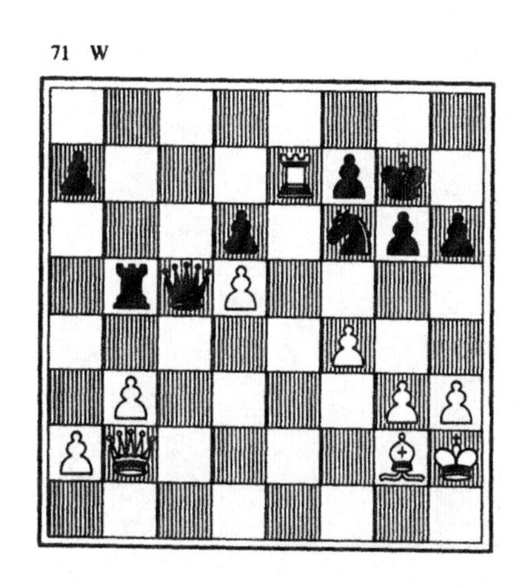

72 B

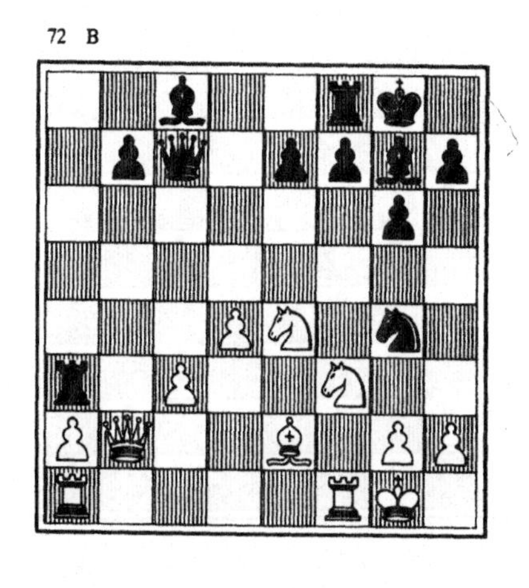

### Solutions to Test 9

65. Romanishin–Poutiainen, Yerevan, 1976.
1 Qg6! Resigns (*1 . . . f×g6* allows *2 Nf6* mate, while *1 . . . B×d5 2 B×d5 Qe7* loses to *3 R×f7 R×f7 4 Rf1*).
66. Euwe–Nestler, Dubrovnik, 1950.
1 Rg5!! Resigns (*1 . . . f×g5* is met by *2 Qh8+ Rg8 3 Rf1+*).
67. Padevsky–Hildebrandt, Gevle, 1956.
1 Q×h6+!! Resigns (*1 . . . K×h6 2 Rh3+ Nh5 3 g5+ Kh7 4 R×h5+ Kg8 5 R×h8* mate).
68. Unzicker–Sanchez, Stockholm, 1952.
1 Rc8!! Resigns (if *1 . . . Q×c8*, then *2 Ne7+*).
69. Brundtrup–Budrich, Berlin, 1954.
1 Bc5 Bb6 2 Qf4+! Resigns.
70. Evans–Bisguier, Philadelphia, 1957.
1 Qa3+Qe7 (on *1 . . . Kg8* there follows *2 B×h7+*) 2 Bc6!! Resigns.
71. Trifunovic–Golombek, Amsterdam, 1954.
1 g4! g5 (*1 . . . Qb4* does not help in view of *2 Re4* followed by *3 g5*) 2 h4, and White wins. (There followed *2 . . . Kg6 3 Be4+ N×e4 4 h5+ Kh7 5 R×f7+* and *6 Qg7* mate.)
72. Bakhir–Nikitin, Moscow, 1956.
1 . . . B×d4+! 2 c×d4 R×f3, and Black wins (*3 Ng3* is answered by *3 . . . R×f1+*).

### Test 10 Positions 73–80

The same theme, but a slightly more difficult test, for which 50 minutes are allowed.

73 B

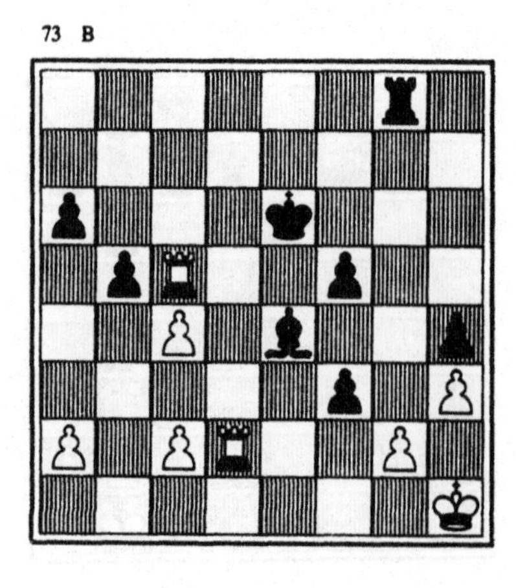

74 B

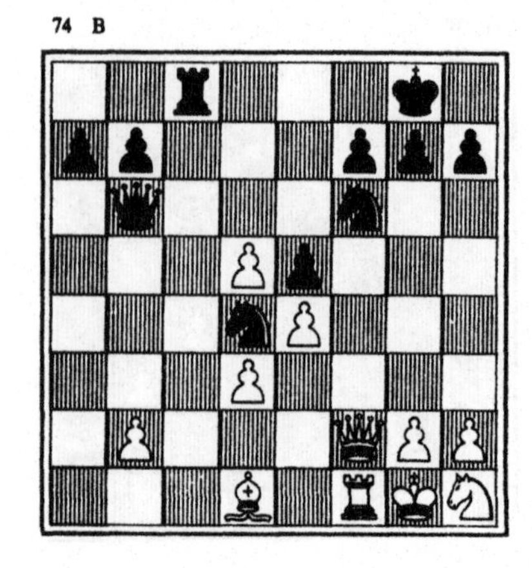

75 W

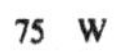

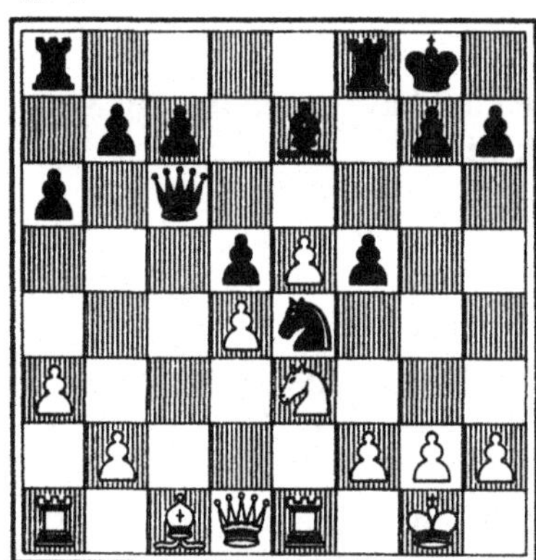

76 B

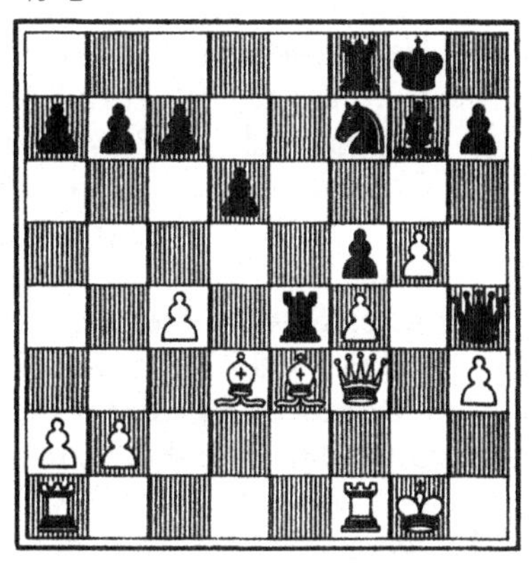

77 W

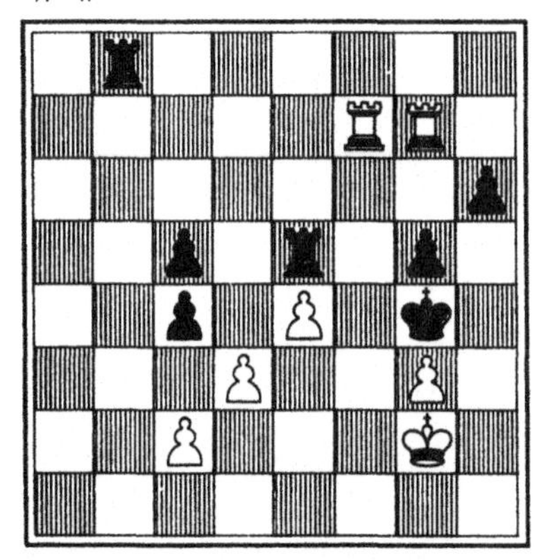

78 W

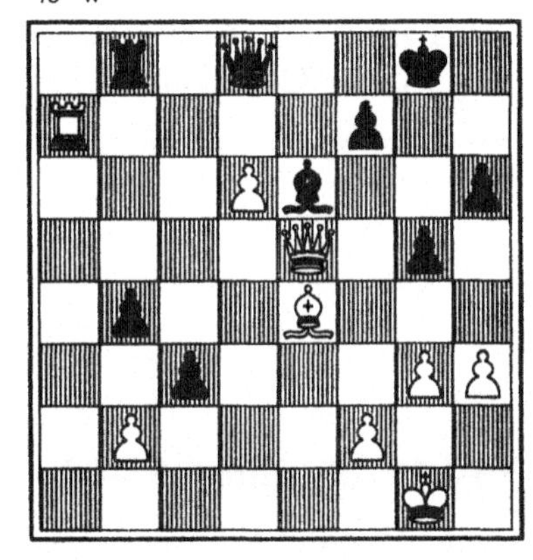

79 W

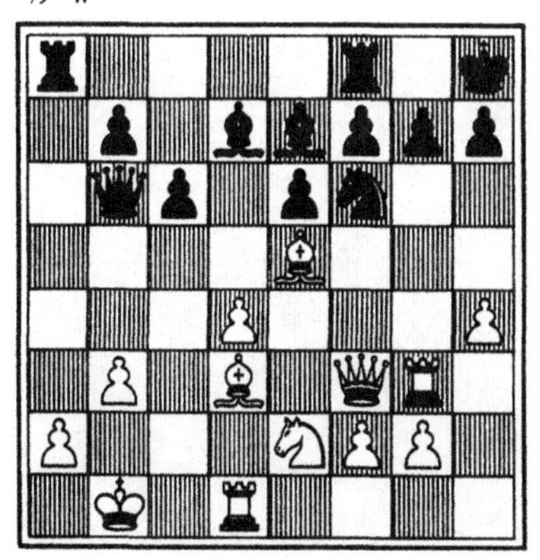

80 W

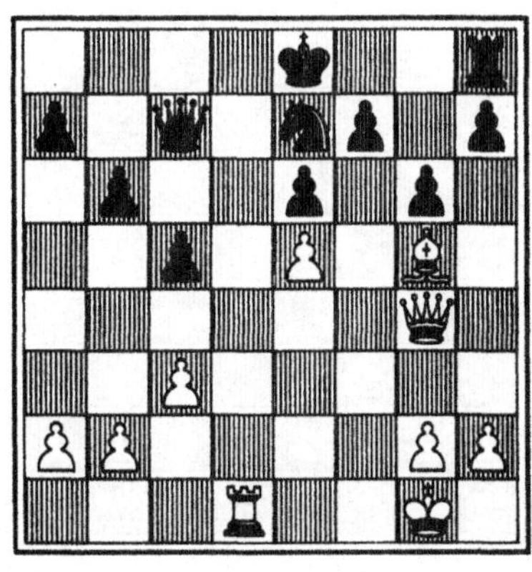

## Solutions to Test 10

73. Hansen–Moller, Oslo, 1962.
1 . . . R×g2 2 R×g2 f2!! White resigns. 2 Rd1 would not have saved the game, on account of 2 . . . f2, while after 2 Rd4 R×c2 Black wins.
74. Bairamov–Gik, Moscow, 1963.
1 . . . Rc2!! 2 B×c2 (on *2 Qe3* there follows *2 . . . Ne2+ 3 Kf2 Ng4+*) 2 . . . Ne2 mate.
75. Keres–Sliwa, Göteborg, 1955.
1 Qb3 Rad8 2 N×f5! R×f5 3 R×e4!!, and White won. There followed 3 . . . Qc4 4 Q×c4 d×c4 5 g4 Rf3 6 Be3.
76. Goldschmidt–Bohm, London, 1973.
1 . . . N×g5! 2 f×g5 R×e3! White resigns (on *3 Q×e3* there follows *3 . . . Bd4*).
77. Durao–Catozzi, Dublin, 1957.
1 Rf4+!! Kh5 2 Rh4+!! g×h4 3 g4 mate.
78. Kasparov–Browne, Banja Luka, 1979.
1 Bh7+! K×h7 2 Q×e6 Resigns.
79. Radulov–Zoderborg, Helsinki, 1961.
1 R×g7!! K×g7 2 Qg4+ Kh8 3 Qh5 Resigns.
80. Lasker, Ed.–Avalla, New York, 1947.
1 Qa4+ Qc6 2 Rd8+!! K×d8 3 Q×c6 Resigns.

## Test 11 Positions 81–88

Continuation of the theme 'The Pin and its exploitation'. The difficulty of this test is approximately the same as that of the previous one. Taking account of the fact that you are already familiar with similar examples, the time for the solving of this test is 40 minutes.

81 B

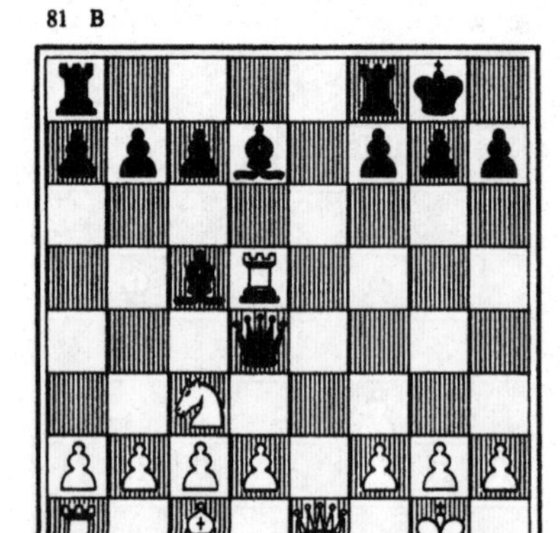

82 W

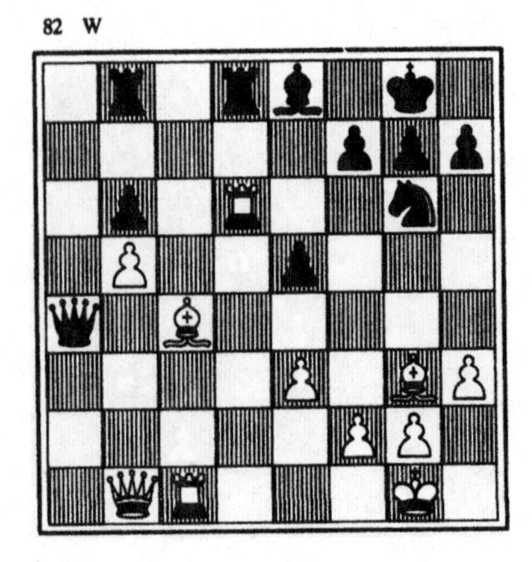

83 W

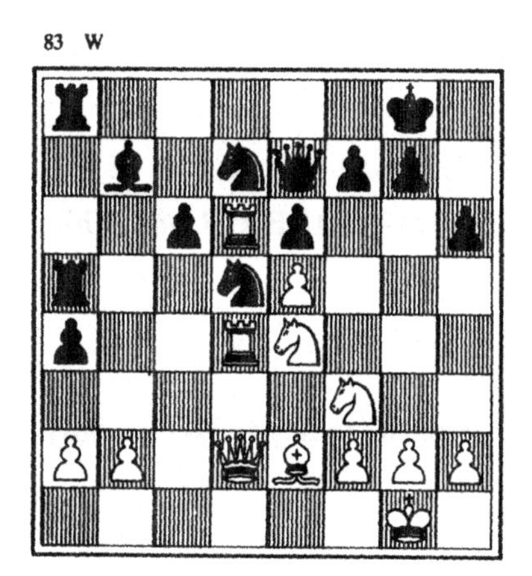

84 W

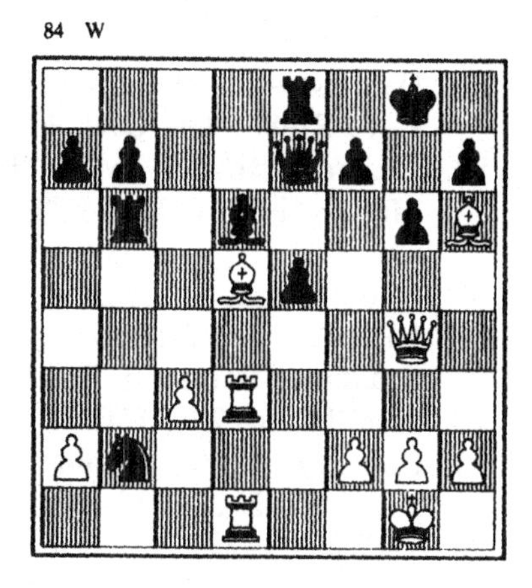

85 B

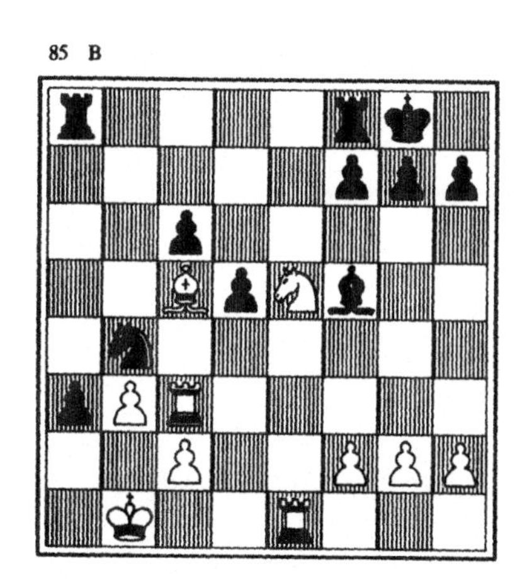

86 W

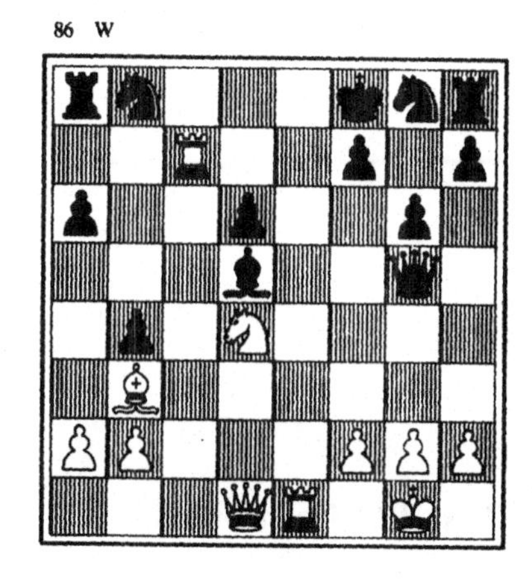

87 B

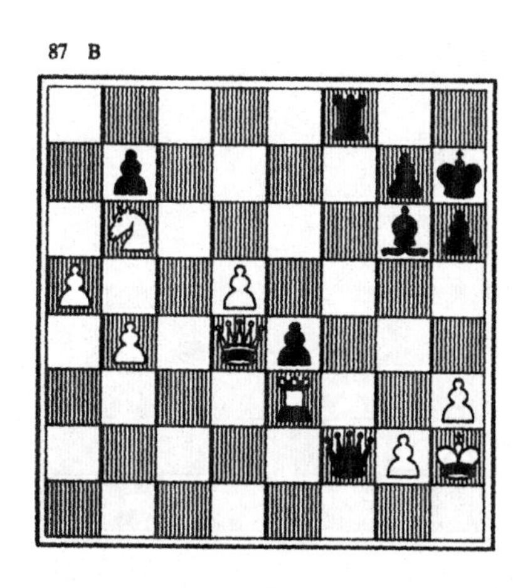

88 W

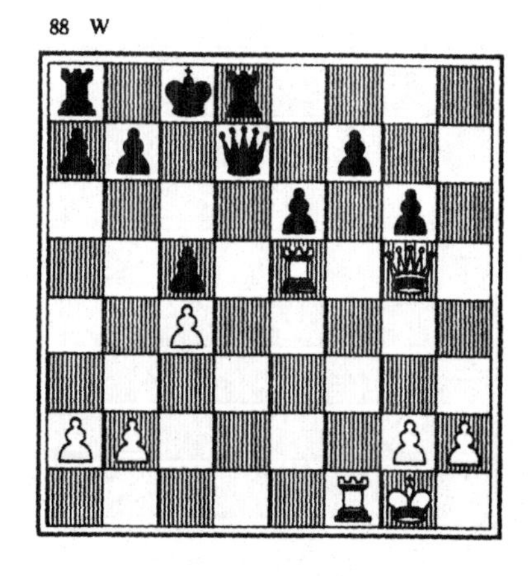

### Solutions to Test 11

81. Danielson–Blomberg, Sweden, 1967.
 1 . . . Rfe8! 2 Qf1 Q×f2+!! 3 Q×f2 Re1 mate.
82. Sakharov–Rovner, Lvov, 1951.
 1 R×g6!! h×g6 2 B×e5 Kf8 (on *2 . . . Rc8* there follows *3 Q×g6!*) 3 B×b8, and White won. On 3 . . . R×b8 there comes 4 Qd3.
83. Holtz–Pangaben, Leipzig, 1960.
 1 R×d7!! Q×d7 2 Nf6+ g×f6 3 Q×h6 Resigns.
84. Kraidman–Bernstein, Tel-Aviv, 1967.
 1 Rf3!! N×d1 2 R×f7 Q×f7 (on *2 . . . Qd8* there follows *3 Rf8* mate) 3 Qd7! Resigns.
85. Hamann–Ornstein, Malmö, 1974.
 1 . . . N×c2! 2 R×c2 Rfe8 3 Bd4 f6! White resigns.
86. Tatarintsev–Zemtsov, Kazan, 1966.
 1 Qf3!! B×b3 (*1 . . . B×f3 2 R×f7* mate) 2 R×f7+!! B×f7 3 Ne6+ Resigns.
87. Quinones–Paoli, Skopje, 1972.
 1 . . . Rf3!! 2 Nc4 Rg3!! 3 Qd2 R×g2+ White resigns.
88. Pichler–Etingen, Montreal, 1967.
 1 R×c5+ Kb8 2 Qe5+ Qd6 3 Rd1!! Resigns.

### Test 12 Positions 89–96

A new theme—'Diversion', one of the most common in practical play. In this test there are eight relatively simple examples. Time for solution 40 minutes.

89 W

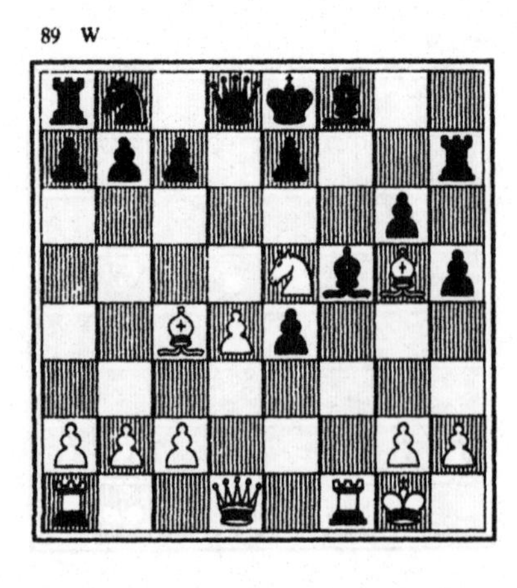

90 W

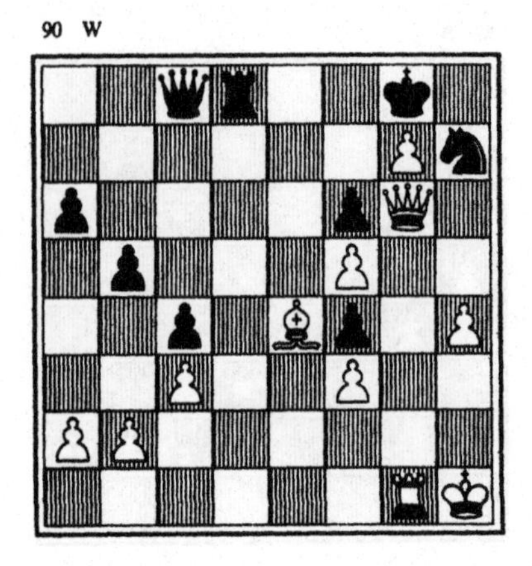

91 W

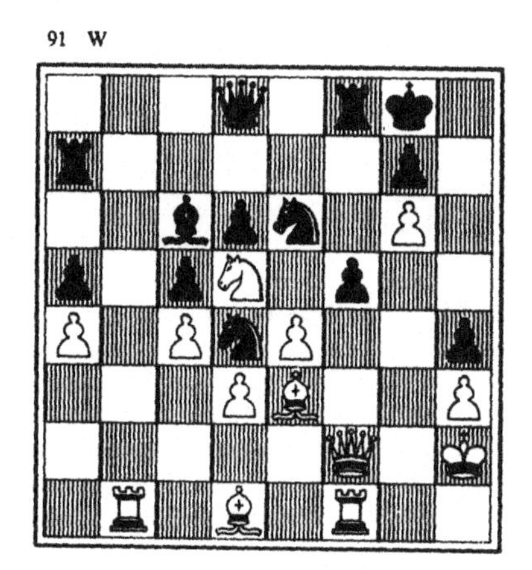

92 W

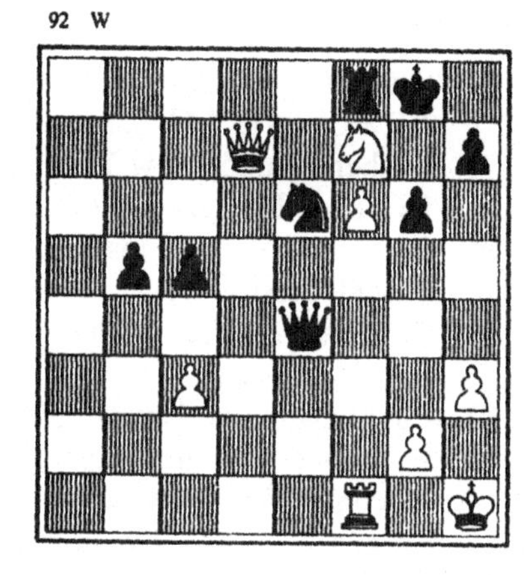

93 B

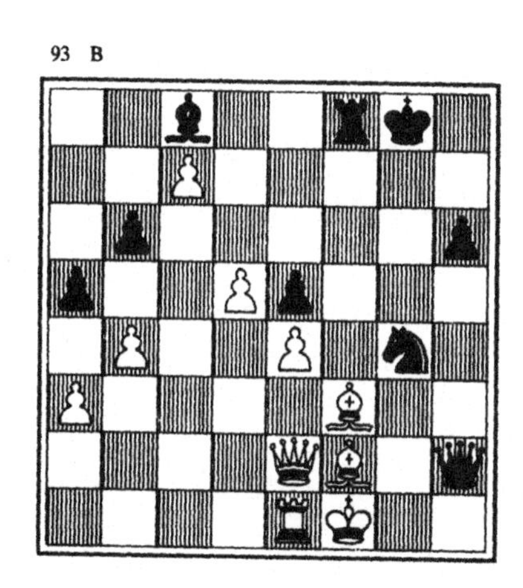

94 W

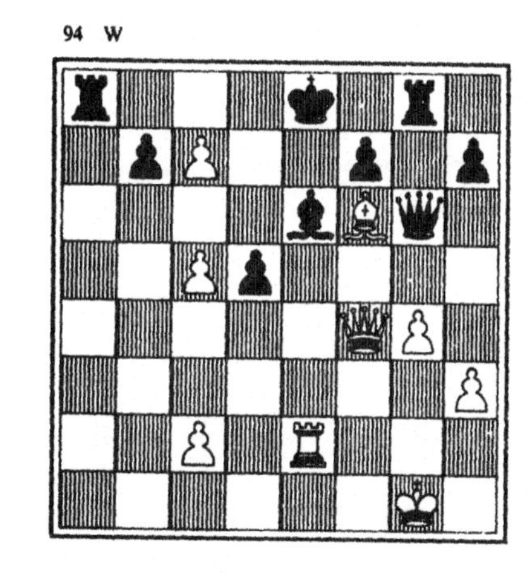

95 B

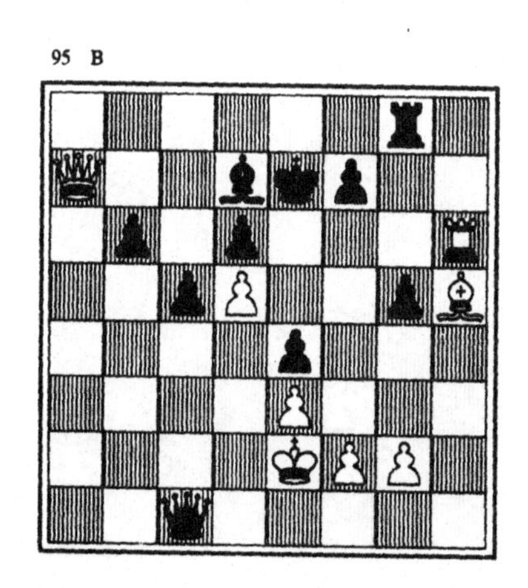

96 B

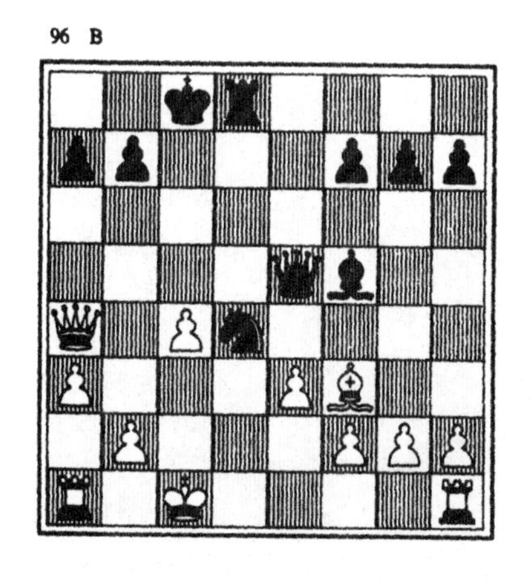

## Solutions to Test 12

89. Shtemberg–Gulnin, USSR, 1968.
 1 R×f5! g×f5 2 Q×h5+! R×h5 3 Bf7 mate.
90. Fischer–Benkö, New York, 1965.
 1 Qe8+!! Resigns (on *1 . . . R×e8* comes *2 Bd5+*, and wins).
91. Botvinnik–Keres, Moscow, 1966.
 1 Rb8!! Resigns (*1 . . . Q×b8* is answered by *2 Q×h4*, with inevitable mate).
92. Reshevsky–Larsen, Palma de Mallorca, 1971.
 1 Ng5!! Resigns.
93. Chekhover–Sokolsky, Leningrad, 1947.
 1 . . . Ba6!! White resigns (*2 b5* is met by *2 . . . B×b5!*).
94. Muchnik–Voronkov, Moscow, 1948.
 1 Qa4+!! R×a4 2 c8=Q mate.
95. Möbius–Hennings, Dresden, 1973.
 1 . . . Ra8!! White resigns (on *2 Q×a8* comes *2 . . . Bb5* mate).
96. Spanier–Lorenz, Hannover, 1965.
 1 . . . Qa5!! White resigns (*2 Q×a5 Nb3* mate, *2 Qd1 Nb3+ 3 Q×b3 Qd2* mate, or *2 Bd1 Ne2+ 3 B×e2 Qd2* mate).

## Test 13 Positions 97–104

The same theme, and a similar degree of difficulty. Therefore the solving time is reduced to 35 minutes.

97 W

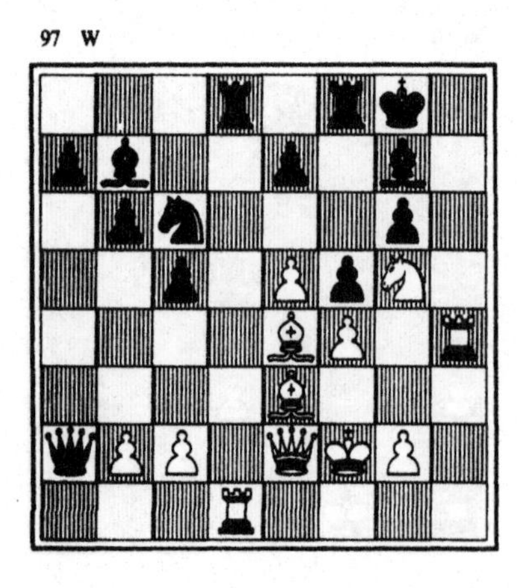

98 B

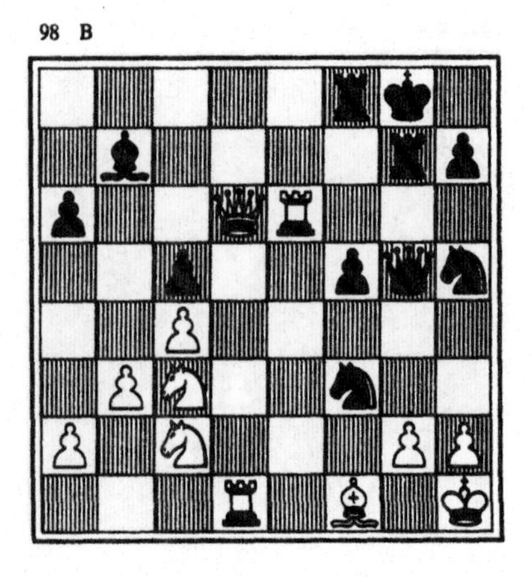

99 W

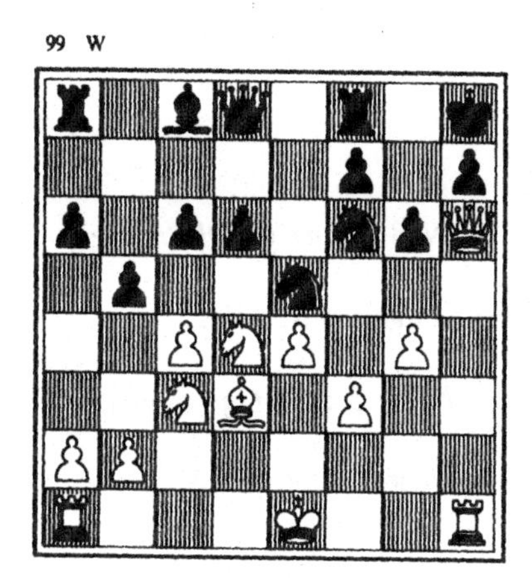

100 B

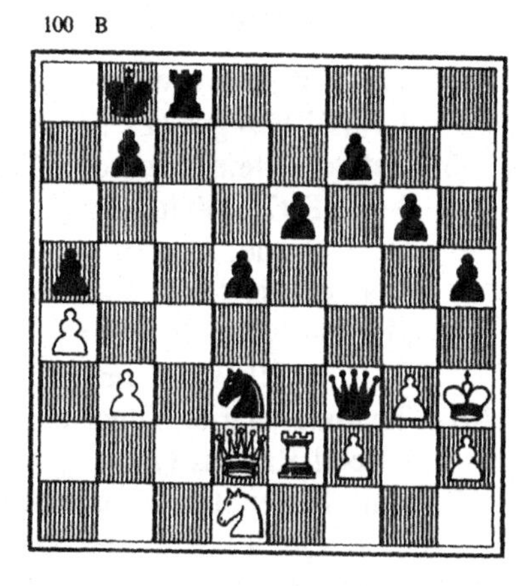

101 W

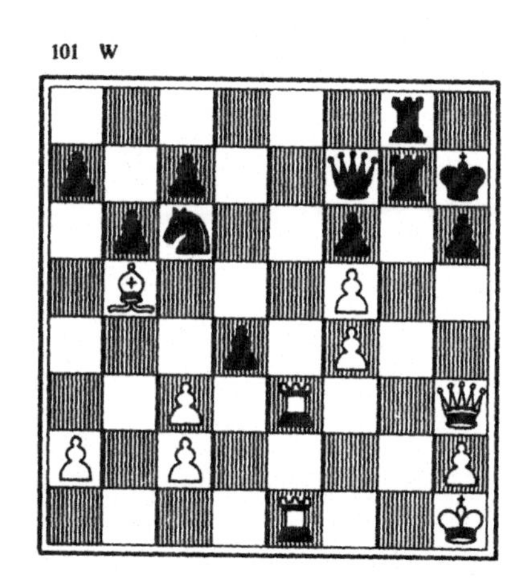

102 B

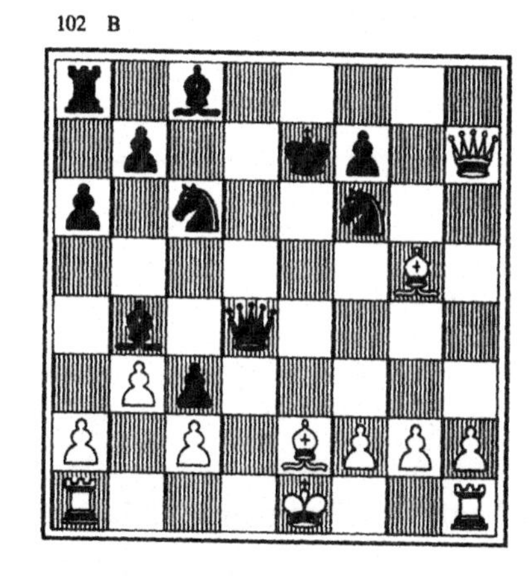

103 W

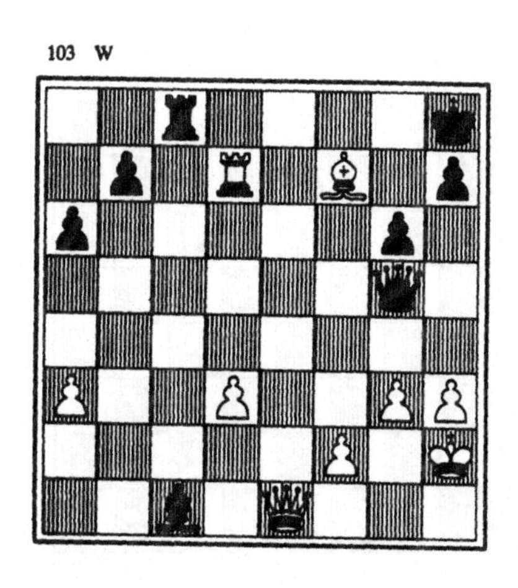

104 W

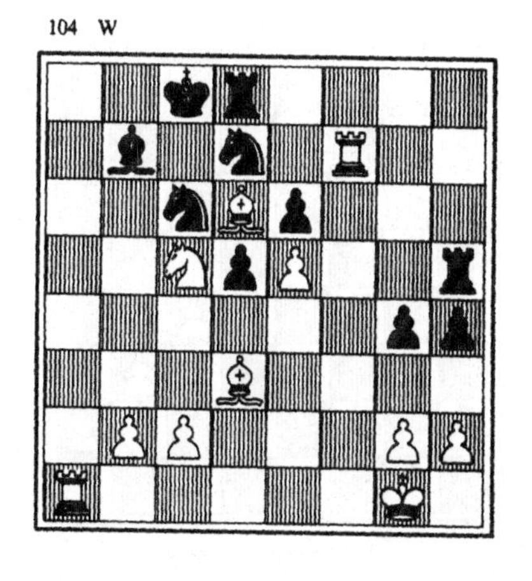

## Solutions to Test 13

97. Tan–Pirc, Beverwijk, 1963.
 1 Ra1!! Resigns (*1 . . . Q×a1 2 Qc4+*).
98. Ustinov–Stein, Moscow, 1965.
 1 . . . Rd7!! White resigns (*2 Q×d7* is met by *2 . . . Ng3+ 3 h×g3 Qh5* mate).
99. Hort–Byrne, R., Varna, 1962.
 1 N×c6!! N×d3+ 2 Kd2 Resigns (there is no defence against *3 Nd5*).
100. Momo–Byrne, R., Varna, 1962.
 1 . . . Rc2!! White resigns (on *2 Q×c2* comes *2 . . . Nf4+ 3 Kh4 Qg4* mate).
101. Pavlovic–Maric, Yugoslavia, 1972.
 1 Bc4!! Resigns (*1 . . . Q×c4* is met by *2 Q×h6+! K×h6 3 Rh3* mate).
102. Hult–Rozenblatt, Stockholm, 1972.
 1 . . . Qd2+! White resigns.
103. Ludolf–Kots, Leningrad, 1962.
 1 Rd8+!! Resigns (*1 . . . R×d8 2 Qc3+*, or *1 . . . Q×d8 2 Qe5+*).
104. Jamieson–Gungaabasar, Nice, 1974.
 1 Ra8+!! Resigns (if *1 . . . B×a8* then *2 Ba6+*, or *1 . . . Ncb8 2 R×b8+! N×b8 3 Rc7* mate).

## Test 14 Positions 105–112

The same theme. The difficulty has increased, but only slightly. Time for solution of this test is 30 minutes.

105 B

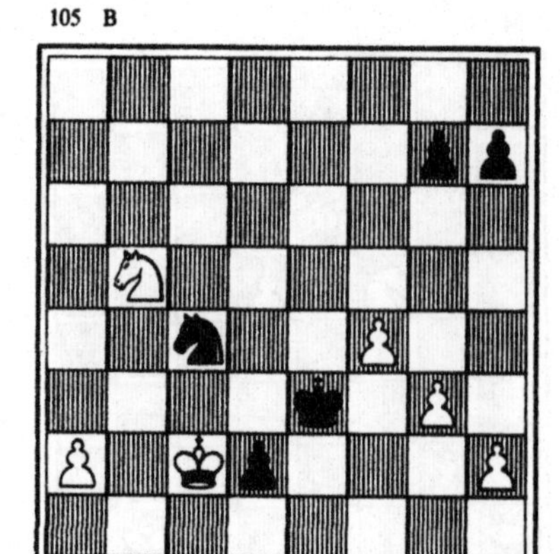

106 W

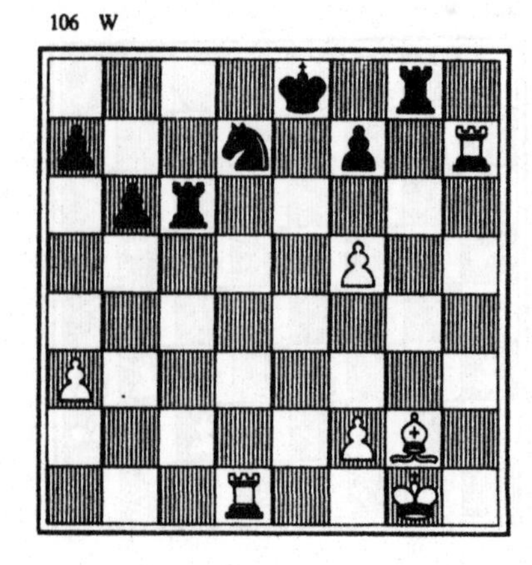

107 B

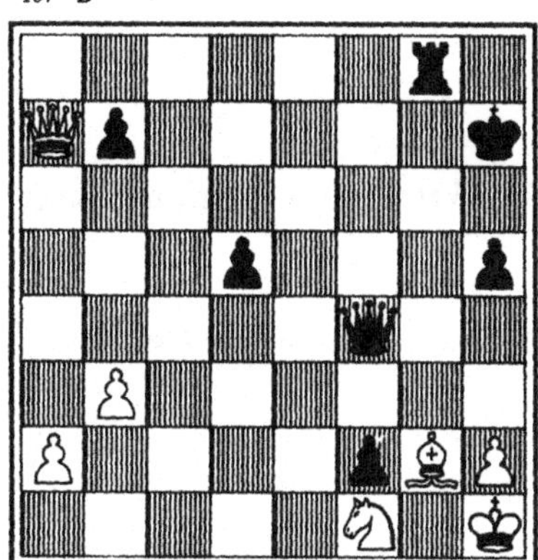

108 B

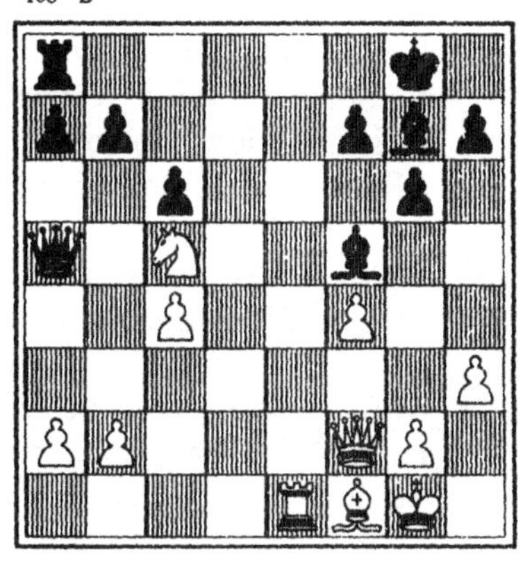

109 W

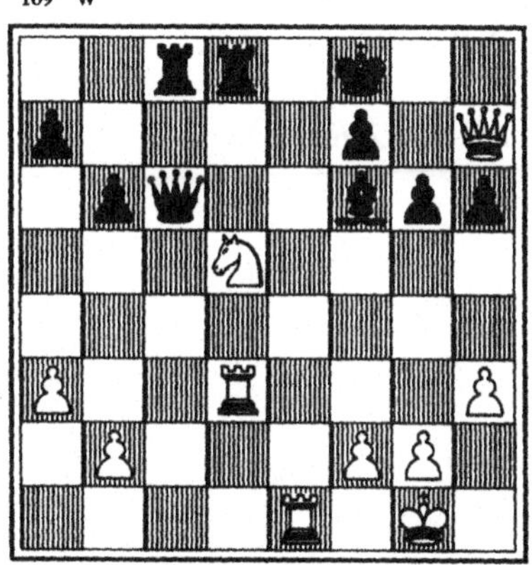

110 B

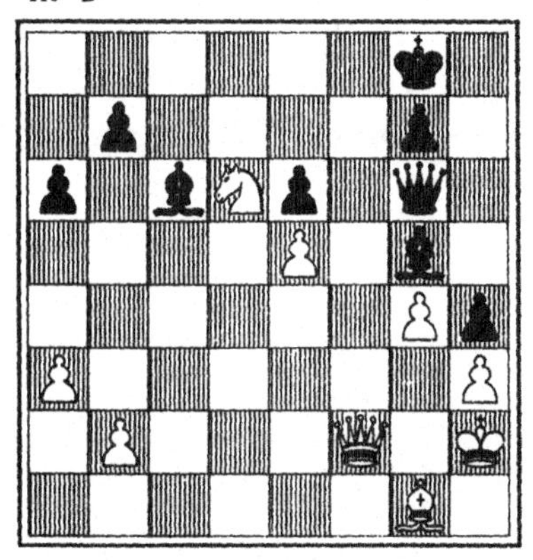

111 W

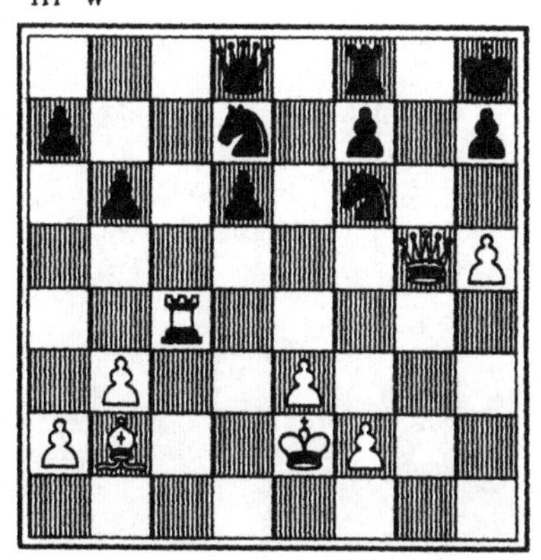

112 W

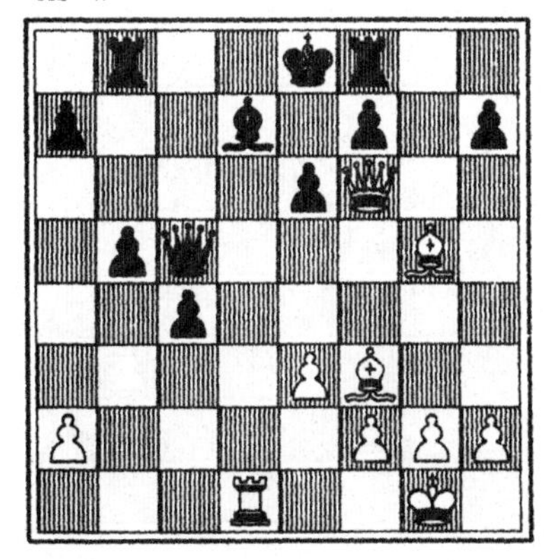

### Solutions to Test 14

105. Barcza–Simagin, Moscow, 1949.
1 . . . Na3+! White resigns (*2 N×a3 Ke2*).
106. Stein–Smyslov, Moscow, 1972.
1 Rh8!!, and White won. After 1 . . . Rg6 2 f×g6 R×h8 3 Bc6 Black came out a piece down, and resigned.
107. Stoltz–Kotov, Stockholm, 1952.
1 . . . Qf3!! White resigns (*2 B×f3* is answered by *2 . . . Rg1* mate, while after *2 Q×b7+ Kh8* there is no perpetual check).
108. Kozma–Alster, Prague, 1952.
1 . . . Bd4!! White resigns.
109. Najdorf–Porat, Amsterdam, 1954.
1 Ne7!! Resigns. The only defence against mate by 2 Qg8 is 1 . . . B×e7, but then comes 2 Qh8 mate.
110. Pantzke–Pakula, Rostock, 1955.
1 . . . Qc2!! White resigns. 2 Q×c2 fails to 2 . . . Bf4 mate, and there is no satisfactory defence.
111. Gunzel–Schwalbe, Berlin, 1966.
1 h6 Rg8 2 Rc8!! Resigns (*2 . . . R×g5 2 R×d8+ Rg8 3 R×d7*).
112. Erbis–Kempf, Stuttgart, 1954.
1 Bc6!! Resigns (*1 . . . Q×c6 2 Qe7* mate, or *1 . . . B×c6 2 Rd8+*).

### Test 15 Positions 113–120

Continuation of the theme of 'Diversion'. Time for thought—35 minutes.

113 W

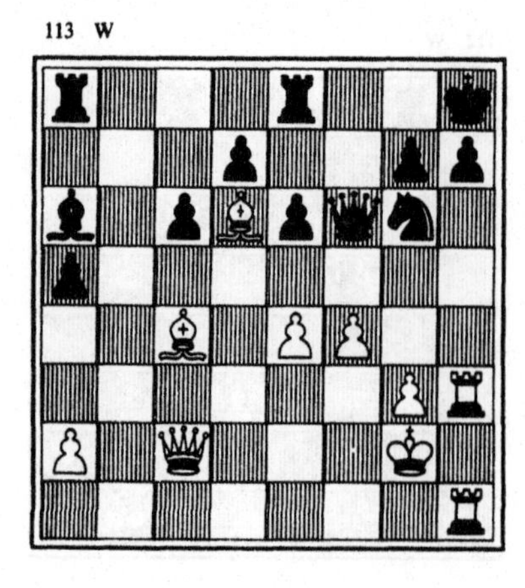

114 B

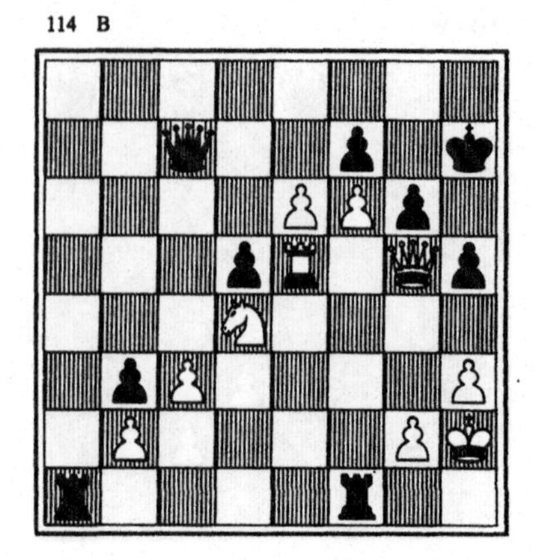

115 B

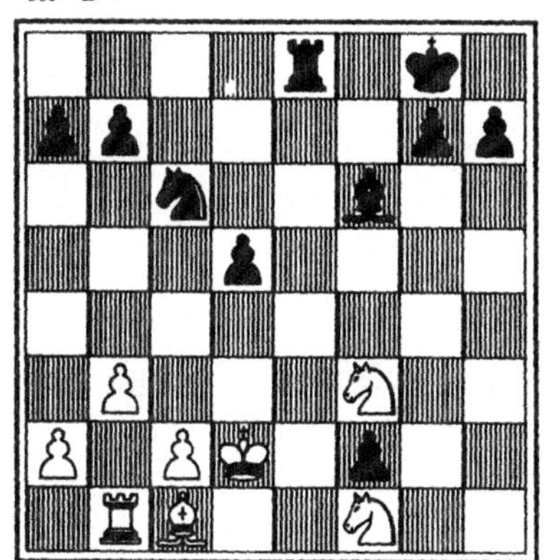

116 W

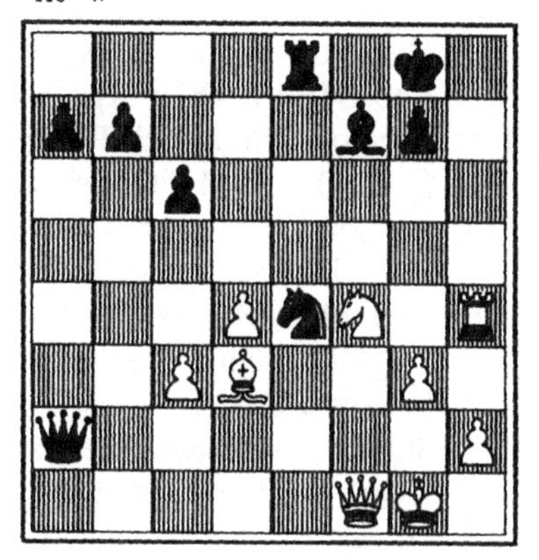

117 W

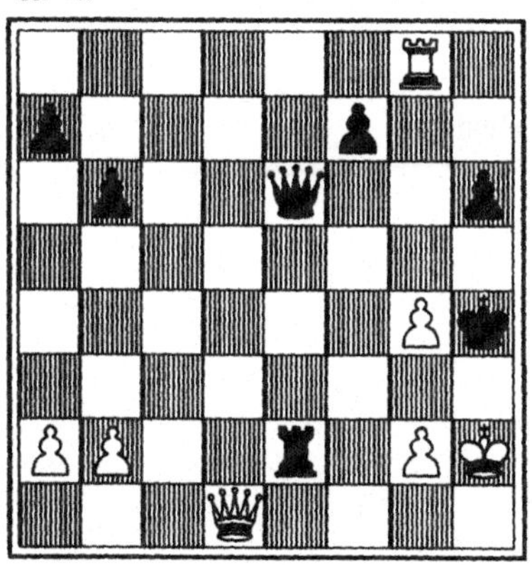

118 W

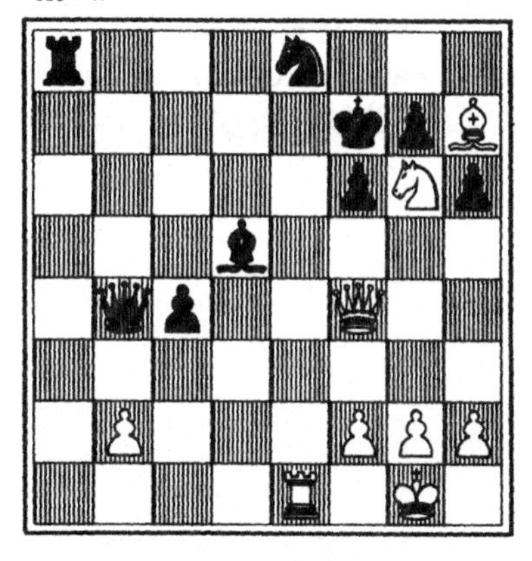

119 W

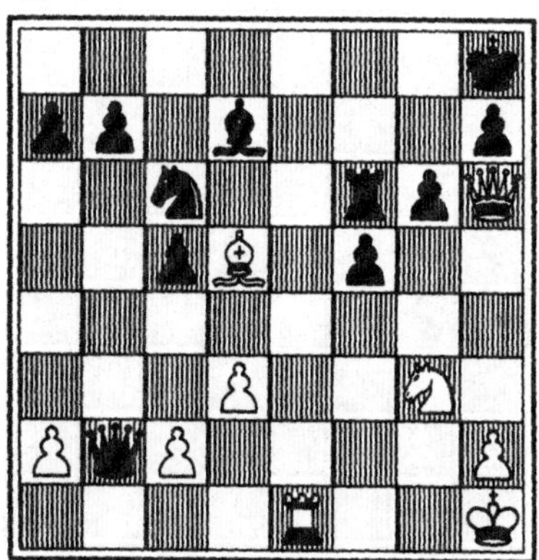

120 W

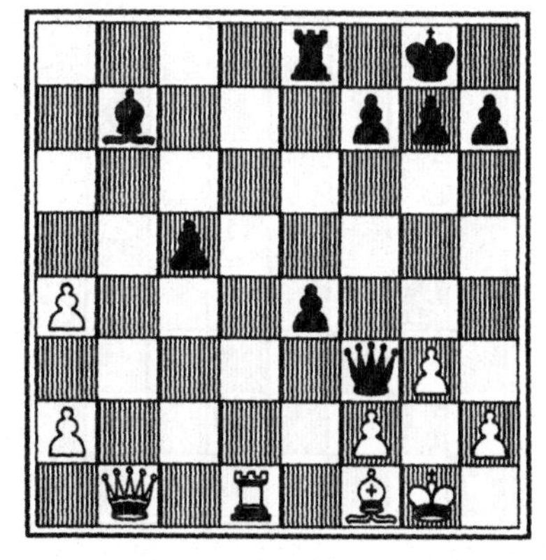

## Solutions to Test 15

113. Gaidarov–Buglak, USSR, 1976.
1 e5 Qf7 2 R×h7+ Kg8 3 Rh8+! Resigns.
114. Lucinovic–Simanski, Poznan, 1953.
1 . . . Q×e5+!! 2 Q×e5 h4! 3 g4 Rf2 mate.
115. Stokloza–Czincel, Krakow, 1965.
1 . . . Re1!! 2 N×e1 Bc3+! White resigns.
116. Golombek–Rossolimo, Venice, 1950.
1 Ng6!! Resigns. The threat is 2 Rh8 mate, and on the only defence 2 . . . B×g6 there follows 3 Bc4+.
117. Stahlberg–Becker, Buenos Aires, 1944.
1 Qe1+!! R×e1 2 g3 mate.
118. Polyak–Kholmov, Riga, 1954 (variation).
1 Qd2!! Qc5 (or *1 . . . Q×d2 2 Re7* mate) 2 Q×d5+, and White wins, since 2 . . . Q×d5 is again answered by 3 Re7 mate. In the game White failed to spot this possibility, and the game ended in a draw.
119. Krutikhin–Chaplinsky, Moscow, 1950.
1 Nh5!! g×h5 2 Rg1! Resigns. Against the two threats of Qg7 mate and Rg8 mate there is no defence.
120. Panchenko–Garcia, Las Palmas, 1978.
1 Qb5! Rb8 (if *1 . . . Rf8*, then *2 Be2!*) 2 Q×b7! Resigns.

## Test 16 Positions 121–128

The final test on the theme 'Diversion'. The time allowed for this test is 35 minutes.

121 W

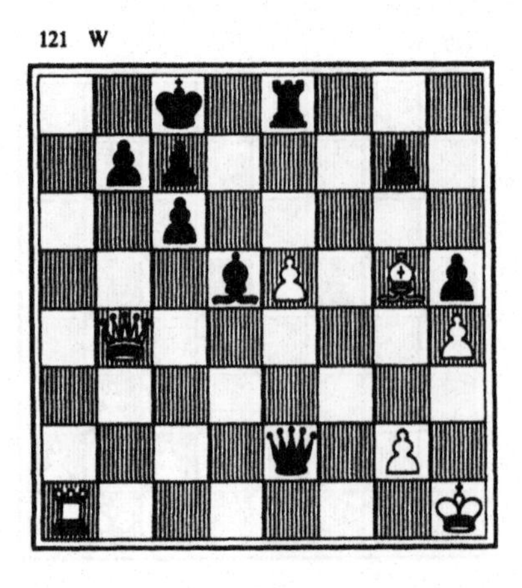

122 W

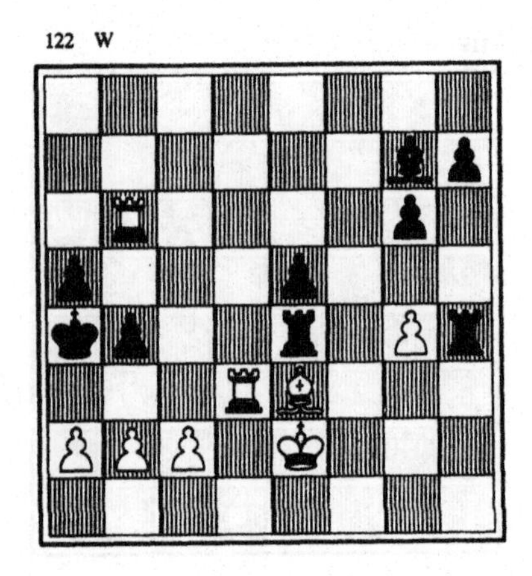

123 B

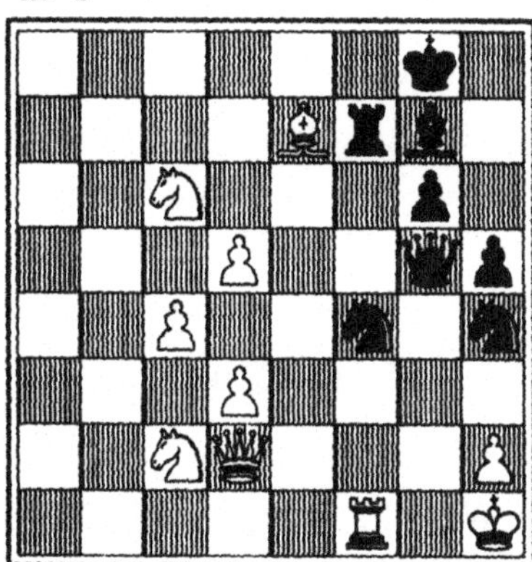

124 W

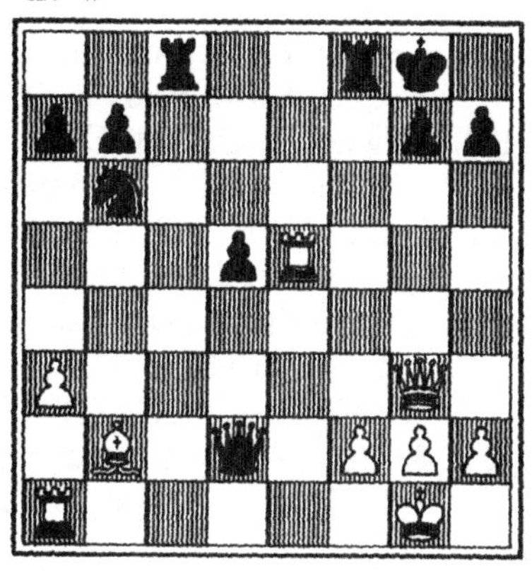

125 B

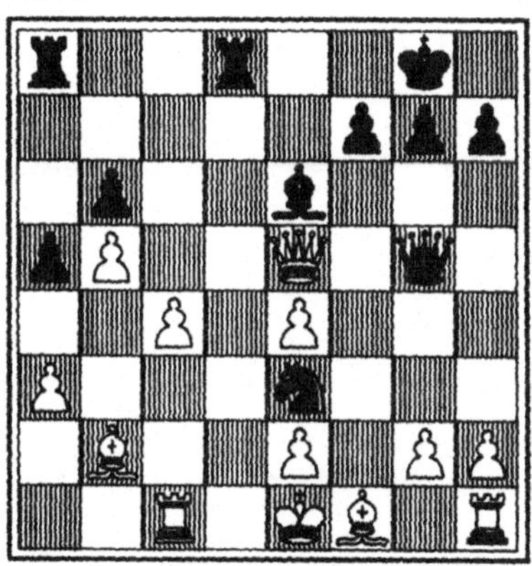

126 W

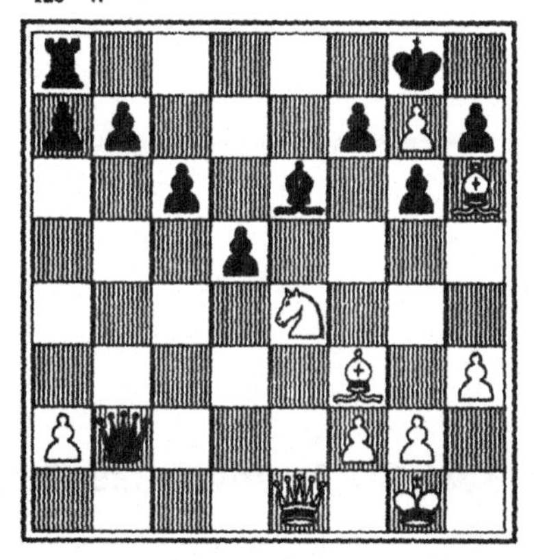

127 B

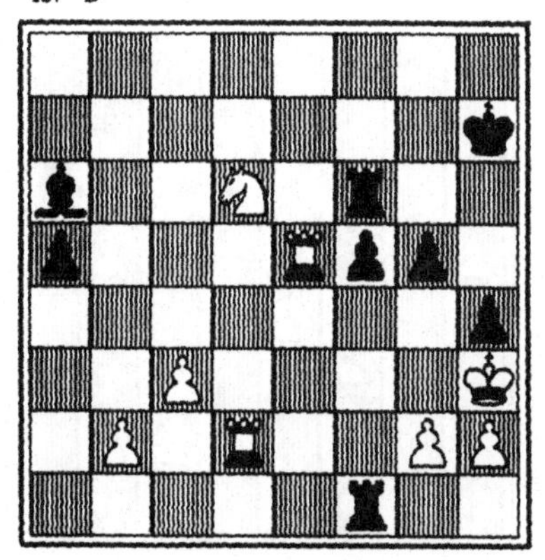

128 W

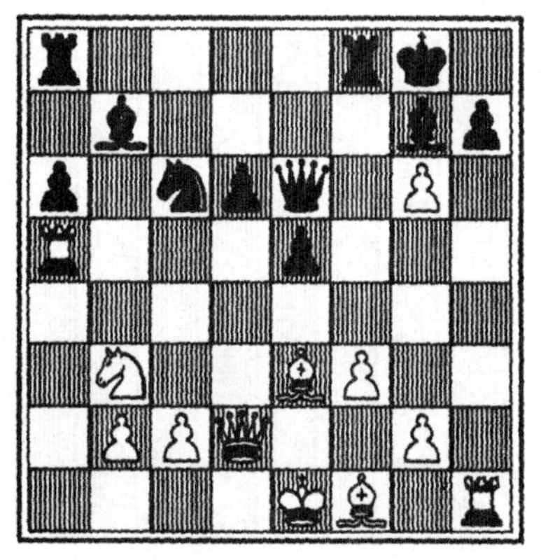

### Solutions to Test 16

121. Georgadze–Kupreichik, Kiev, 1973.
 1 Ra8+ Kd7 2 Rd8+!! Resigns.
122. Shablinsky–Ushkal, Corr., 1974.
 1 Ra3+!! b×a3 2 b3 mate.
123. Evans–Grefe, USA, 1973.
 1 . . . Nh3!! 2 Qe2 Qd2!! White resigns.
124. Lukacs–Blackstock, Budapest, 1977.
 1 Re2! Qh6 2 Re6! g6 3 Qe5 (threatening *4 Re7*; if *3 . . . Rf5 4 Q×f5*, or *3 . . . Nc4 4 Q×d5*) 3 . . . Nd7 4 Q×d5 Resigns.
125. Kurtesch–Flesch, Budapest, 1966.
 1 . . . Rd1+!! 2 R×d1 (on *2 Kf2* there follows *2 . . . Ng4+*) 2 . . . Nc2+ 3 Kf2 Qe3 mate.
126. Wallis–Horseman, Nottingham, 1954.
 1 Qb4!! Qa1+ (if *1 . . . Q×b4* then *2 Nf6* mate) 2 Bd1!! Resigns.
127. Man–Papp, Budapest, 1956.
 1 . . . R×d6!! 2 R×d6 Rf3+!! 3 g×f3 Bf1 mate.
128. Adorjan–Fuller, London, 1975.
 1 Q×d6! Q×d6 2 Bc4+ Rf7 3 B×f7+ Kf8 4 Bc5 h×g6 5 Bc4! Resigns.

## Test 17 Positions 129–136

A new theme, which occurs in practice almost as frequently as the previous one. The theme goes by the name of 'Decoy'. The positions are relatively simple. Time for solution of the whole test—40 minutes.

129 B

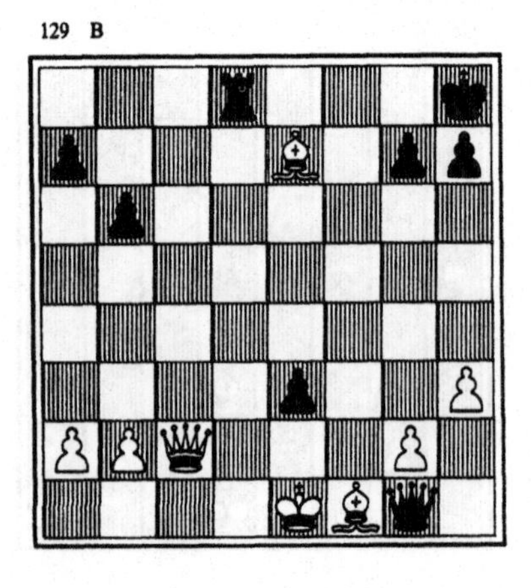

130 W

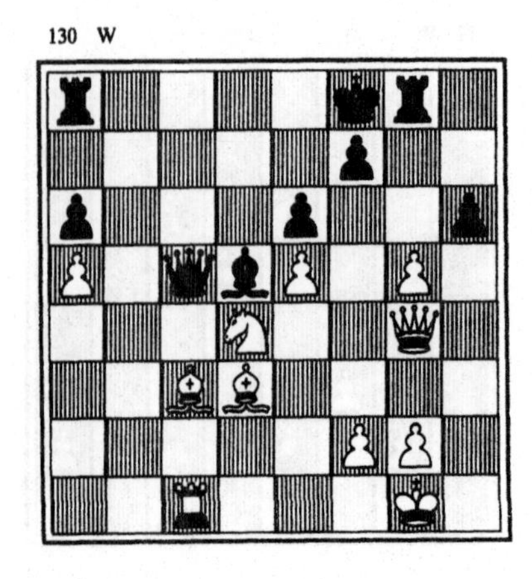

131 W

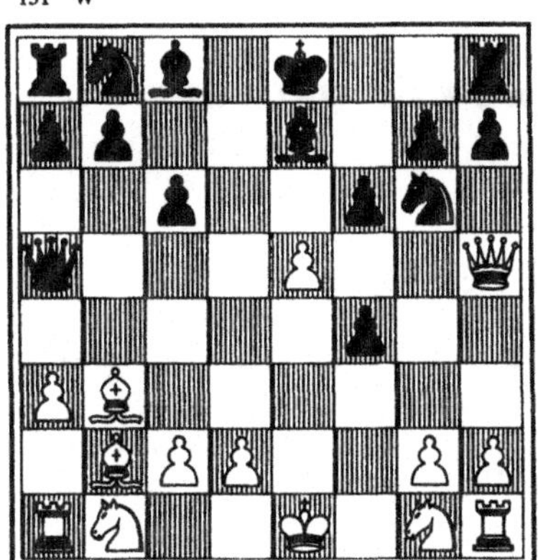

132 W

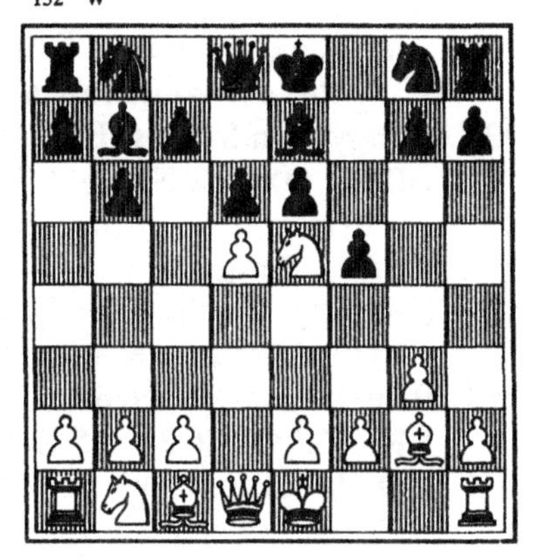

133 W

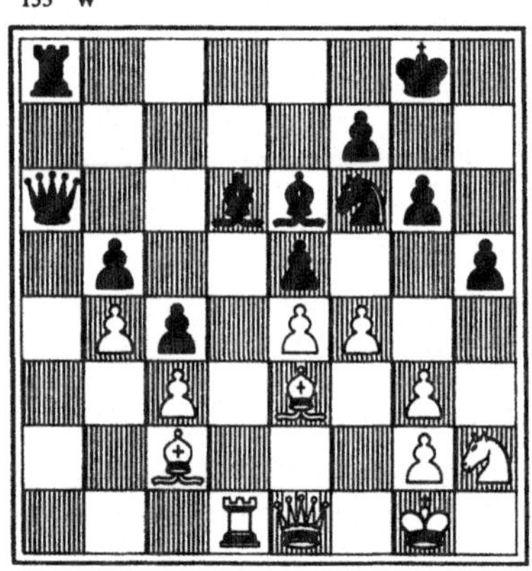

134 B

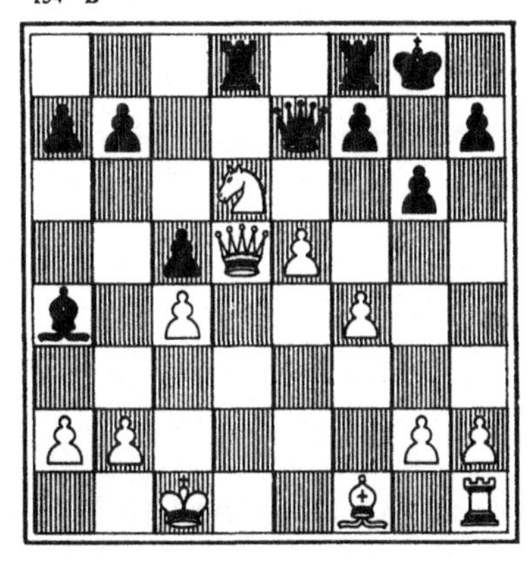

135 W

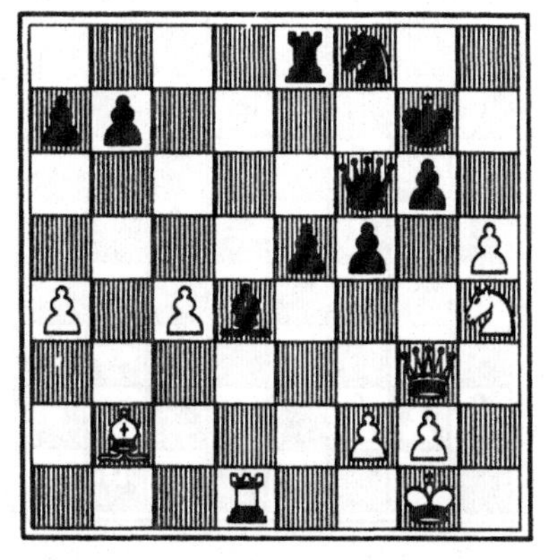

136 W

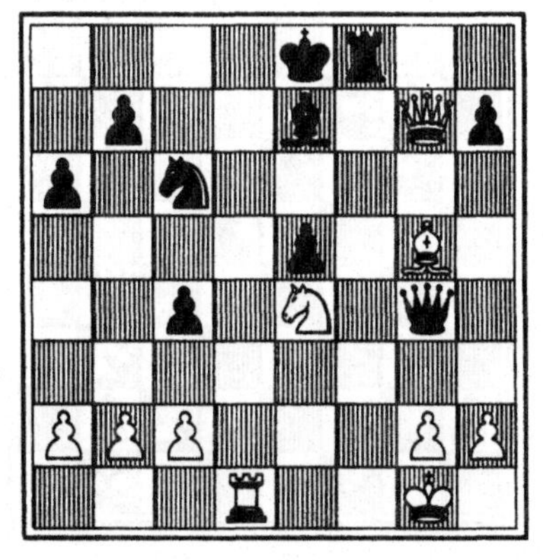

## Solutions to Test 17

129. Zeek–Link, Flensburg, 1959.
1 . . . Rd1+!! White resigns (*2 Q×d1 Qf2* mate, or *2 K×d1 Q×f1* mate).
130. Szilágyi–van Steenis, Budapest, 1949.
1 Bd4!! Q×b4 2 N×e6+! Resigns.
131. Katalymov–Ilivitsky, Frunze, 1959.
1 Bf7+! Resigns (*1 . . . K×f7 2 e6+*, or *1 . . . Kf8 2 B×g6*).
132. Zaverbny–Gumlius, Brussels, 1953.
1 Nf7!! K×f7 2 d×e6+, and White won the exchange and the game.
133. Blau–Donner, Wageningen, 1958.
1 R×d6!! Q×d6 2 f×e5 Resigns (*2 . . . Q×e5 3 Bf4!*).
134. Estrada–Gligoric, Varna, 1962.
1 . . . R×d6! 2 Q×d6 Rd8! White resigns.
135. Averbakh–Penrose, London, 1954.
1 R×d4!! f4 (or *1 . . . e×d4 2 B×d4 Q×d4 3 N×f5+!*) 2 R×f4! Resigns.
136. Walther–Bhend, Zurich, 1964.
1 Rd8+!! K×d8 (*1 . . . B×d8 2 Nd6* mate, or *1 . . . N×d8 2 Q×e7* mate) 2 B×e7+ Resigns.

## Test 18 Positions 137–144

Compared with the previous test, this is somewhat more difficult. Time for thought 45 minutes.

137 B

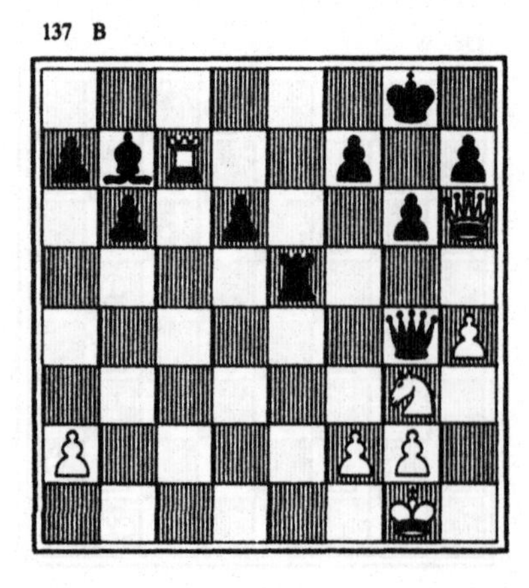

138 B

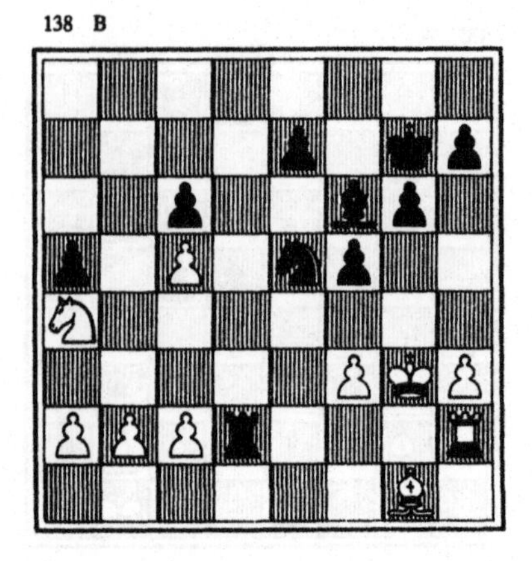

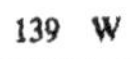

139 W

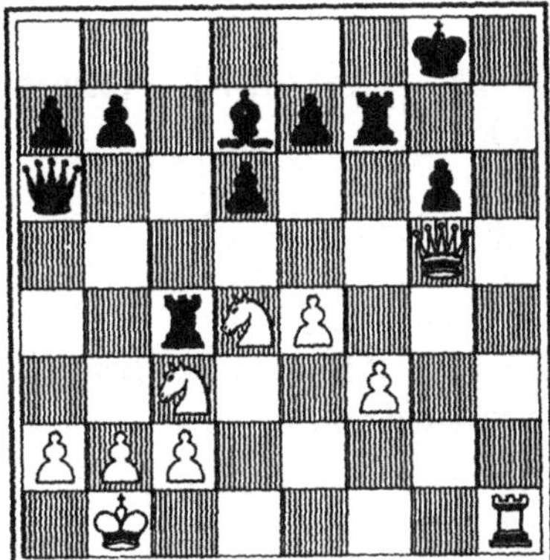

140 B

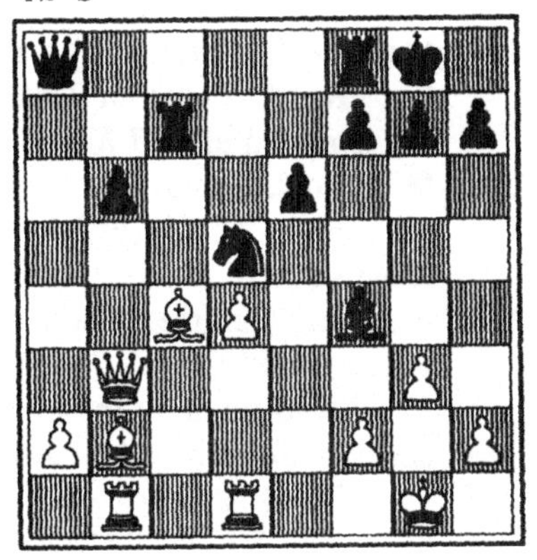

141 W

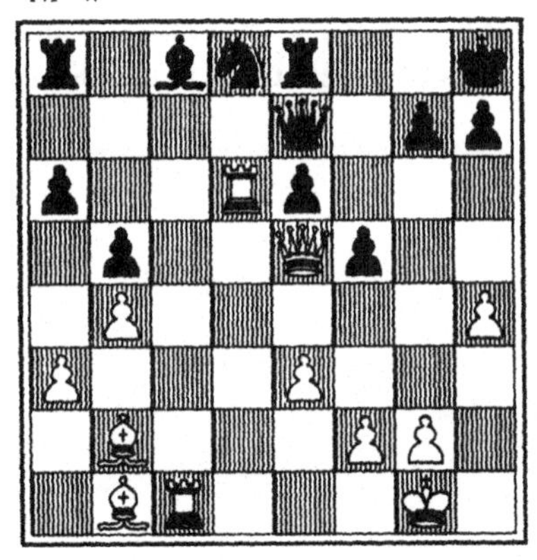

142 W

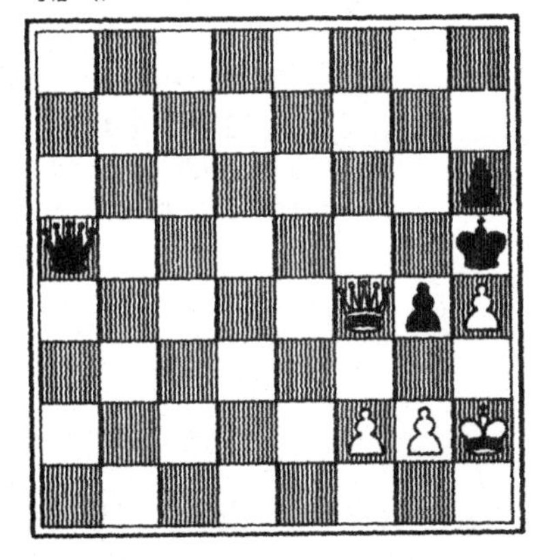

143 B

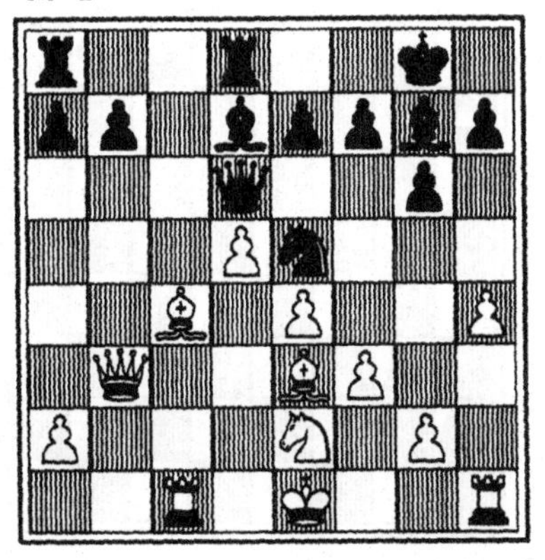

144 B

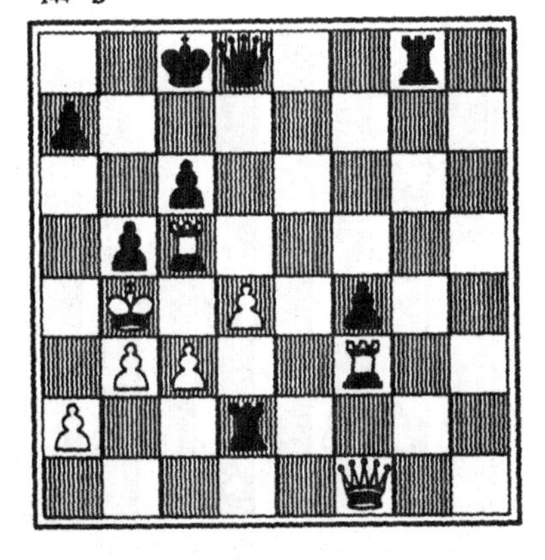

## Solutions to Test 18

137. Madler–Uhlmann, Aschersleben, 1963.
1 . . . Re1+! 2 Kh2 (or *2 Nf1 R×f1+ 3 K×f1 Qd1* mate) 2 . . . Rh1+!! White resigns (he is mated after *3 K×h1 Qh3+ 4 Kg1 Q×g2* mate).
138. Milyutin–Lazarev, Kiev, 1968.
1 . . . Bh4+!! 2 Kf4 (or *2 K×h4 N×f3+ 3 Kg3 N×h2 4 B×h2 f4+!*) 2 . . . Nc4!! White resigns (there is no defence against *3 . . . e5* mate).
139. Essegern–Kummer, Halle, 1969.
1 Ne6!! Rf6 (if *1 . . . B×e6*, then *2 Q×g6+ Rg7 3 Qe8* mate) 2 Rh8+!! Resigns (if *2 . . . K×h8*, then *3 Qh6+*, or *2 . . . Kf7 3 Rf8+ K×e6 4 Qd5* mate).
140. Lisitsyn–Smyslov, Moscow, 1944.
1 . . . R×c4!! 2 Q×c4 Ne3!!, and Black wins. On 3 f×e3 there follows 3 . . . B×e3+ 4 Kf1 Qf3+ 5 Ke1 Qf2 mate.
141. Muffang–Defos, Corr., 1948.
1 Rc7!! Q×c7 2 R×d8! Resigns.
142. van Steenis–Handke, Detmold, 1953.
1 Qf7+! K×h4 2 Qg6!! Resigns (*2 . . . Qe5+* is met by *3 g3+ Q×g3+ 4 f×g3* mate).
143. Naranja–Portisch, Siegen, 1970.
1 . . . b5!! 2 Bd3 (*2 B×b5* is answered by *2 . . . Rab8 3 a4 a6*) 2 . . . Qb4+ White resigns. On 3 Q×b4 comes 3 . . . N×d3+ and 4 . . . N×b4, while if 3 Kf1 or 3 Kd1, then 3 . . . Q×b3 4 a×b3 N×d3.
144. Silversen–Podgorny, Corr., 1949.
1 . . . Qa5+!! 2 K×a5 R×a2+ 3 Kb4 a5 mate.

### Test 19 Positions 145–152

Similar to the previous test in complexity; time for solving 40 minutes, and for a correct solution score 40 points.

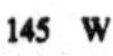
145 W

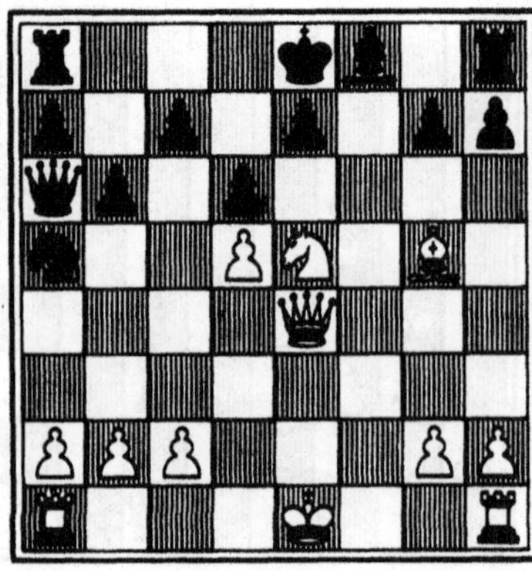

146 W

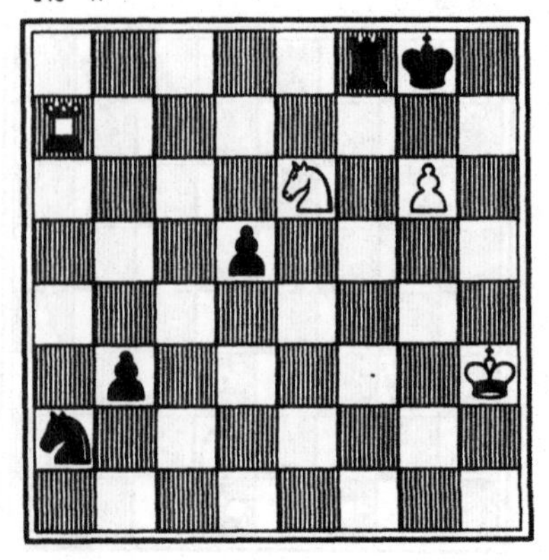

147 W

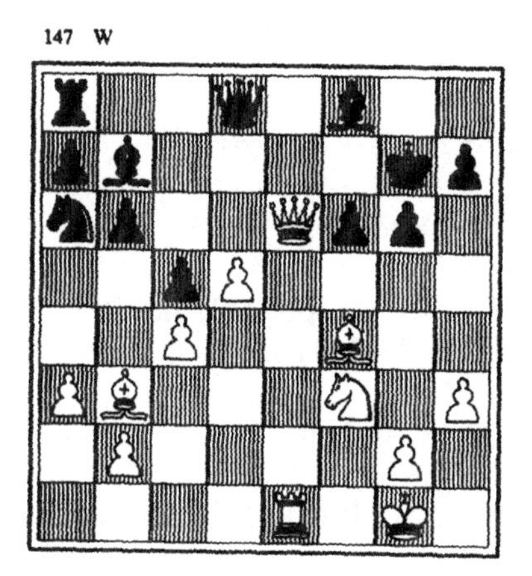

148 W

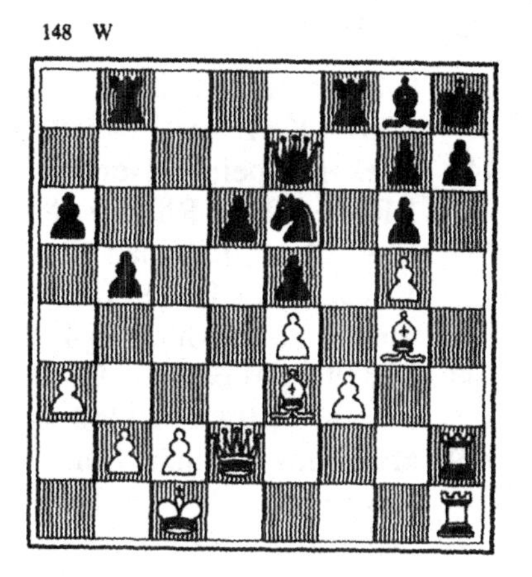

149 W

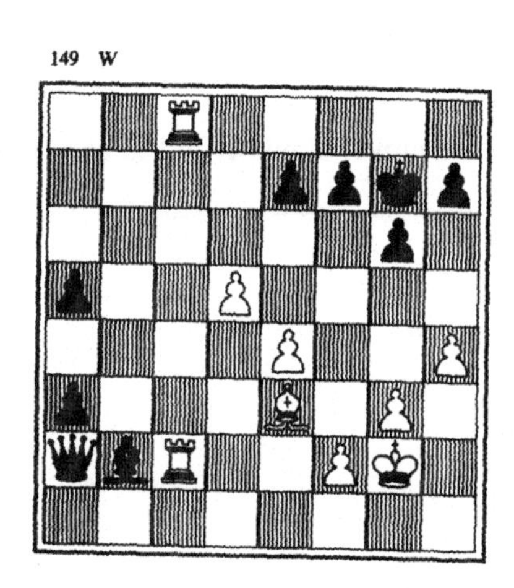

150 W

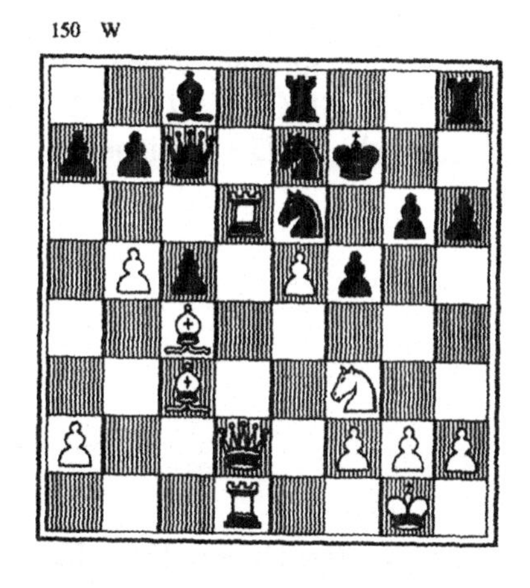

151 W

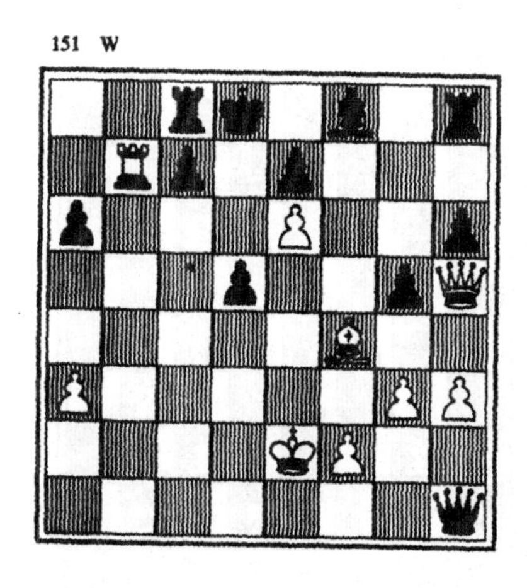

152 W

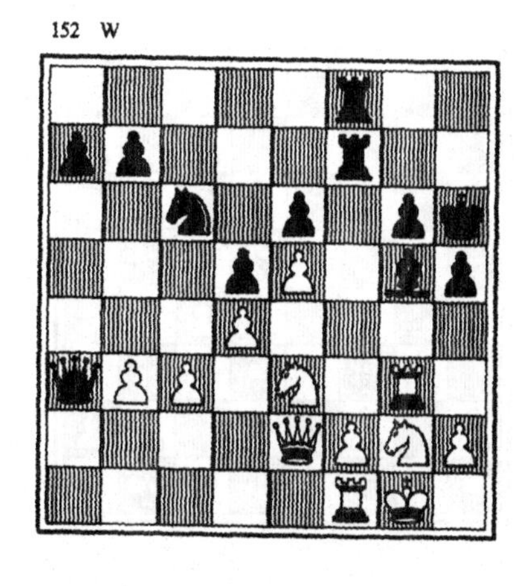

## *Solutions to Test 19*

145. Sokolsky–Kofman, Kiev, 1948.
1 Nf7!! K×f7 (or *1 . . . Rg8 2 Q×h7*) 2 Rf1+ Ke8 3 R×f8+ Resigns.
146. Bilek–Kuijpers, Beverwijk, 1966.
1 Rg7+ Kh8 2 Rh7+ Kg8 3 Rh8+!! Resigns (*3 . . . K×h8 4 g7+*).
147. Uusi–Etruk, Estonian Ch., 1976.
1 Ne5! Qe8 2 Bh6+! (in the game the less strong *2 Qd7+* was played), and White wins: 2 . . . K×h6 3 Ng4+, or 2 . . . Kh8 3 Q×e8 R×e8 4 N×g6+.
148. Kimelfeld–Bukulin, Moscow Ch., 1976.
1 R×h7+! B×h7 2 Qh2 Kg8 3 Q×h7+ Kf7 4 Q×g6+! Resigns.
149. Maksimov–Oleinik, Corr., 1977.
1 Rg8+! Kf6 (*1 . . . K×g8 2 Bh6 f5 3 Rc8+ Kf7 4 Rf8* mate) 2 Bd4+ e5 3 Rc6+ Ke7 4 Bc5+ Kd7 5 Ra6! followed by 6 Ra7 mate.
150. I. Zaitsev–Bonch-Osmolovsky, Moscow, 1969.
1 B×e6+ B×e6 2 R×e6! K×e6 3 Q×h6!! Resigns (if *3 . . . R×h6*, then *4 Ng5* mate, while on *3 . . . Q×e5* there follows *4 Ng5+ Kf6 5 Rd6* mate).
151. Winz–Videla, Mendoza, 1955.
1 B×c7+! R×c7 2 Qe8+!! K×e8 3 Rb8+ Resigns.
152. Pavlov–Stolyar, Varna, 1970.
1 R×g5! K×g5 2 Qd2! Q×b3 (desperation, but other moves similarly fail to save Black) 3 Nf5+ Resigns.

## Test 20 Positions 153–160

A new theme, 'Interference'. The time allotted for this test is 45 minutes.

153 B

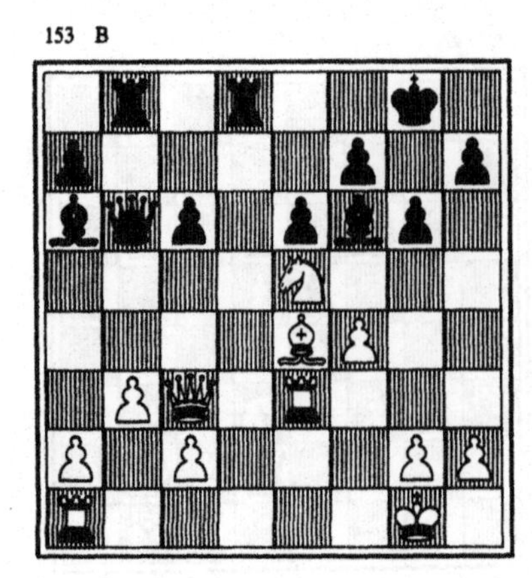

154 W

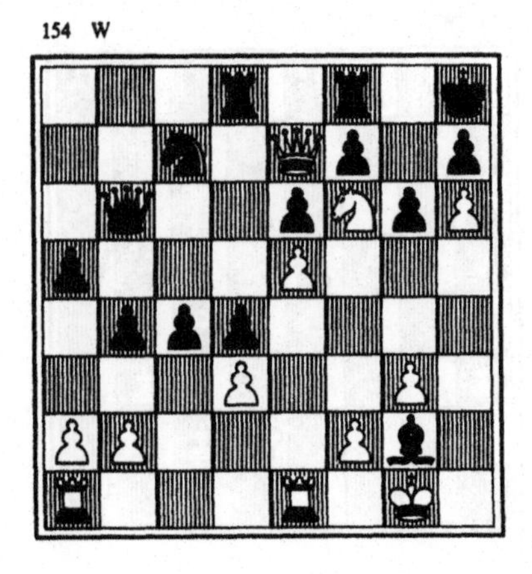

155 W

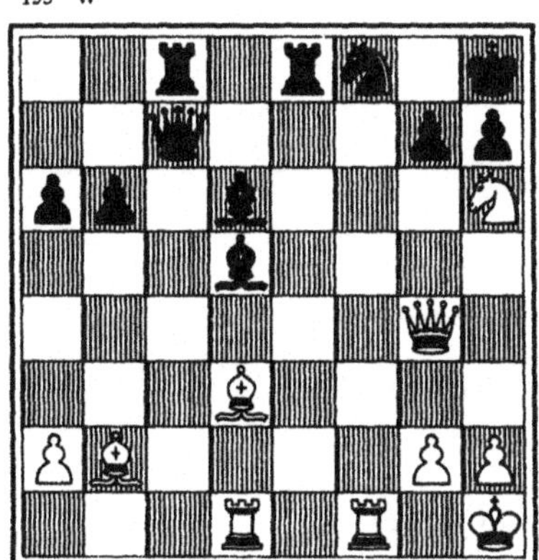

156 W

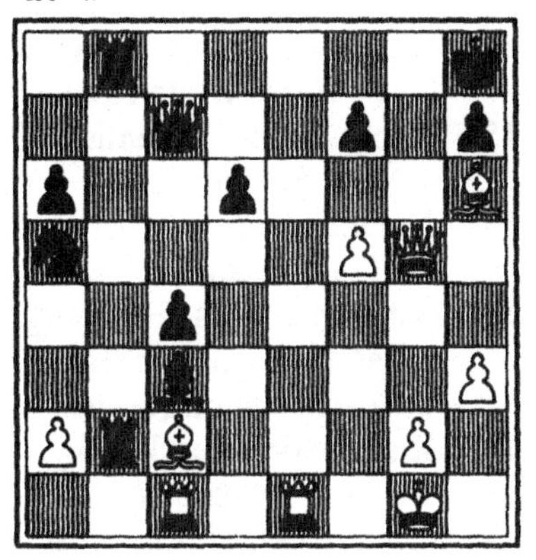

157 W

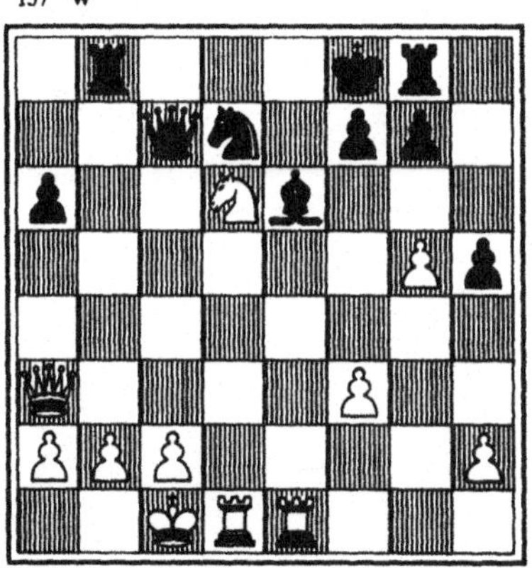

158 B

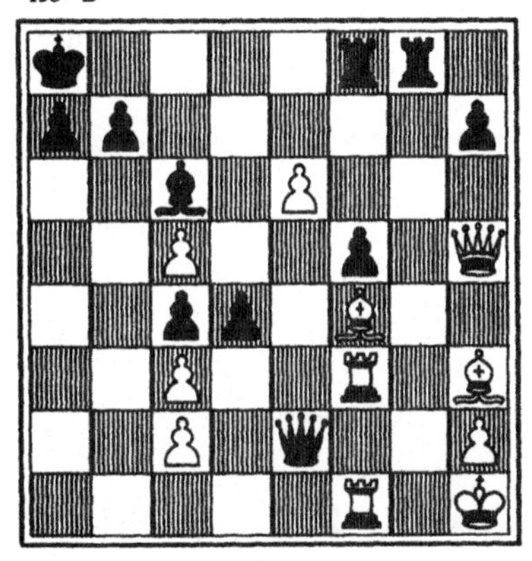

159 B

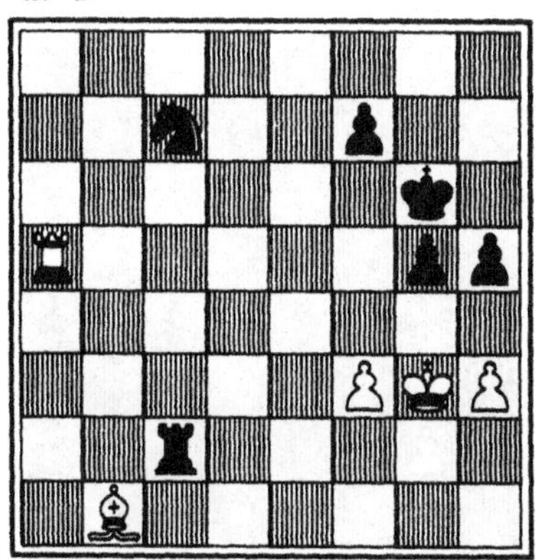

160 W

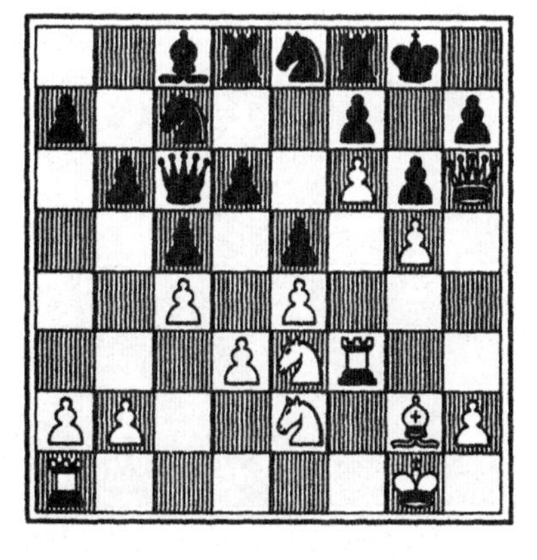

## *Solutions to Test 20*

153. Kaminsky–Osnos, Leningrad, 1968.
   1 . . . Bd3!! White resigns.
154. Zilbershtain–Dementiev, Grozny, 1968.
   1 Ne8!! Resigns.
155. Najdorf–Matanovic, Mar del Plata, 1961.
   1 Nf7+!! Resigns.
156. Sämisch–Ahues, Hamburg, 1946.
   1 Re5!! Resigns. The immediate 1 f6 does not work on account of 1 . . . Qc5+, with the exchange of queens.
157. Kupreichik–Tseshkovsky, 44th USSR Ch., 1976.
   1 Nc8+! Resigns (*1 . . . Nc5 2 Q×c5+! Q×c5 3 Rd8* mate).
158. Lilienthal–Ragozin, Moscow, 1946.
   1 . . . Rg4!! White resigns (*2 B×g4 Q×f1* mate, or *2 Q×g4 f×g4*, and wins).
159. Tavernier–Grodner, Charleville, 1952.
   1 . . . h4+! 2 Kg4 f5+! 3 R×f5 Rg2 mate.
160. Reshevsky–Persitz, Haifa, 1958.
   1 Nf5!! Resigns. On 1 . . . g×f5 there follows 2 Rh3!, while after 1 . . . B×f5 2 e×f5 there is no defence against Rh3.

## Test 21 Positions 161–168

We repeat the theme of 'Interference', but the test is significantly more difficult. Time to complete it 60 minutes.

161 W

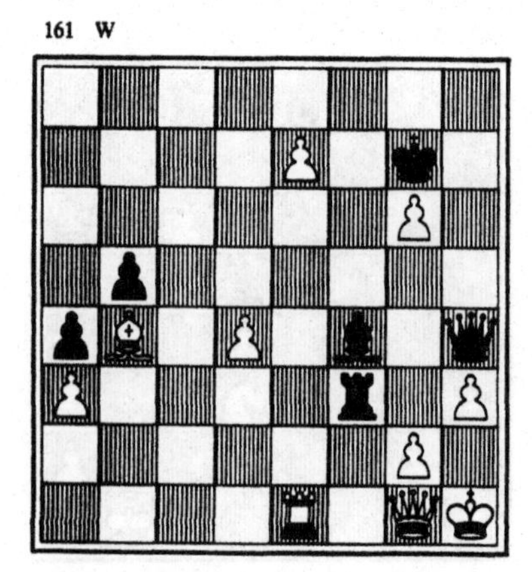

162 B

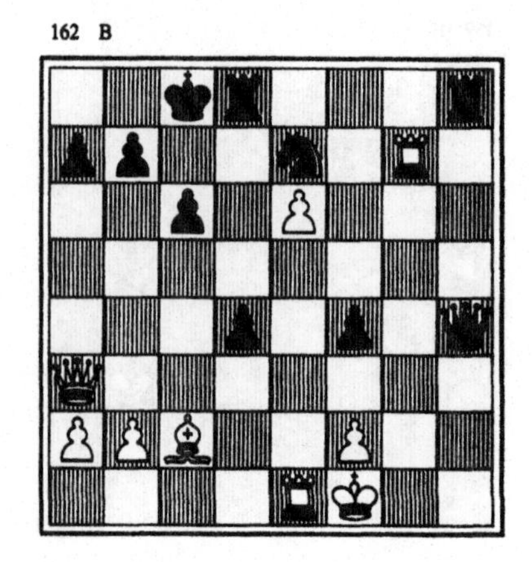

163 W

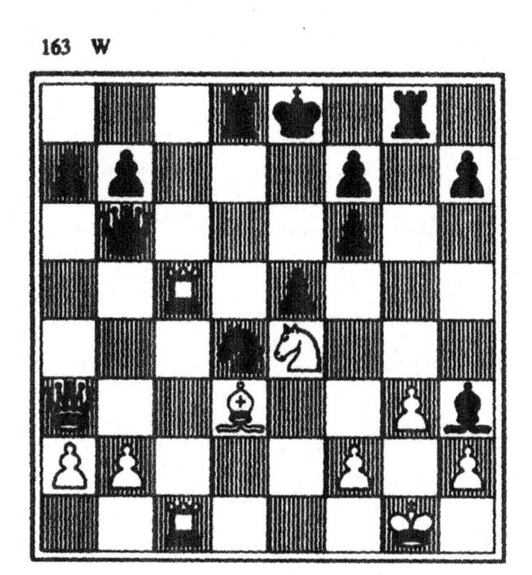

164 W

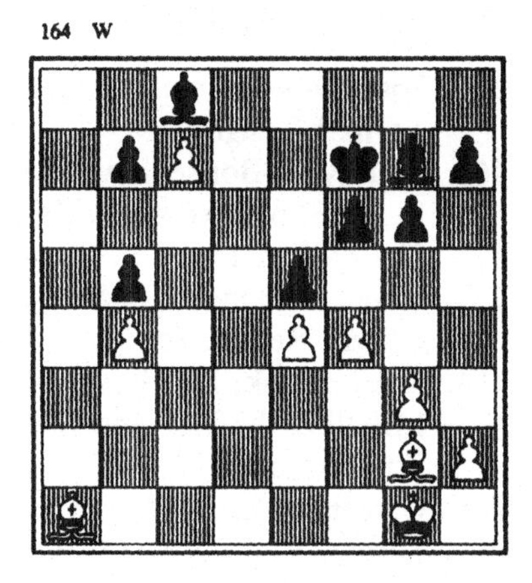

165 W

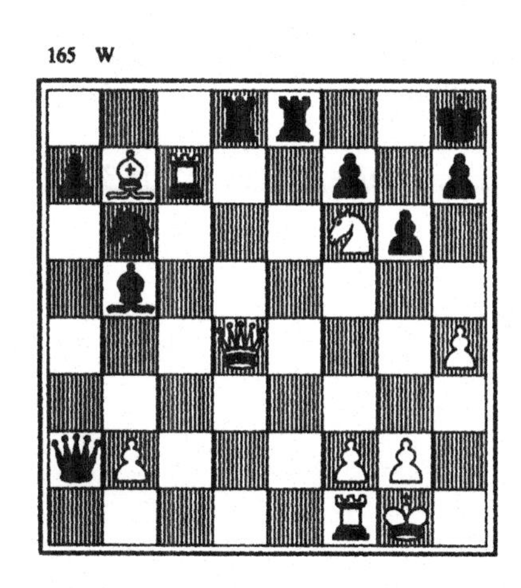

166 W

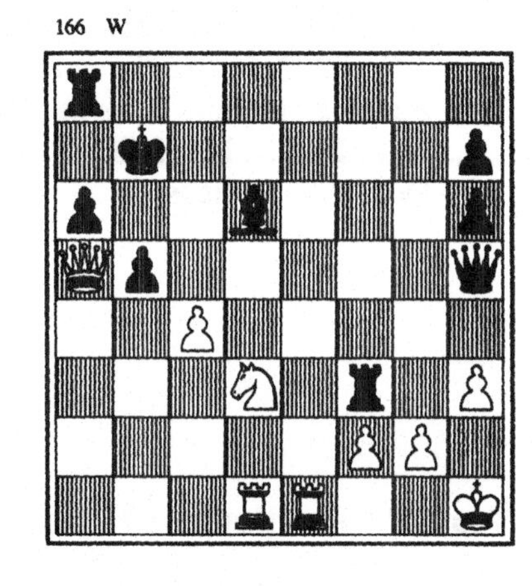

167 B

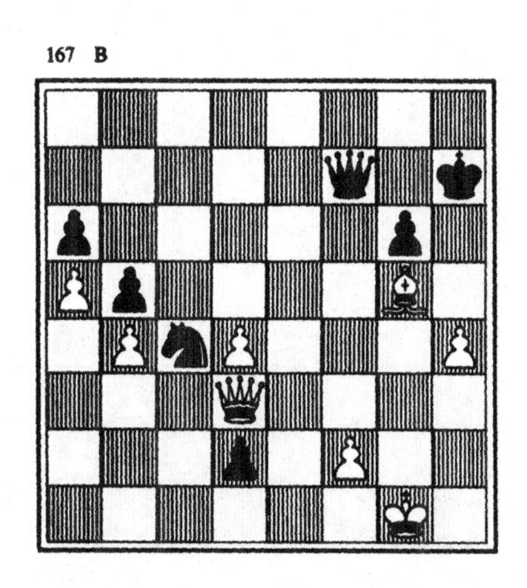

168 B

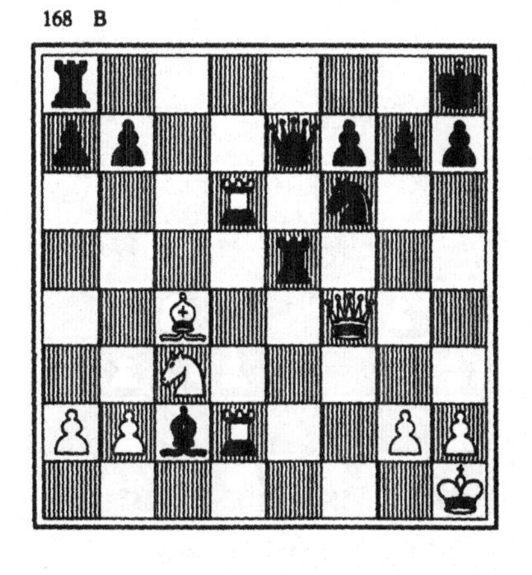

## Solutions to Test 21

161. Spassky–Korchnoi, Moscow, 1955.
1 Qh2!! Resigns.
162. Zhuravlev–Borisenkov, Moscow, 1949.
1 . . . d3! White resigns. On 2 B×d3 there comes 2 . . . f3! 3 Re3 (or *3 Q×e7 Qh3+ 4 Kg1 Qh1* mate) 3 . . . Qh1+4 Rg1 Q×g1+ 5 K×g1 Rdg8+ 6 Kf1 Rh1 mate.
163. Stanchev–Bankov, Sofia 1948.
1 Rc6!! Resigns (on *1 . . . b×c6* there follows *2 N×f6* mate).
164. Shashin–Gik, Kharkov, 1967.
1 Bh3!! B×h3 2 f5!, and White wins. In the game there followed 1 . . . f5 2 B×e5, and White won.
165. Urseanu–Anstasiadi, Bucharest, 1960.
1 Bd5!! R×d5 2 R×f7! Resigns.
166. Ragozin–Bronstein, Moscow, 1945.
1 Nf4!! R×f4 (or *1 . . . B×f4 2 Re7+Kc6 3 Re6+ Kc5 4 Rd5+*) 2 R×d6 Qf7 3 Qb6+ Resigns.
167. Sulim–Ioffe, USSR, 1976.
1 . . . Qf5! 2 Qe2 Ne3! and wins: 3 f×e3 (or *3 B×e3*) 3 . . . Qb1+ and 4 . . . d1=Q, or 3 Q×d2 Qg4+. In the game Black missed this possibility.
168. Fuchs–Korchnoi, Yerevan, 1965.
1 . . . Bd3!! 2 B×d3 (if *2 R6×d3* or *2 R2×d3*, then *2 . . . Re1+!*) 2 . . . Q×d6 3 Bf1 Qc5 White resigns.

## Test 22 Positions 169–176

We make the acquaintance of a new theme—'Defence-elimination'. Solving time 45 minutes, and with the proviso that everything is solved, add 40 points to your score.

169 B

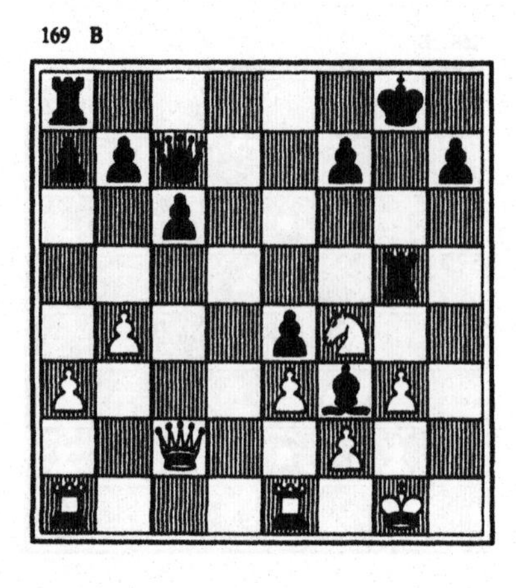

170 W

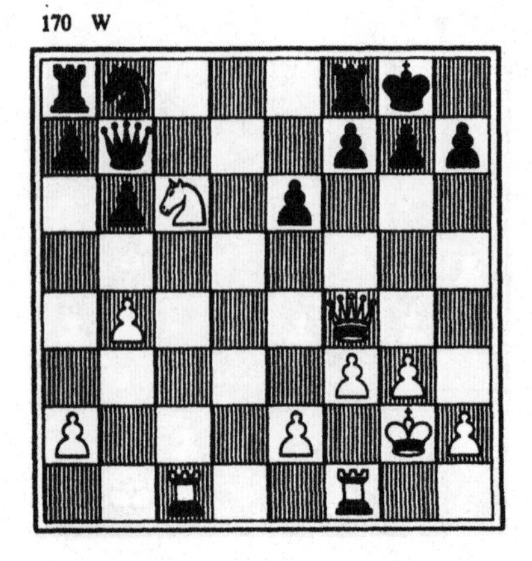

171 W

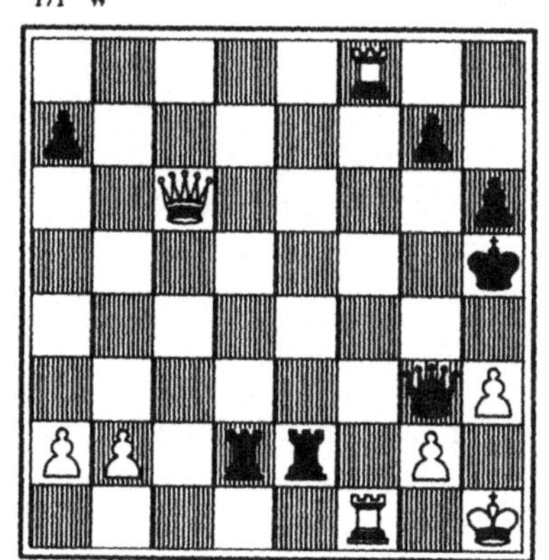

172 W

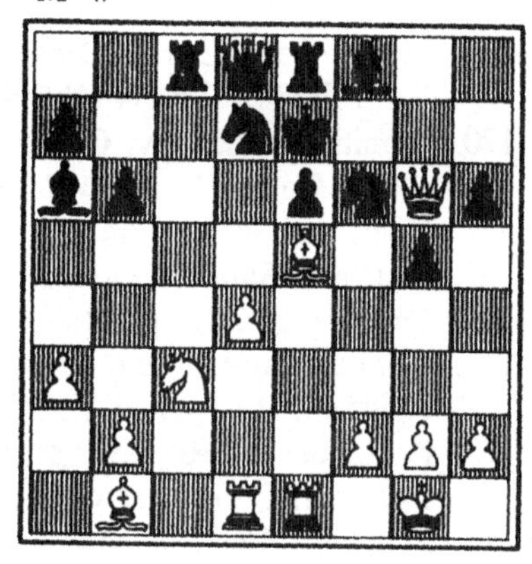

173 W

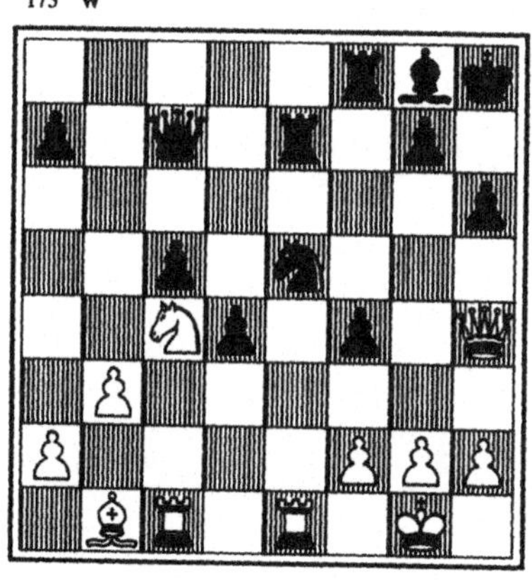

174 W

175 W

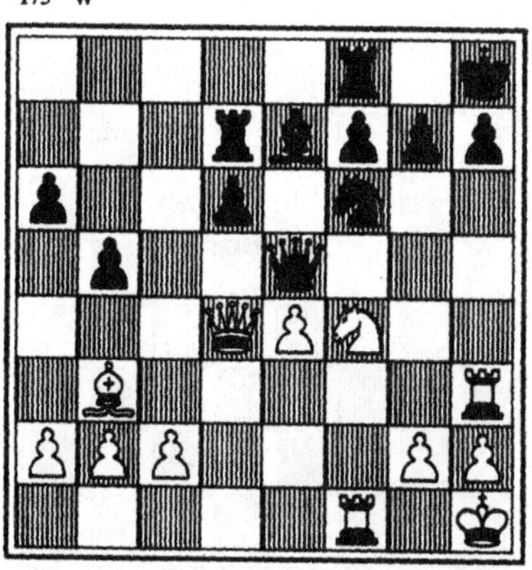

176 W

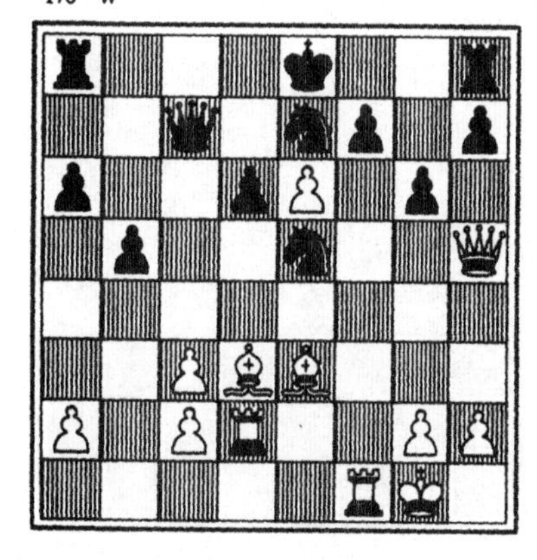

## Solutions to Test 22

169. Moush–Peer, Zurich, 1960.
1 . . . Q×f4!! 2 e×f4 Rh5 White resigns.
170. Lipnitsky–Sokolsky, Odessa, 1949.
1 Nd8! Qe7 (if *1 . . . R×d8*, then *2 Rc7*, while on *1 . . . Qd5* there follows *2 Rfd1!*) 2 Qe4!, and White won.
171. Shtirberg–Sabinin, Novosibirsk, 1971.
1 R1f5+ g5 2 R×g5+!! Resigns.
172. Donner–Dunkelblum, Beverwijk, 1964.
1 Nd5+!! Resigns. If 1 . . . e×d5, then 2 B×f6++, or 1 . . . N×d5 2 Qh7+!
173. Kottnauer–E. Richter, Bratislava, 1948.
1 Q×e7!! Q×e7 2 N×e5 Resigns.
174. Echeveri–Raisa, Varna, 1962.
1 R×e5!! d×e5 2 Qf6! Resigns.
175. Wade–Boxall, England, 1953.
1 B×f7! R×f7 (or *1 . . . Q×d4 2 Ng6* mate) 2 Ng6+ Resigns.
176. Tal–Suetin, Tbilisi, 1969.
1 Q×e5!! d×e5 2 e×f7+ Resigns. If 2 . . . Kf8, then 3 Bh6+, while 2 . . . Kd8 or 2 . . . Kd7 is answered by 3 Bf5+.

## Test 23 Positions 177–184

We continue working on the previous theme, but the test is more difficult. Therefore the time for solution is 50 minutes.

177 B

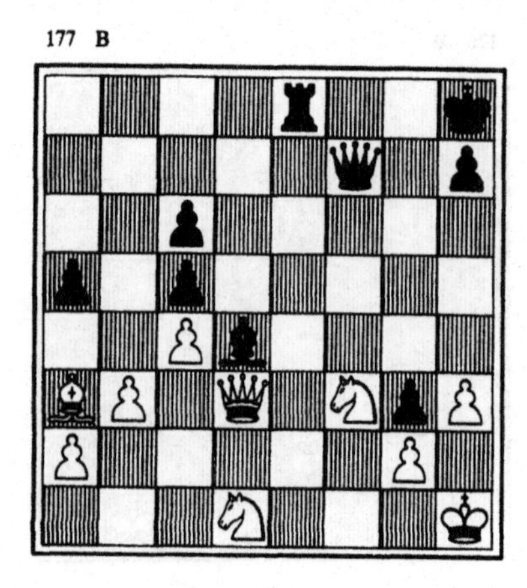

178 B

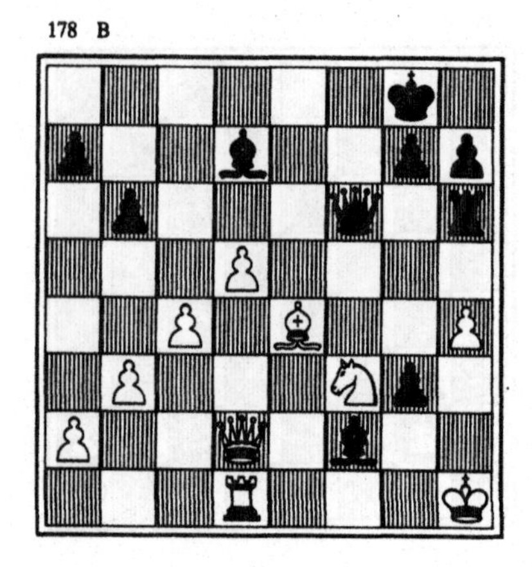

179 W

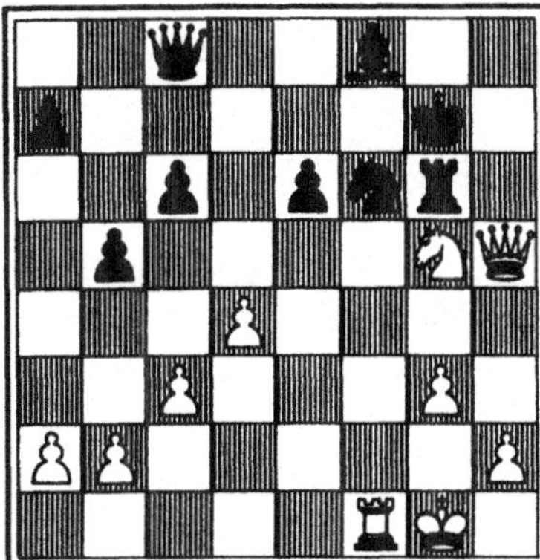

180 W

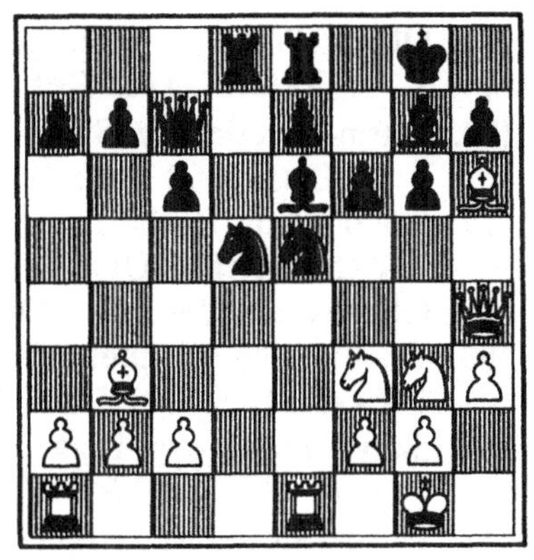

181 W

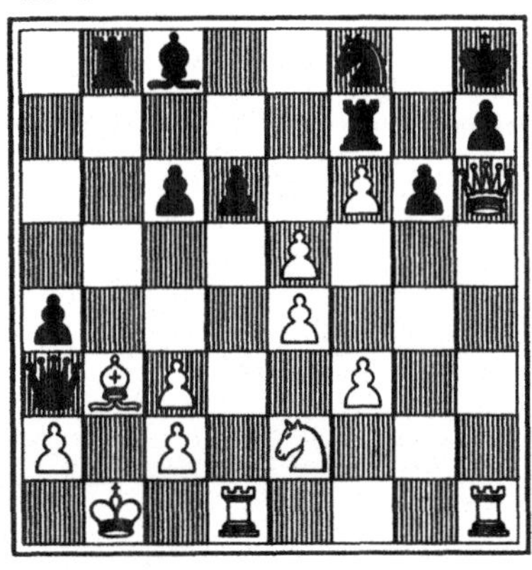

182 B

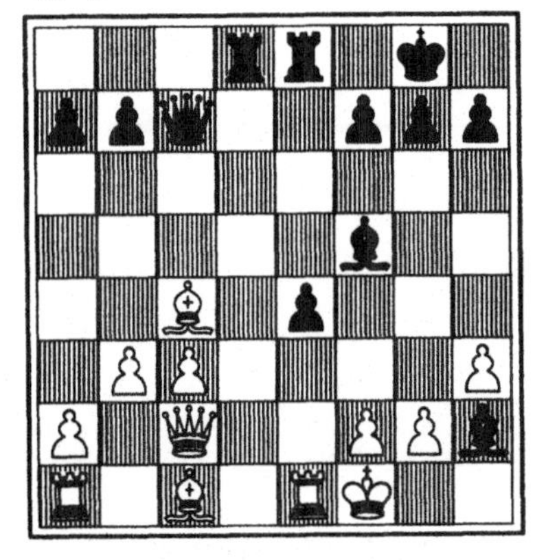

183 W

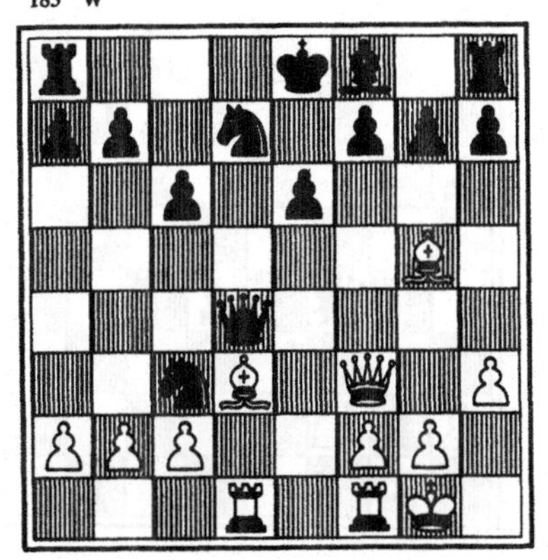

184 W

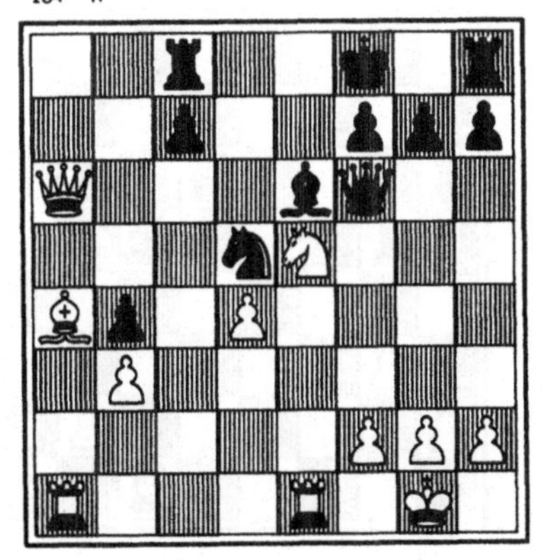

## Solutions to Test 23

177. Oberle–Pfister, Würzburg, 1958.
 1 . . . Q×f3!! 2 g×f3 Re1+ 3 Kg2 Rg1 mate.
178. Estrin–Boleslavsky, Sverdlovsk, 1946.
 1 . . . Q×f3+!! 2 B×f3 R×h4+ 3 Kg2 Bh3+ White resigns.
179. Slobodnikov–Buzhdizhan, Moscow, 1966.
 1 R×f6!! K×f6 2 Qf3+! K×g5 3 Qf4+ Resigns. On 2 . . . Kg7 there would have followed 3 Qf7+ Kh6 4 Qh7+ K×g5 5 Qh4+ Kf5 6 Qf4 mate.
180. Tal–Timman, Skopje, 1972.
 1 R×e5!! f×e5 2 Ng5 Bf6 3 N×e6 Resigns.
181. Skuya–Rozenberg, Riga, 1962.
 1 Q×f8+!! R×f8 2 R×h7+!! K×h7 3 Rh1+ Resigns.
182. Fiordeli–Melchior, Argentina, 1954.
 1 . . . e3!! 2 Q×f5 Q×c4+!! 3 b×c4 e2+ 4 R×e2 Rd1+ White resigns.
183. Veresov–Dementey, Minsk, 1966.
 1 Bg6!! Ne2+ 2 Q×e2 Qe5 3 B×f7+! Resigns (*3 . . . K×f7 4 R×d7+*).
184. Friedrich–Bantleon, Hannover, 1967.
 1 Nd7+! B×d7 2 Q×c8+! B×c8 3 Re8 mate.

## Test 24 Positions 185–192

A new theme—'Square-vacation'. The test is set for 50 minutes.

185 W

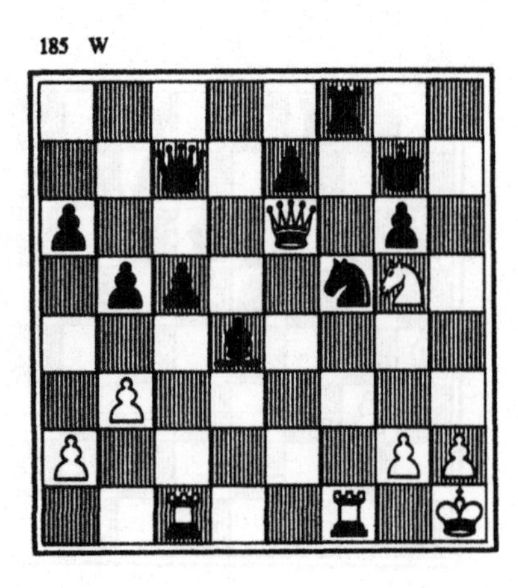

186 W

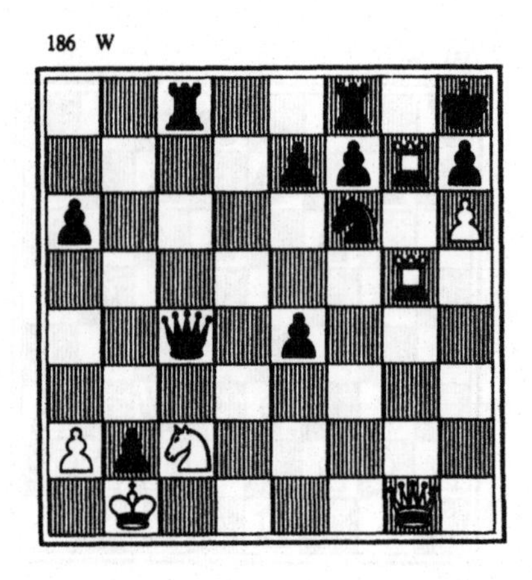

187 B

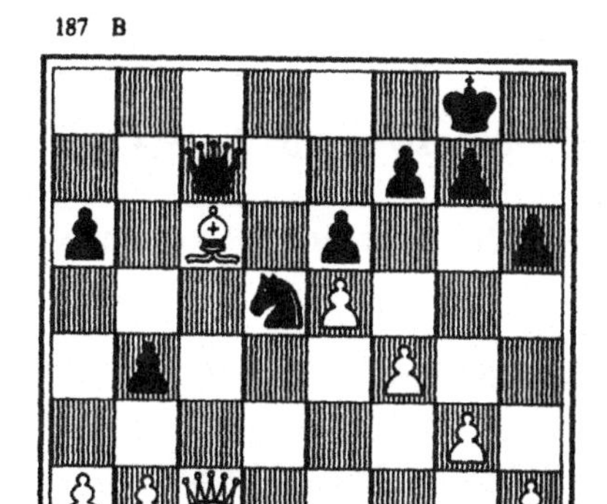

188 B

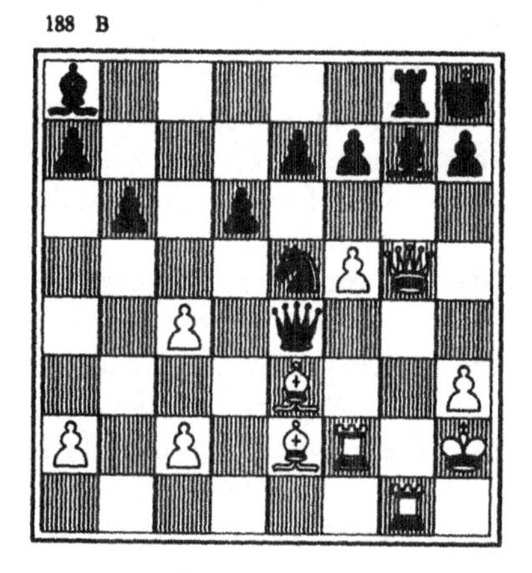

189 B

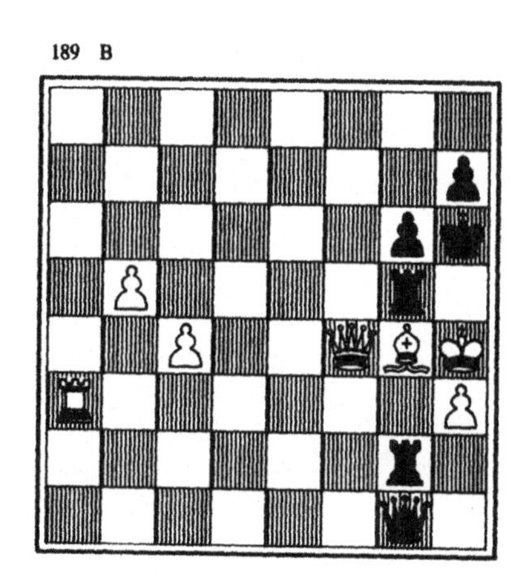

190 B

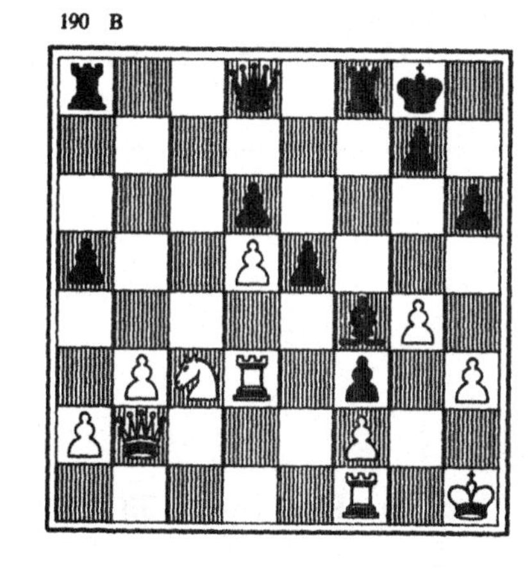

191 W

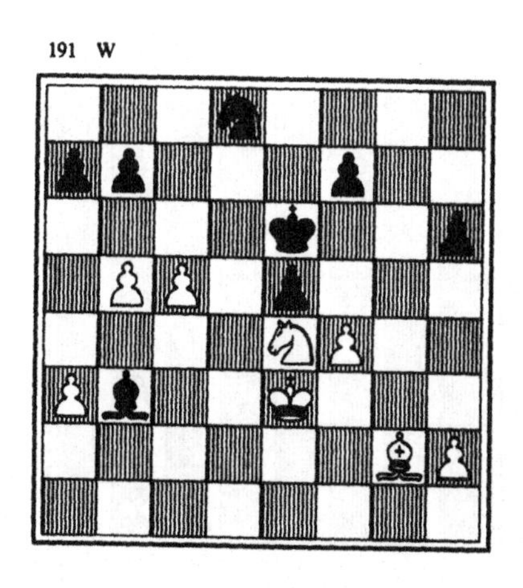

192 W

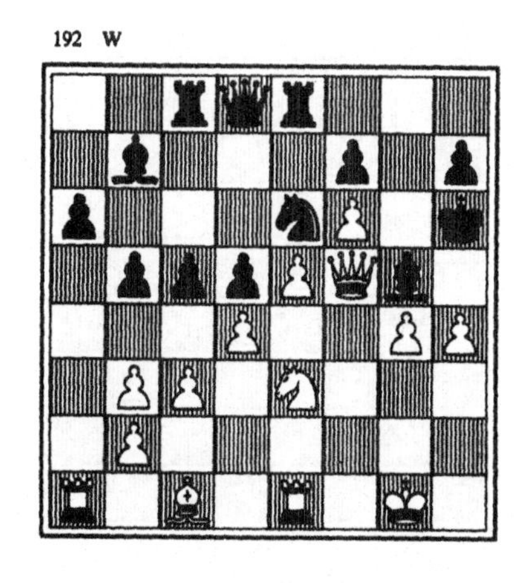

## *Solutions to Test 24*

185. Tal–Parma, Bled, 1961.
1 Q×f5! Resigns (*1 . . . R×f5* and *1 . . . g×f5* are both answered by *2 Ne6+*).
186. Heemsoth–Heisenbutter, West Germany, 1958.
1 Rc5!! Resigns. Against the threats of 2 R×h7+ and 3 Qg7 mate, and 2 R×c4, there is no defence.
187. Prokhorovich–Ravinsky, Moscow, 1958.
1 . . . b3!! White resigns (on *2 a×b3* there follows *2 . . . Nb4!*).
188. Ravinsky–Simagin, Moscow, 1947.
1 . . . Ng4+!! White resigns (any capture on g4 is answered by *2 . . . Be5+!*).
189. Georgadze–Kuindzhi, Tvilisi, 1973.
1 . . . Qf2+!! 2 Q×f2 Rh5+!! White resigns (on *3 B×h5* there follows *3 . . . g5* mate).
190. Rutgen–Petz, Corr., 1956.
1 . . . e4!! 2 N×e4 Be5 White resigns. Against 3 . . . Qh4 there is no defence.
191. Smyslov–Szabó, Hastings, 1954/5.
1 c6! e×f4+ 2 K×f4 Resigns. On 2 . . . b×c6 comes 3 Nc5+, while if the bishop moves there follows 3 c7.
192. Hallen–Bauer, Switzerland, 1959.
1 Q×g5+!! N×g5 2 Nf5+ Kg6 3 h5 mate.

## Test 25 Positions 193–200

We make the acquaintance of a very common device bearing the name of ‘Line-opening’. This theme occurs very often in practical games. The test is fairly easy—time 45 minutes.

193 B

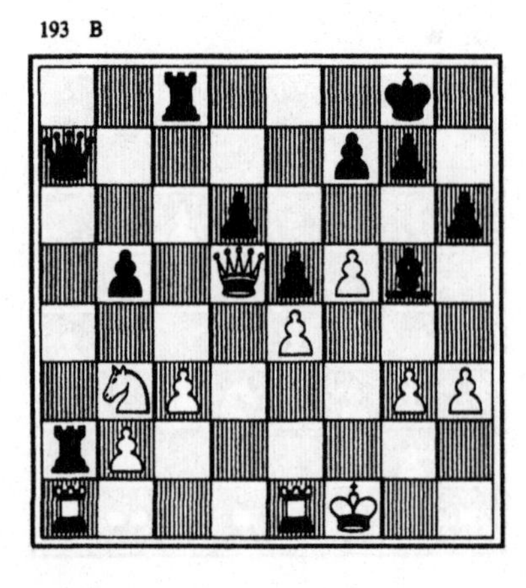

194 B

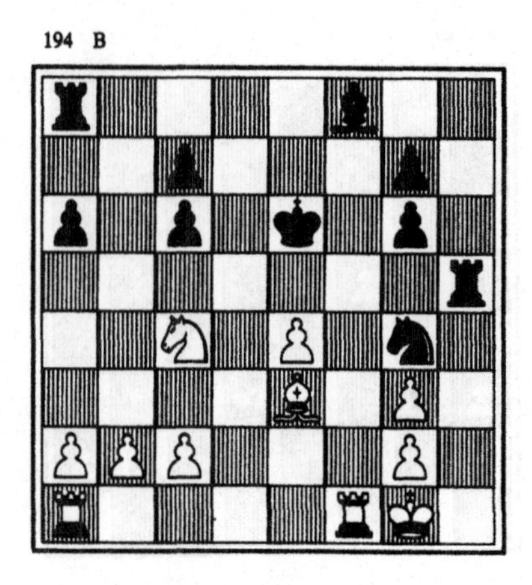

195 B

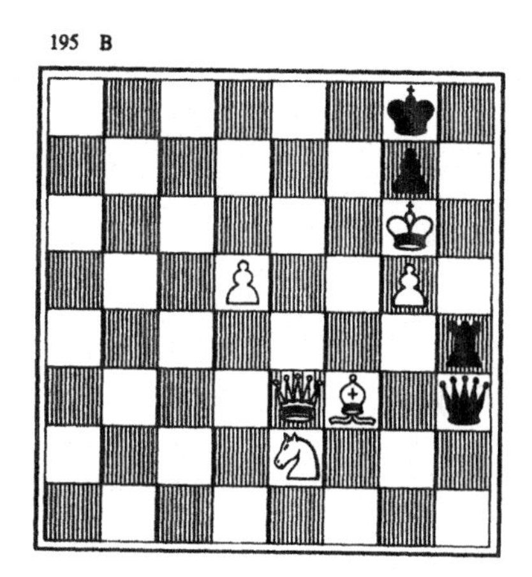

196 W

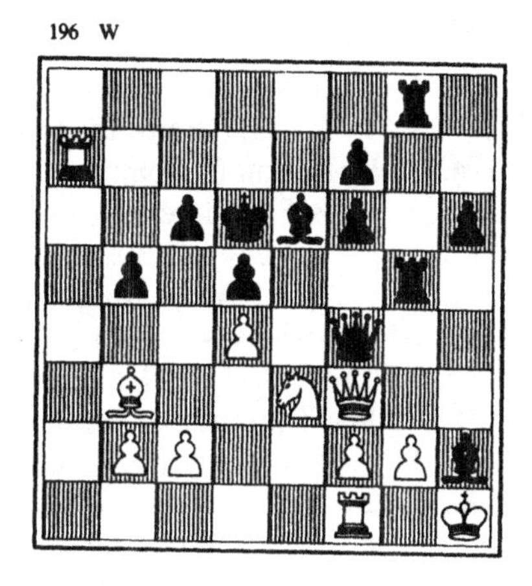

197 B

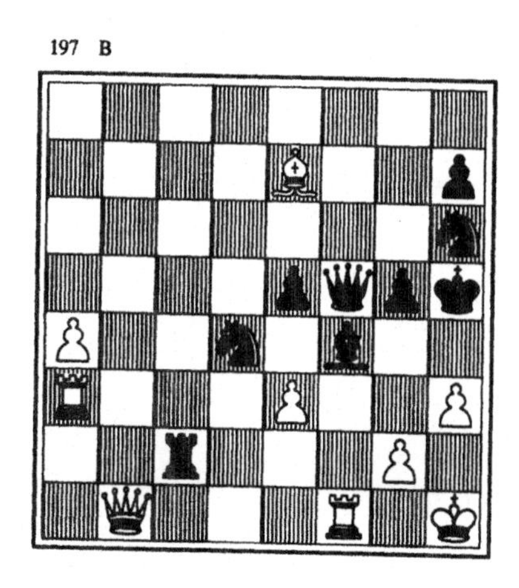

198 B

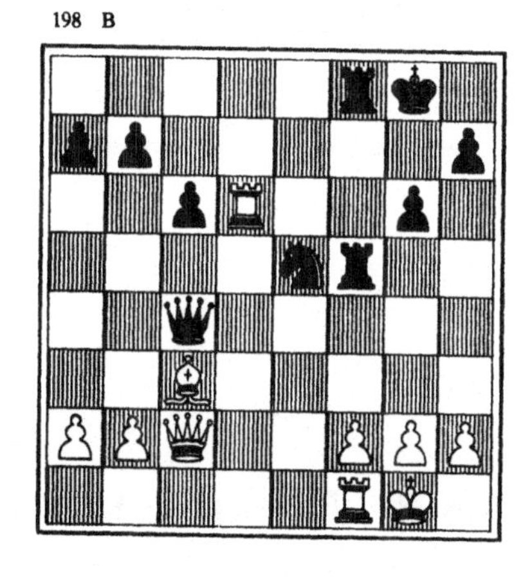

199 W

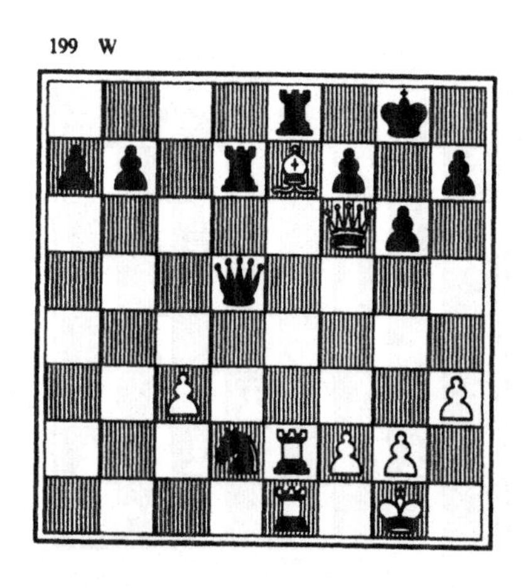

200 W

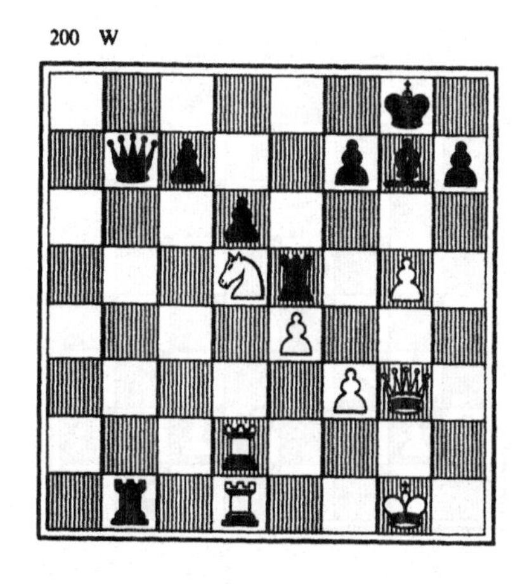

## Solutions to Test 25

193. Unzicker–Fischer, Varna, 1962.
1 . . . R×c3!! White resigns.
194. Dely–Kerkhoff, Sombor, 1966.
1 . . . Bc5!! White resigns (on *2 B×c5* comes *2 . . . Rah8!*).
195. Váragyi–Lengyel, Budapest, 1963.
1 . . . Re4!! White resigns (*2 Q×e4 Qh7* mate).
196. Khodko–Nosov, Lipetsk, 1956.
1 Nf5+!! B×f5 2 Qc3! Resigns (*2 . . . Ke6 3 Q×c6+*).
197. Malich–Ljubojevic, Amsterdam, 1972.
1 . . . Q×h3+!! White resigns. On 2 g×h3 there follows 2 . . . Rh2+ 3 Kg1 Ne2 mate.
198. Szabó–Ivkov, Bath, 1973.
1 . . . Nf3+!! White resigns (*2 g×f3 Rg5+ 3 Kh1 Q×f1* mate).
199. Butnoryus–Gutman, Riga, 1974.
1 Qh8+!! Resigns (*1 . . . K×h8* is met by *2 Bf6+* and *3 R×e8* mate).
200. Tsvetkov–Pachman, Hilversum, 1947.
1 Nf6+!! Kh8 2 Q×e5! Resigns (on *2 . . . d×e5* there follows *3 Rd8+ Bf8 4 R×f8+ Kg7 5 Rg8* mate).

## Test 26 Positions 201–208

The same theme as in the previous test, but more difficult. Time for the solution of this test is 50 minutes.

201 W

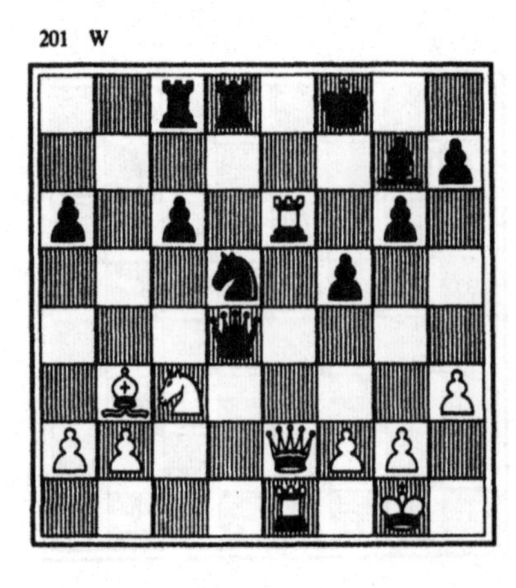

202 W

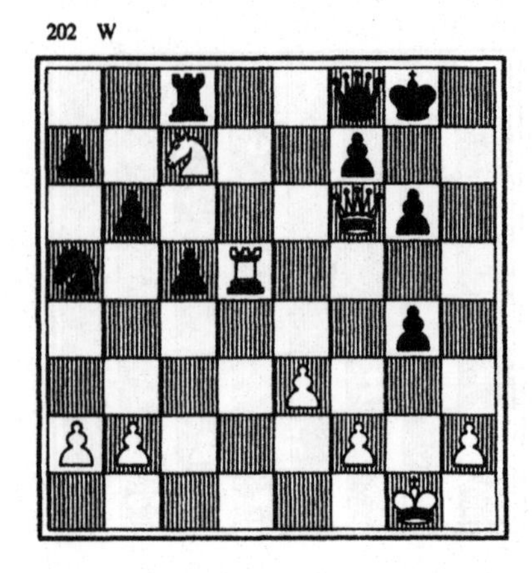

203 B

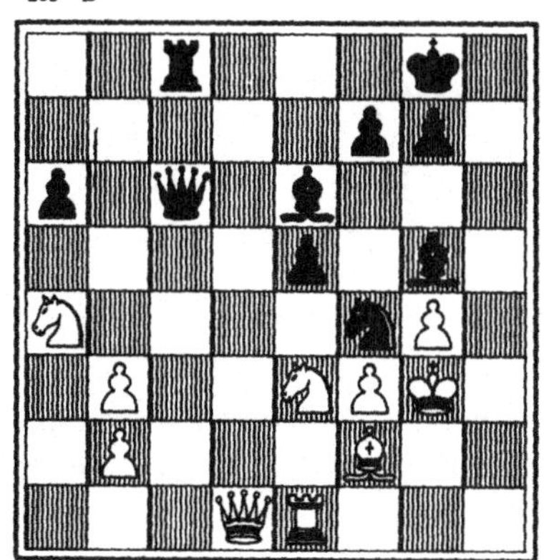

204 B

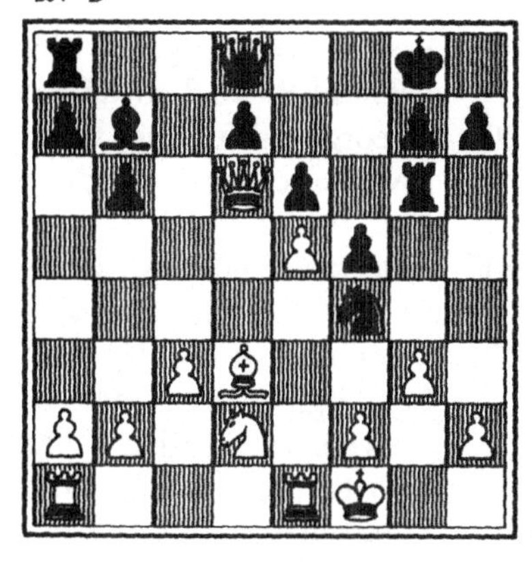

205 W

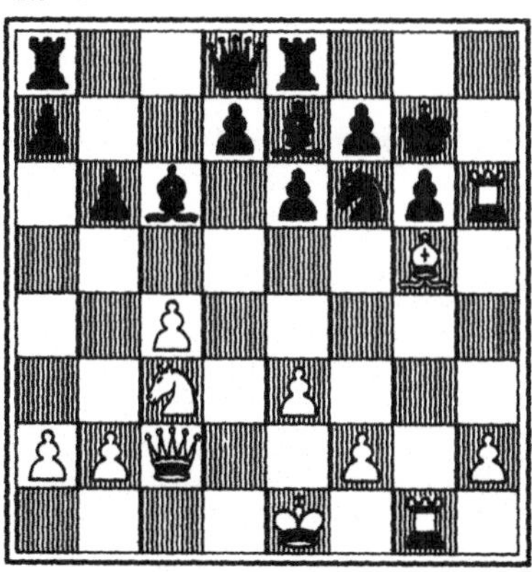

206 W

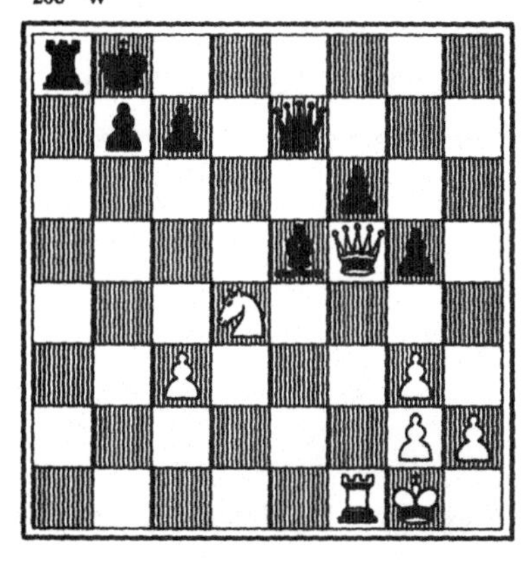

207 W

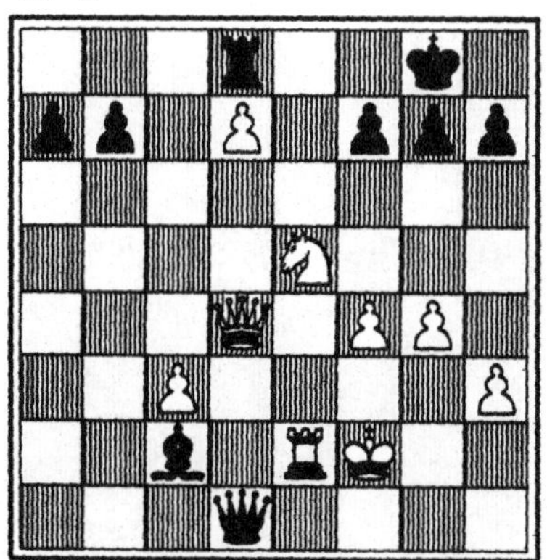

208 W

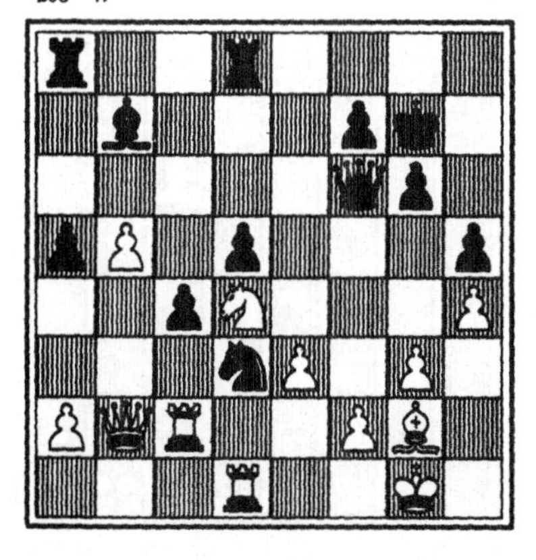

### Solutions to Test 26

201. Hort–Larsen, Lugano, 1968.
 1 R×c6! R×c6 2 B×d5 Resigns (if *2 . . . Rc7*, then *3 Qe6!*).
202. Gheorghiu–Muhring, Halle, 1966.
 1 Ne6!! Rc6 (on *1 . . . f×e6* there follows *2 Q×g6+ Qg7 3 Q×e6+*, while if *1 . . . Qh6*, then *2 Rh5!*) 2 Rh5! Resigns (if *2 . . . g×h5*, then *3 Qg5+* and *4 N×f8*).
203. Adashev–Guldin, Moscow, 1959.
 1 . . . B×b3!! 2 Q×b3 Qh6! White resigns.
204. Krasnov–Averkin, Novosibirsk, 1969.
 1 . . . Bg2+ 2 Kg1 Qh4!! White resigns. If 3 g×h4, then 3 . . . Nh3 mate, while on 3 g×f4 comes 3 . . . Bf3+ 4 Kf1 Qh3 mate. In addition, Black threatens 3 . . . Q×h2+ 4 K×h2 Rh6+ 5 Kg1 Rh1 mate.
205. Bobotsov–Kolarov, Varna, 1971.
 1 R×g6+!! f×g6 2 Bh6+!! Resigns.
206. Domulis–Shtaerman, Daugavpils, 1972.
 1 Nc6+! b×c6 2 Rb1+ Ka7 3 Qf2+ Resigns.
207. Tolush–Ravinsky, Leningrad, 1950.
 1 Nc6!! Q×e2+ 2 K×e2 b×c6 3 Qe5! Resigns.
208. Benkö–Inei, Budapest, 1949.
 1 R×d3! c×d3 2 Ne6+! f×e6 3 Rc7+ Resigns.

### Test 27 Positions 209–216

Theme: 'Utilization of Open Files'. Closely linked to the previous theme, and virtually a continuation of it. Time for solution of these positions—50 minutes.

209 W

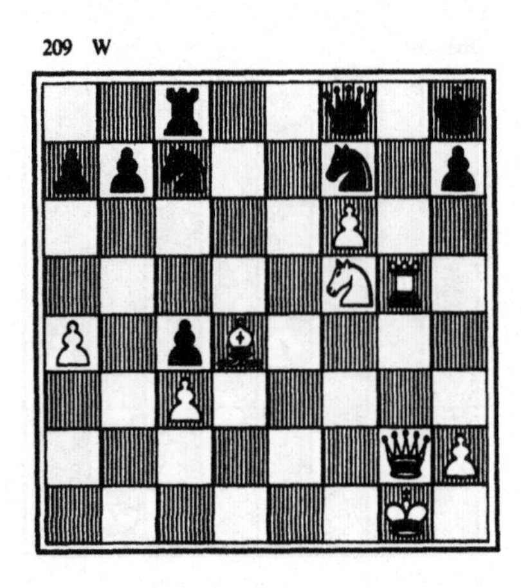

210 W

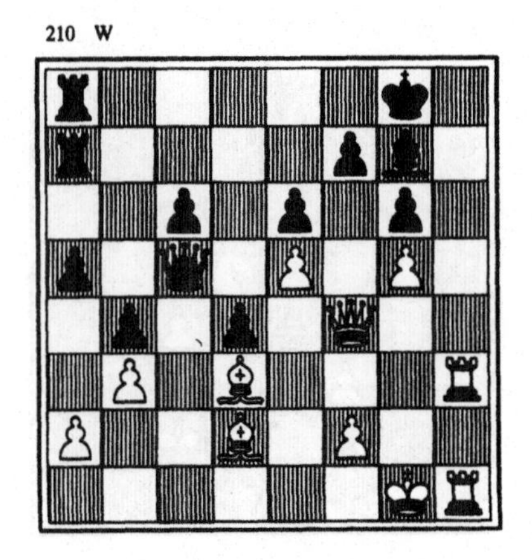

211 W

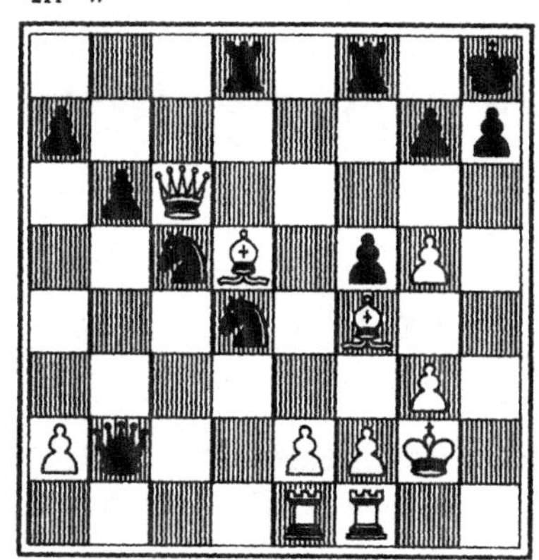

212 B

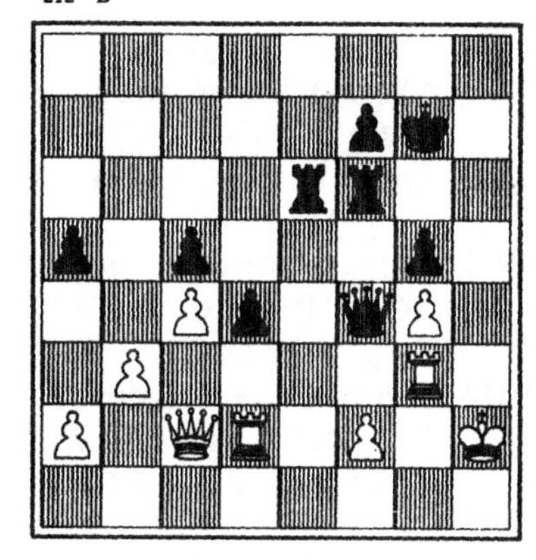

213 W

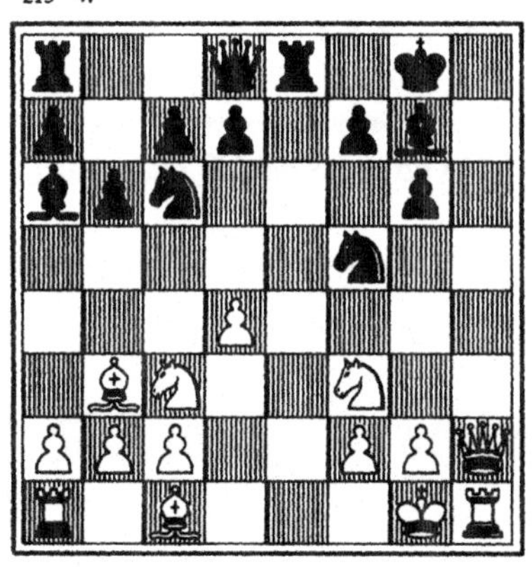

214 W

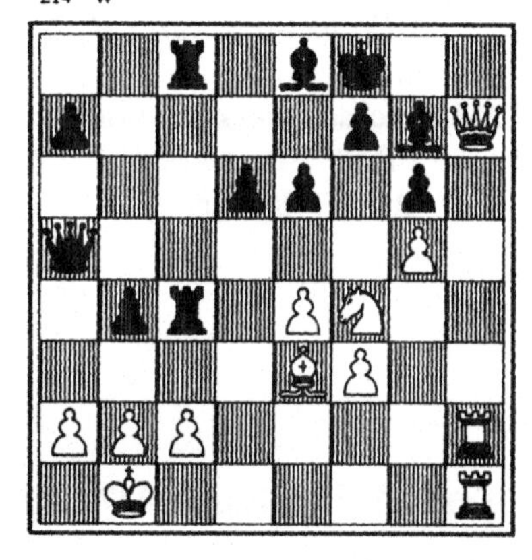

215 W

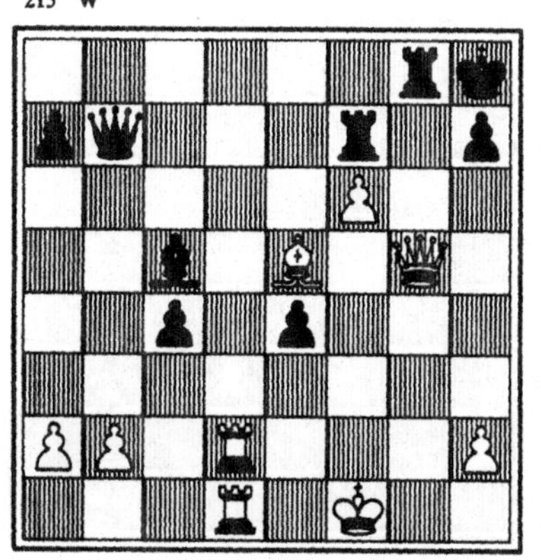

216 W

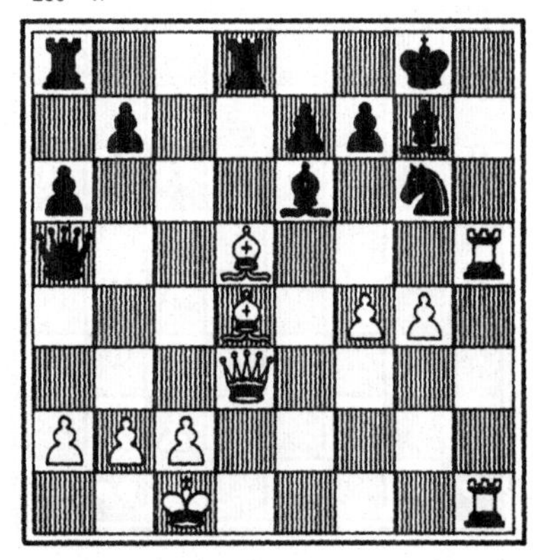

## *Solutions to Test 27*

209. Virtanen–Bjorkqvist, Corr., 1974.
1 Rg8+!! Resigns (on *1 . . . Q×g8* there follows *2 Qg7+!! Q×g7 3 f×g7+ Kg8 4 Ne7* mate).
210. Szabó–Bakonyi, Debrecen, 1951.
1 Qf6!! Resigns.
211. Darga–Duckstein, Lucerne, 1963.
1 Qg6!! Resigns. After 1 . . . R×d5 there follows 2 Rh1 Kg8 3 R×h7 Rf7 4 R×g7+! R×g7 5 Qe8+ Kh7 6 Rh1 mate.
212. Polugayevsky–Smyslov, Moscow, 1960.
1 . . . Re1! 2 Kg2 (forced, since *2 . . . Rh6+ 3 Kg2 Rhh1* was threatened) 2 . . . Re3!! White resigns. The threat is 3 . . . R×g3+ 4 f×g3 Qf1+, and on 3 Qd1 there follows 3 . . . R×g3+ 4 f×g3 Qe4+ 5 Kg1 Rf3.
213. Ritov–Malevinsky, Leningrad, 1969.
1 Bg5 Qc8 2 Bf6!! Resigns.
214. Rigó–Sápi, Hungary, 1967.
1 Q×g7+!! K×g7 2 Rh8! Resigns (against *3 R1h7* mate there is no defence).
215. Korpás–Bokor, Miskolc, 1972.
1 Q×g8+!! K×g8 2 Rg2+ Resigns (*2 . . . Kh8 3 Rd8+ Bf8 4 R×f8+! R×f8 5 f7* mate).
216. Dickson–Perkins, Edinburgh, 1958.
1 Rh8+! B×h8 (if *1 . . . N×h8*, then *2 Qh7+ Kf8 3 Q×h8+ B×h8 4 R×h8* mate) 2 Q×g6+ Resigns.

## Test 28 Positions 217–224

The same theme as in the previous test, but considerably more difficult. Time for solution 60 minutes.

217 W

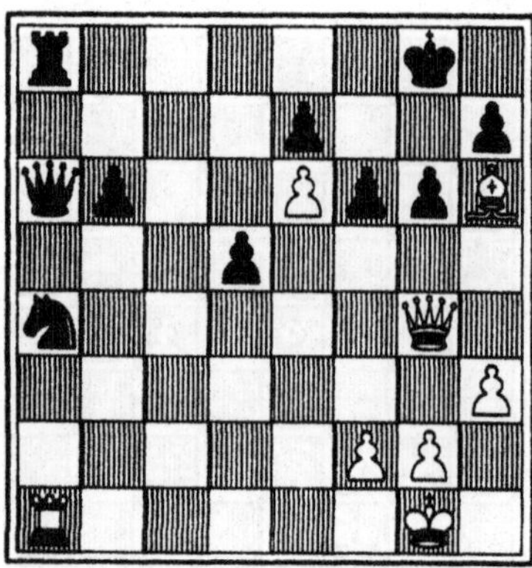

218 B

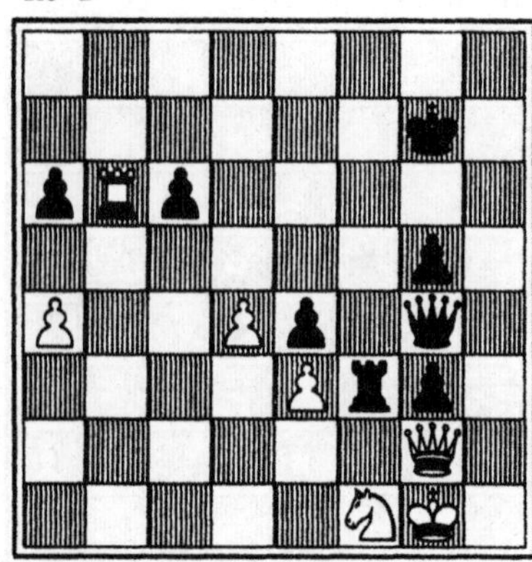

219 W

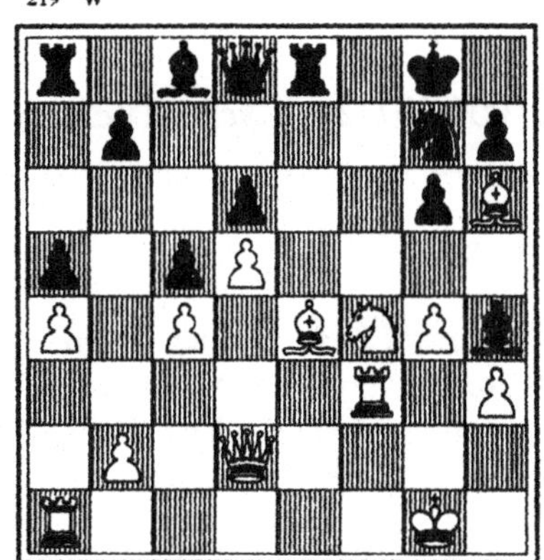

220 B

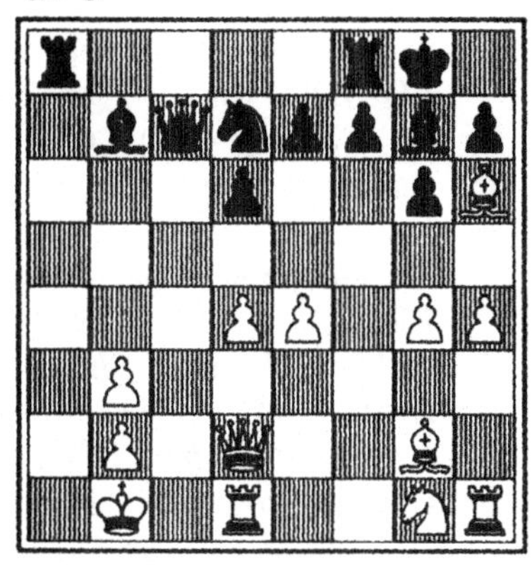

221 W

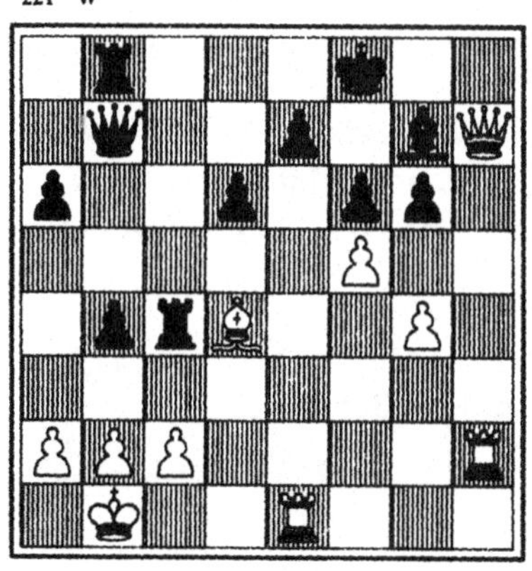

222 W

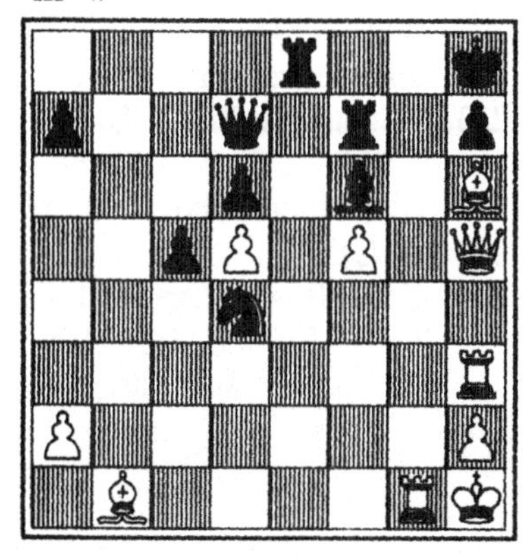

223 W

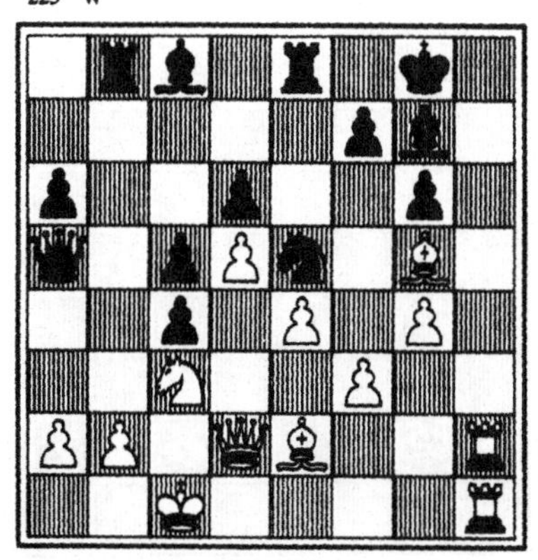

224 W

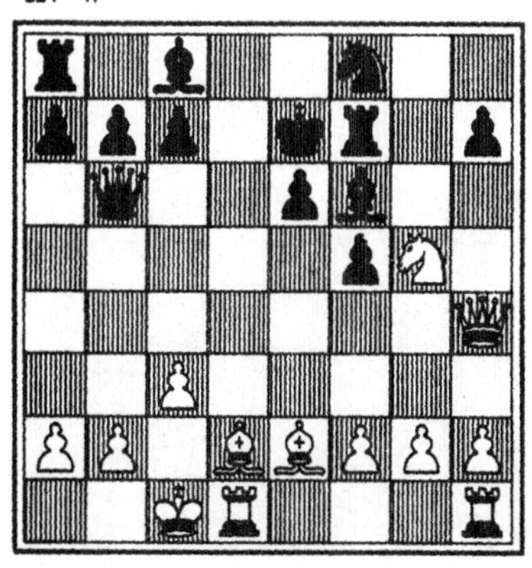

## Solutions to Test 28

217. Tseitlin–Lerner, Leningrad, 1974.
1 Qb4! Ra7 (or *1 . . . Qa7 2 R×a4 Q×a4 3 Q×e7*) 2 Rc1! Qb7 (*2 . . . Nc5 3 R×c5!*, or *2 . . . b5 3 Q×b5!*) 3 Q×e7!! Resigns.
218. Bankov–Lusmyagi, Parnu, 1974.
1 . . . Rf2 2 Qh1 R×f1+!! 3 K×f1 Qd1+ White resigns.
219. Hort–Popov, Varna, 1969.
1 Raf1!! R×e4 (*1 . . . Be7* is similarly inadequate, in view of *2 B×g7 K×g7 3 Nh5+ g×h5 4 Rf7+* and *5 Qh6!*, while other continuations are answered in the same way) 2 B×g7! K×g7 3 Nh5+!! Resigns (on *3 . . . g×h5* there follows *4 Rf7+ Kh8 5 Qh6 Qg8 6 R×h7+! Q×h7 7 Rf8* mate).
220. Gassanov–Arakelov, Baku, 1960.
1 . . . B×h6 2 Q×h6 Ra1+!! 3 K×a1 Qc2! White resigns (against *4 . . . Ra8* there is no defence).
221. Martens–Milotsky, Stuttgart, 1961.
1 Reh1 e5 (on *1 . . . R×d4* there follows *2 Q×g7+*) 2 Qh8+! Kf7 3 Q×g7+! Resigns.
222. Ivanko–Dolezal, Prague, 1955.
1 Bg7+!! R×g7 2 R×g7 Q×g7 (if *2 . . . K×g7*, then *3 Q×h7+* and *4 Q×d7*) 3 Q×e8+ Resigns. 2 . . . Re1+ would not have helped—3 Rg1!, when White comes out the exchange ahead.
223. Neybut–Kirillov, Riga, 1956.
1 Rh8+!! B×h8 2 R×h8+ K×h8 3 Bf6+ Kh7 4 Qg5!!, and White wins. On 4 . . . B×g4 there follows 5 f×g4 Nd3+ 6 B×d3 Re5 7 Qh4+ Rh5 8 g×h5 g5 9 Q×g5 Rg8 10 Qf5+.
224. Kobr–Bogac, Czechoslovakia, 1958.
1 Bh5! Rg7 2 Be3 Qa5 (the same move follows after *2 . . . Qb5*) 3 Qa4!! Q×a4 (*3 . . . Qe5* fails to save the game after *4 Qb4+ c5 5 B×c5+*) 4 Bc5 mate.

## Test 29 Positions 225–232

We meet the theme 'Diagonal-opening'. The test is relatively simple. Time—40 minutes.

225 B

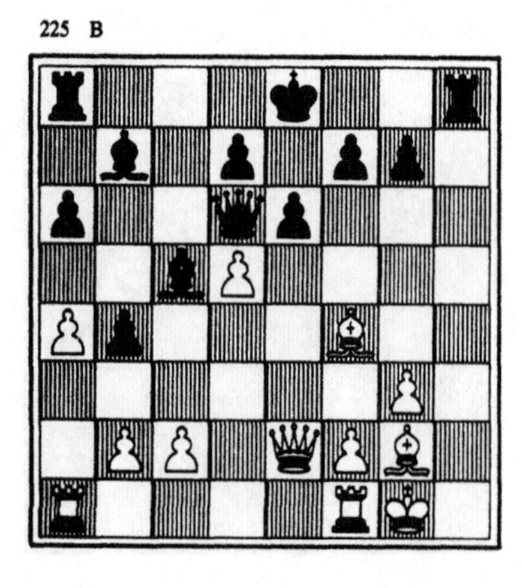

226 W

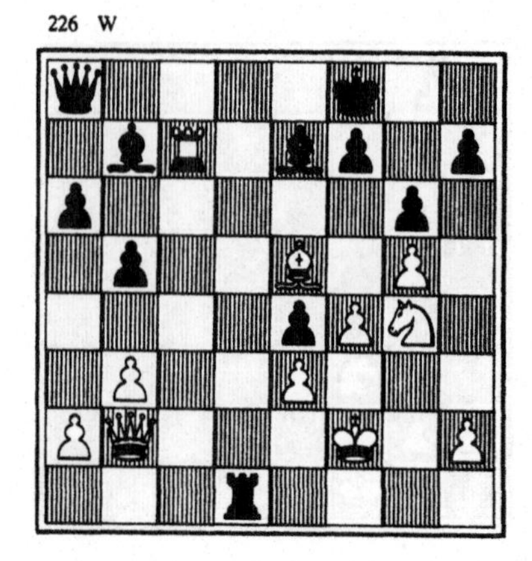

227 W

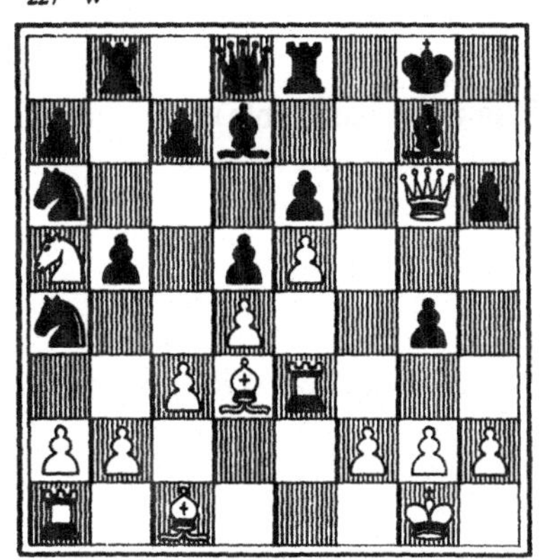

228 B

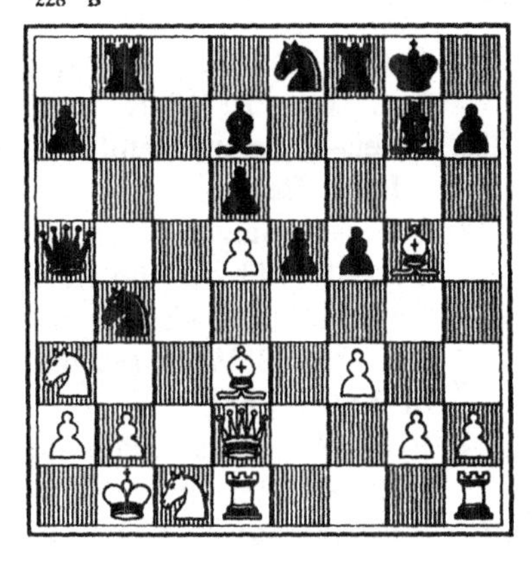

229 W

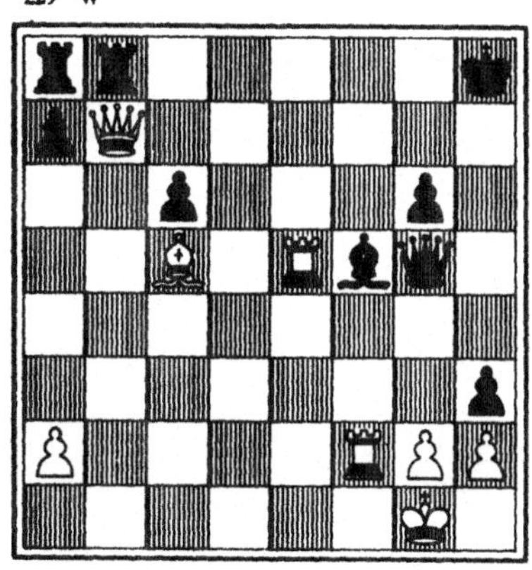

230 W

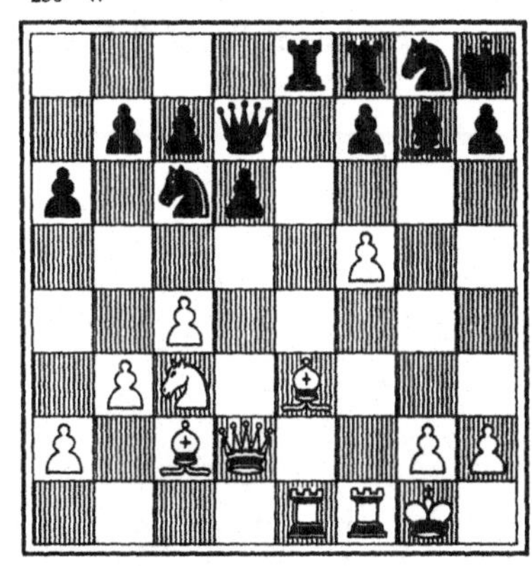

231 B

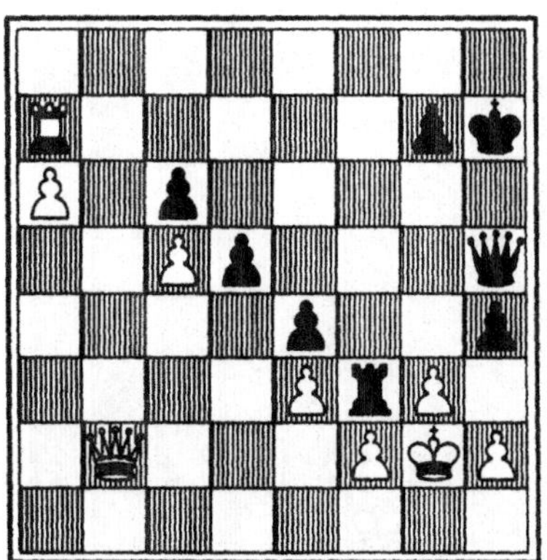

232 W

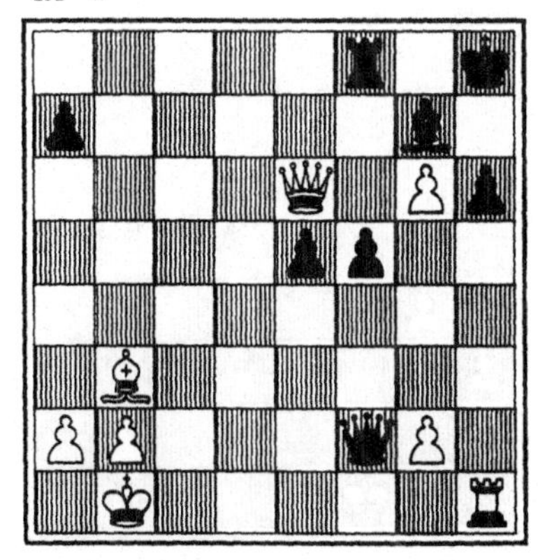

### Solutions to Test 29

225. Gutop–Roshal, Moscow, 1963.
1 . . . Q×d5!! White resigns (after *2 B×d5 B×d5*, mate is inevitable).
226. Alfeis–Torman, Hamburg, 1949.
1 Bd6!! Resigns.
227. Sokolsky–Saigin, Kiev, 1950.
1 Rf3!! g×f3 2 B×h6 Resigns.
228. Lorente–Alba, Castilia, 1959.
1 . . . N×d3! White resigns. If 2 Q×a5, then 2 . . . R×b2+ 3 Ka1 e4! 4 R×d3 Rb4+, or 2 Q×d3 e4!!.
229. Pytel–Wisznewski, Poland, 1967.
1 Re8+!! Resigns.
230. Krecmar–Sajger, Corr., 1948–9.
1 f6!! N×f6 (if *1 . . . B×f6*, then *2 Qd3*) 2 R×f6! Resigns (since *2 . . . B×f6* fails to *3 Qd3!*).
231. Caberel–Eliskases, Mar del Plata, 1949.
1 . . . h3+! 2 Kg1 Rf7! White resigns (on *3 R×f7* there follows *3 . . . Qd1* mate).
232. Wade–Kuijpers, England, 1972.
1 R×h6+!! B×h6 2 Q×e5+ Resigns (*2 . . . Bg7 3 Qh2+*, and mates).

### Test 30 Positions 233–240

Continuation of the previous theme. Slightly more complicated, but not a great deal so. Time for the test—40 minutes.

233 B

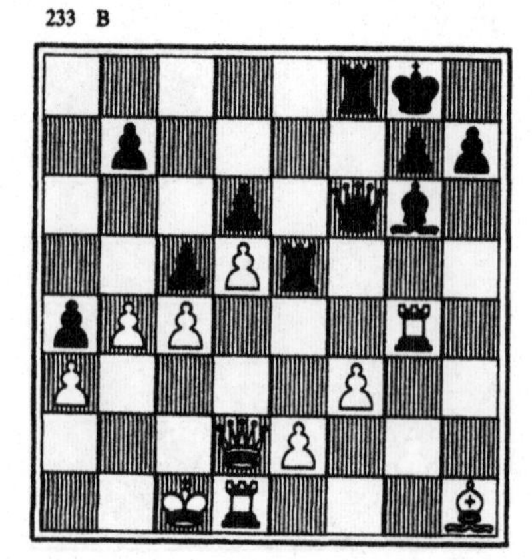

234 W

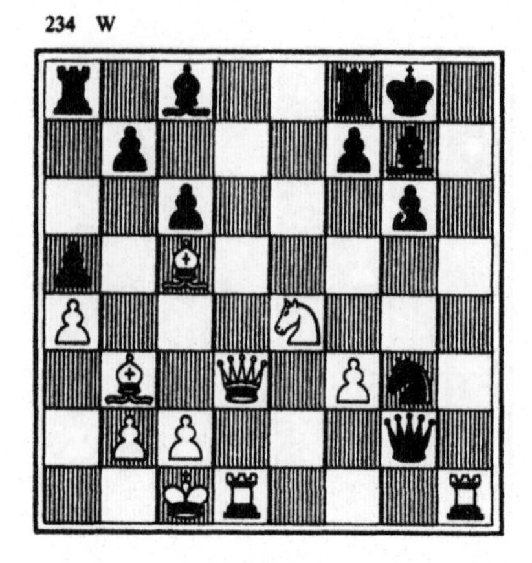

235 B

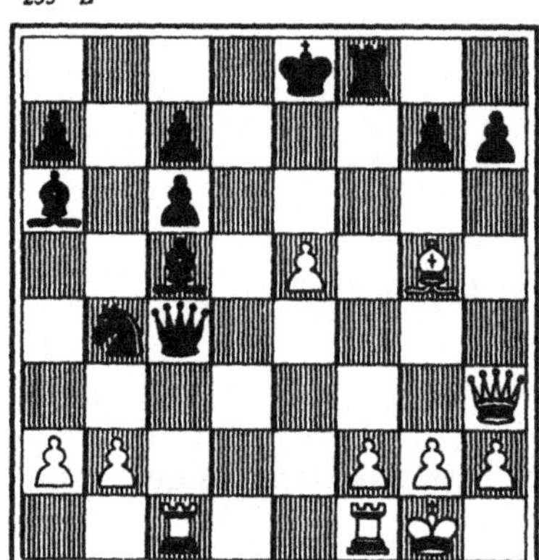

236 W

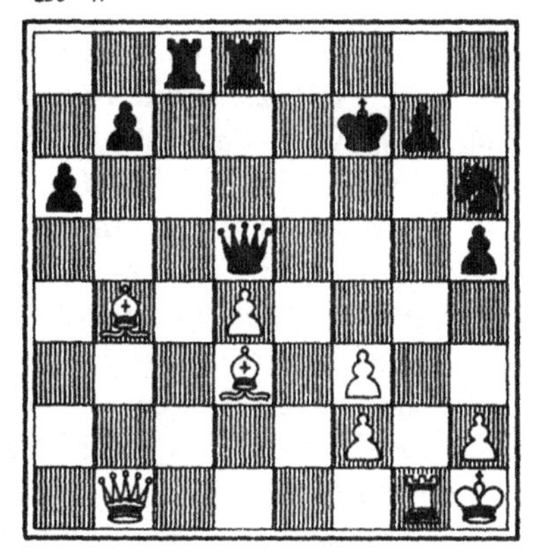

237 W

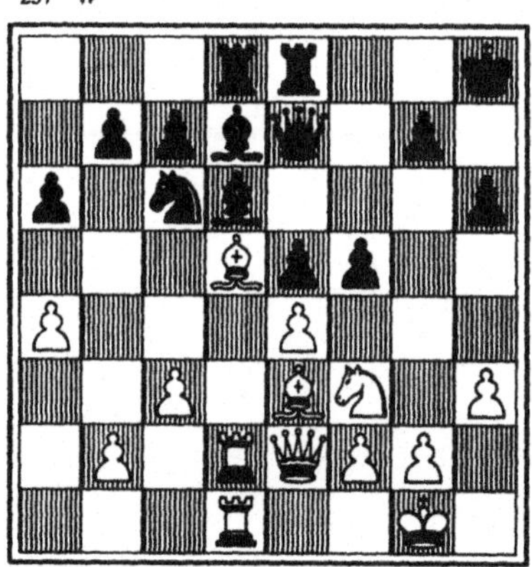

238 B

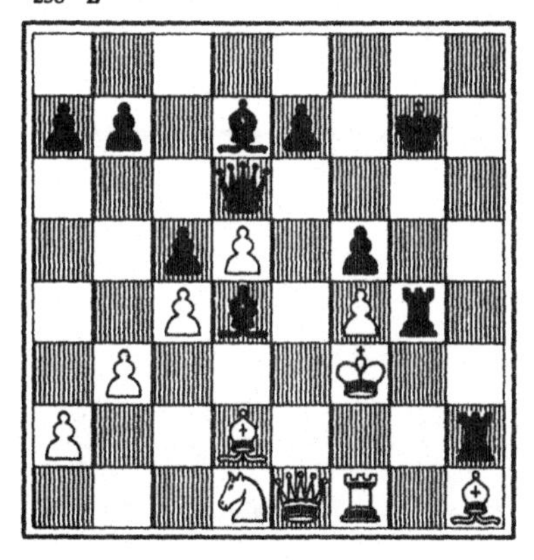

239 W

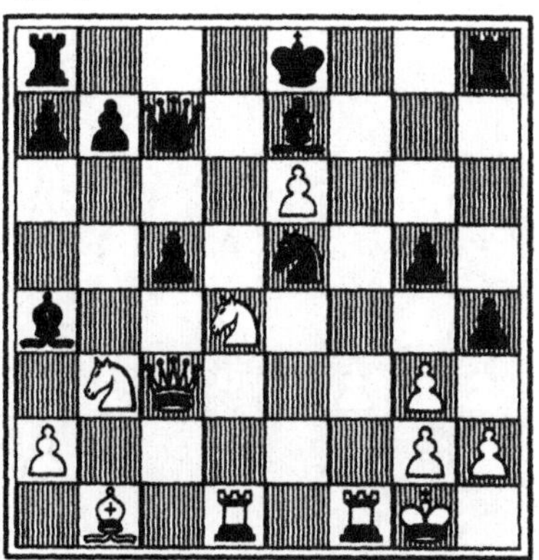

240 W

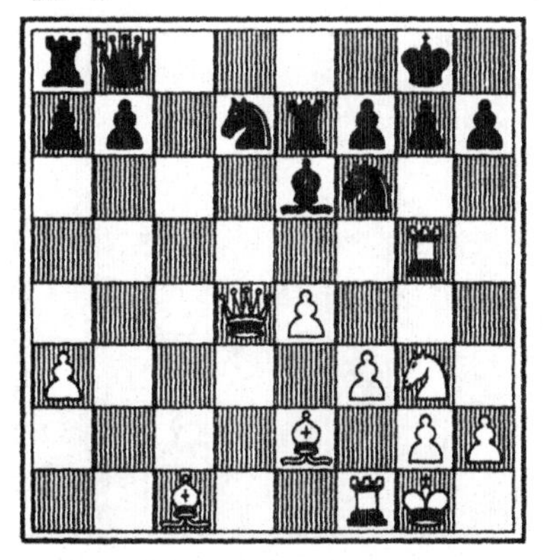

### Solutions to Test 30

233. Trifunovic–Ragozin, Moscow, 1947.
1 . . . R×e2!! White resigns (*2 Q×e2 Qc3+*).
234. Reshevsky–Yanovsky, Lugano, 1968.
1 Nf6+!! B×f6 2 Q×g6+ Bg7 3 Qh7 mate.
235. Messing–Forintos, Budapest, 1968.
1 . . . R×f2!! 2 R×c4 Rf3+ White resigns (*3 R×c5 R×f1* mate).
236. Nilsen–Lindholm, Stockholm, 1947.
1 Bc4!! R×c4 2 Qg6+ Kg8 3 Q×g7 mate.
237. Lukovnikov–Sergeev, Voronezh, 1974.
1 Bg5!! h×g5 2 N×e5!! Resigns. Black has a choice between losing his queen and being mated.
238. Chepukaitis–Osnos, Leningrad, 1970.
1 . . . Q×d5+!! 2 c×d5 Rh3+ White resigns (since *3 Ke2 Bb5* is mate).
239. Bramaier–Broistadt, Magdeburg, 1972.
1 Nb5!! B×b5 2 Q×e5!! Resigns.
240. Botvinnik–Keres, The Hague, 1948.
1 R×g7+!! K×g7 2 Nh5+ Kg6 (if *2 . . . Kh8*, then *3 Bg5!*, or *2 . . . Kf8 3 N×f6*) 3 Qe3! Resigns.

## Test 31 Positions 241–248

The theme 'Utilization of Open Diagonals' is an integral continuation of the previous theme. The examples are fairly difficult. Time for their solution—55 minutes.

241 B

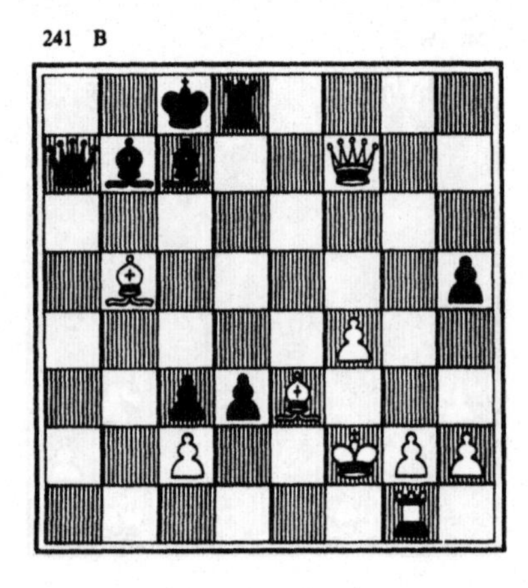

242 B

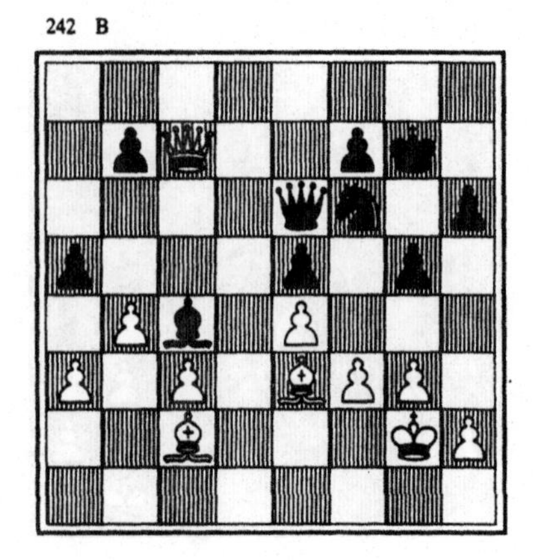

243 B

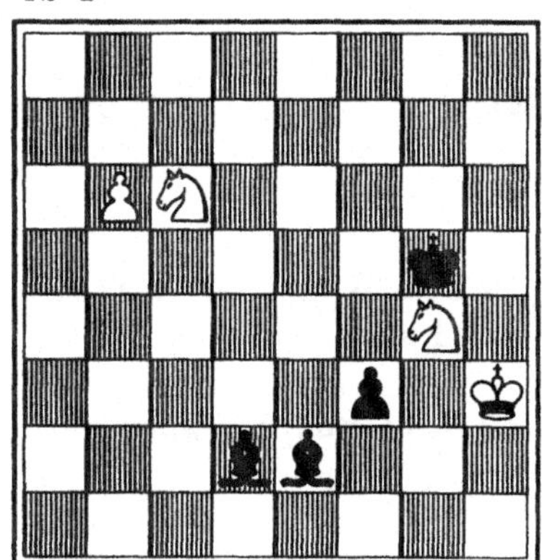

244 B

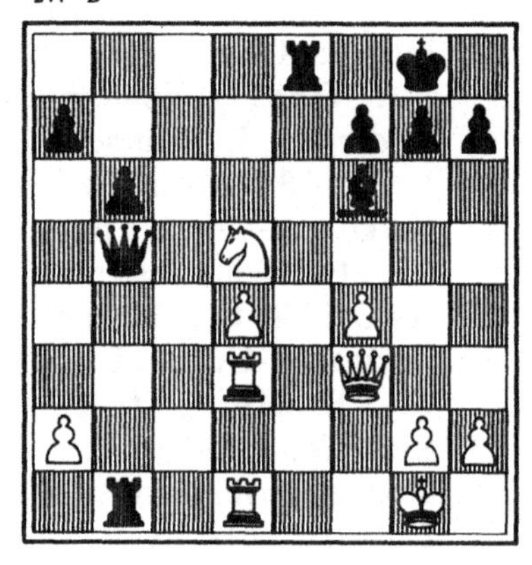

245 W

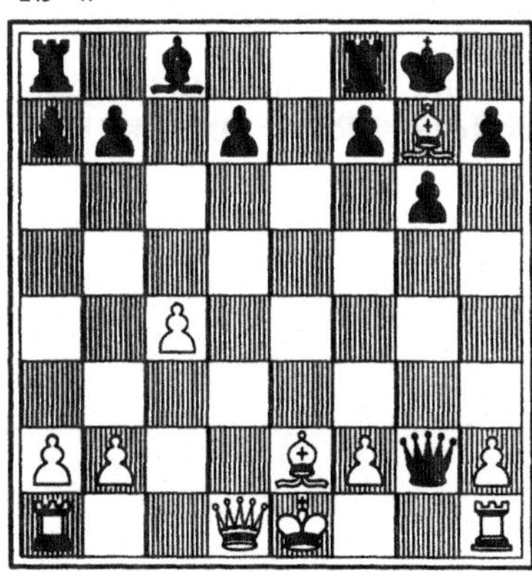

246 W

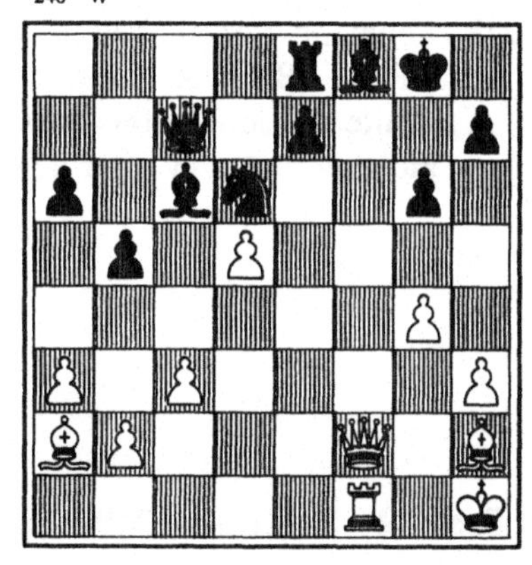

247 W

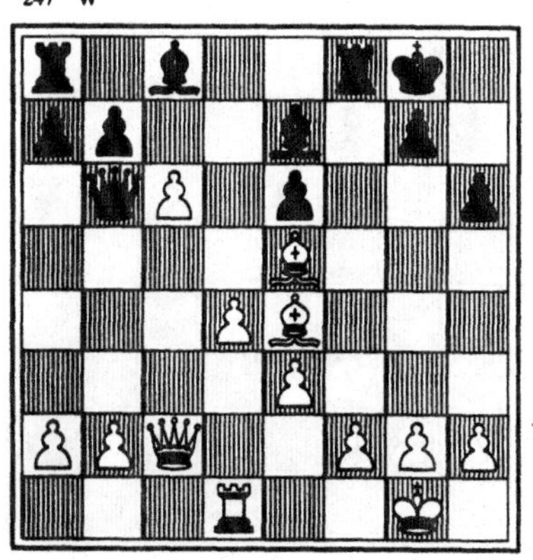

248 W

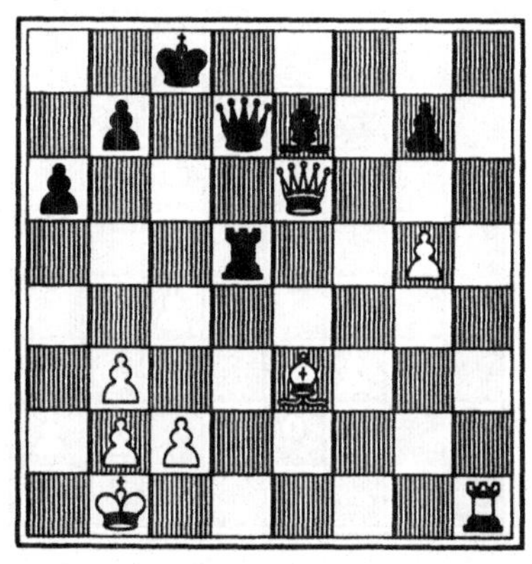

## Solutions to Test 31

241. Mikenas–Gusev, Ashkhabad, 1957.
1 . . . Q×e3+!! White resigns (*2 K×e3 Bb6* is mate).
242. Andersson, U.–Hartston, Hastings, 1972/3.
1 . . . Qh3+!! White resigns.
243. Karkosyan–Osnos, Frunze, 1973.
1 . . . Bf4! White resigns. If 2 Nh2 (*2 b7 Bf1* mate), then 2 . . . B×h2! 3 K×h2 f2 4 b7 f1=Q 5 b8=Q Qf2+ 6 Kh3 (*6 Kh1 Bf3* mate) 6 . . . Bf1 mate.
244. Tukmakov–Gufeld, Dnepropetrovsk, 1962.
1 . . . B×d4+!! 2 Kf1 (*2 R×d4 Re1+ 3 Kf2 Rf1+*, or *2 Ne3 Q×d3*, and wins) 2 . . . Re3!! White resigns.
245. Gaprindashvili–Servaty, Dortmund, 1974.
1 Qd4!! Q×h1+ (on *1 . . . f6* there would have followed *2 B×f8*) 2 Kd2 Q×a1 3 Qf6!! Resigns.
246. Ferrer–Hartston, J., Menorca, 1973.
1 d×c6+ Kh8 (or *1 . . . e6 2 B×d6* and *3 Qf7+*) 2 Be5+ Bg7 3 Qf8+! Resigns.
247. Stradalov–Charushin, Corr., 1955.
1 Bh7+! Kh8 2 B×g7+!! K×g7 3 Qg6+ Kh8 4 Bg8! Resigns.
248. Lehmann–Pomar, Palma de Mallorca, 1966 (variation).
1 Rh8+! Bd8 2 R×d8+!! K×d8 3 Bb6+ Kc8 4 Qg8+, and White wins. In the game White overlooked this possibility, and played 1 Qe4 Rd1+ 2 R×d1 Q×d1+3 Ka2. He won, but only after a further . . . 50 moves.

## Test 32 Positions 249–256

In this test you meet a new theme: 'Blocking', i.e. the blocking of some square or other. The test is of moderate difficulty, and the time allotted is 45 minutes.

249 W

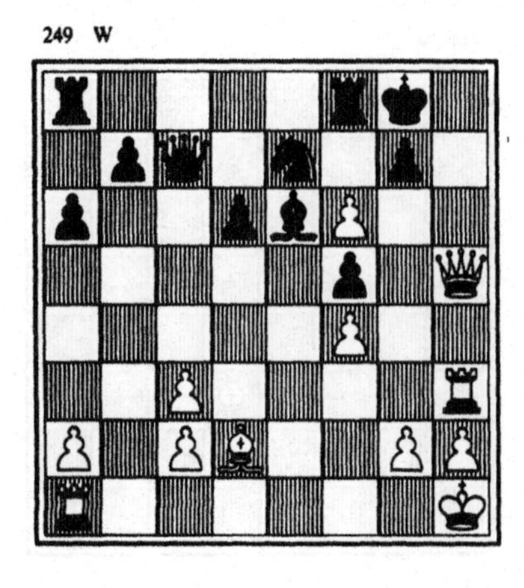

250 B

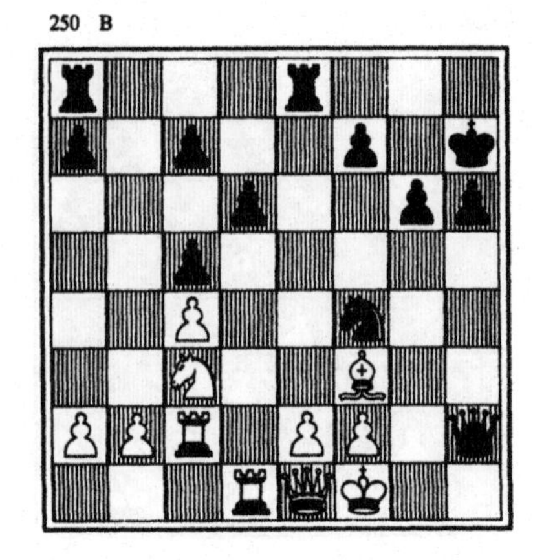

251 B

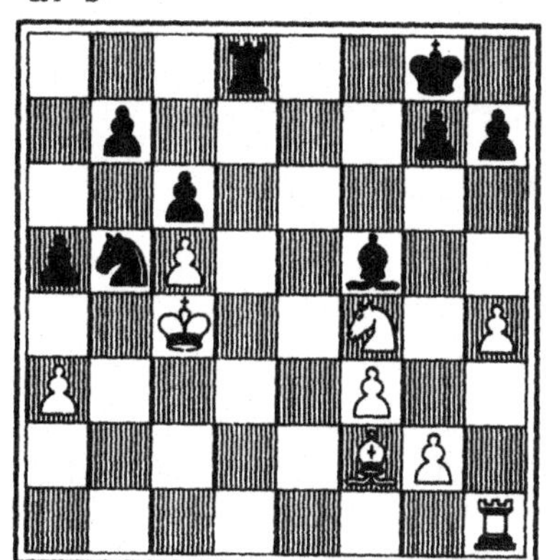

252 W

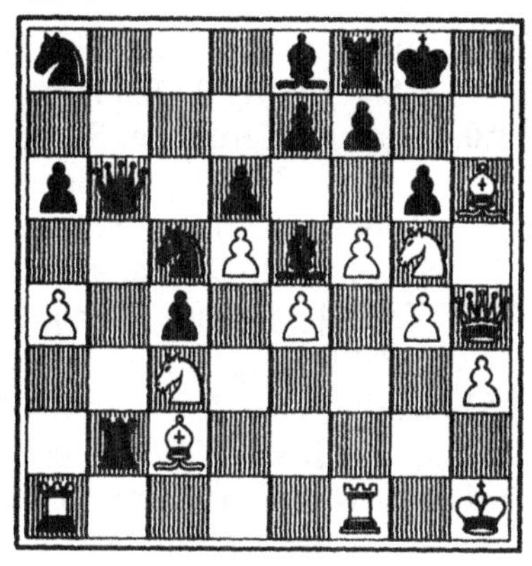

253 B

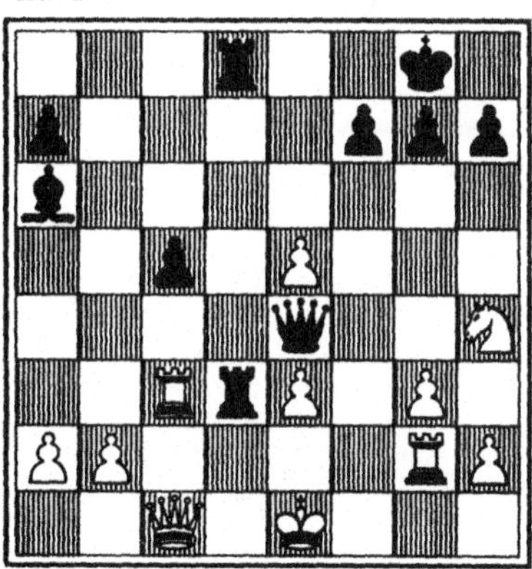

254 B

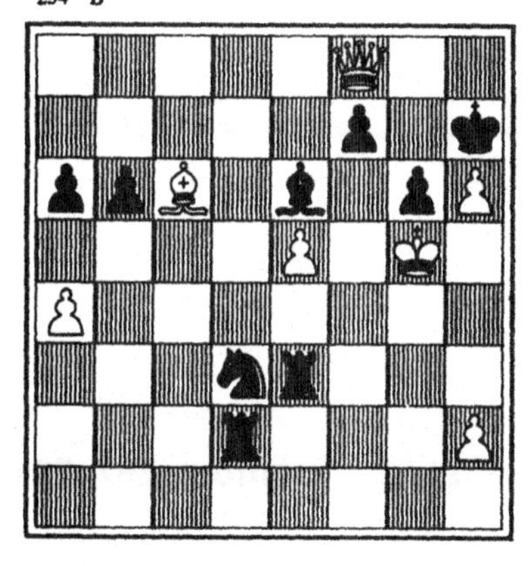

255 W

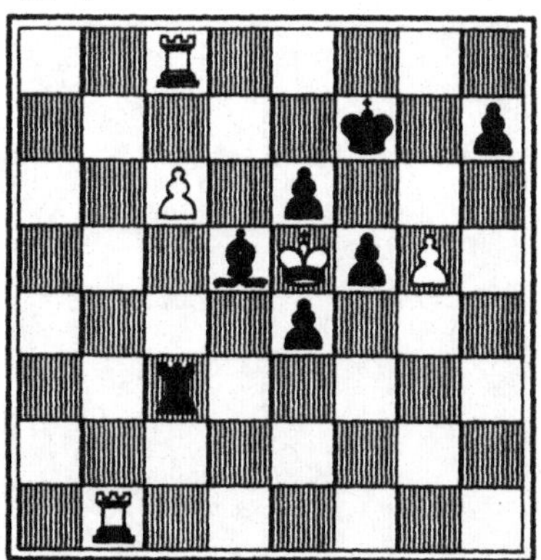

256 W

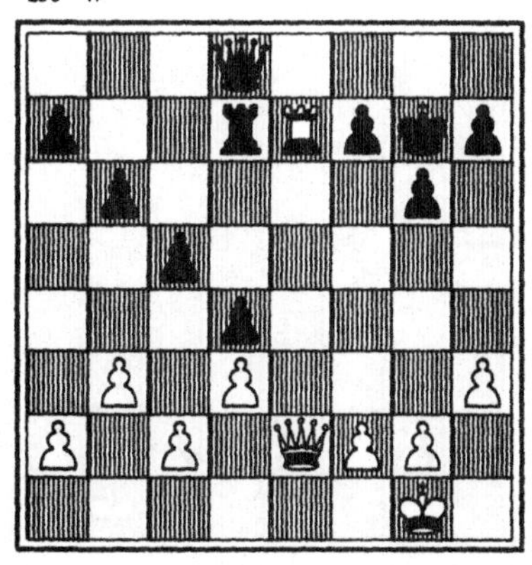

### *Solutions to Test 32*

249. Springer–Ebersbach, Berlin, 1958.
 1 f7+!! R×f7 2 Qh8 mate.
250. Fridman–Ternblom, Stockholm, 1973.
 1 . . . Re3!! White resigns. If immediately 1 . . . Nh3, then 2 e3!.
251. Kopylov–Karlson, Irkutsk, 1961.
 1 . . . Rd3!! 2 N×d3 Be6 mate.
252. Valund–Martens, Vesco, 1958.
 1 Bg7!! K×g7 2 f6+!! B×f6 3 Qh7 mate.
253. Saidy–Padevsky, Varna, 1958.
 1 . . . Q×e3+!! White resigns (on *2 Q×e3* comes *2 . . . Rd1+* and *3 . . . Rf1* mate).
254. Kilander–Ceki, Corr., 1966–7.
 1 . . . f6+!! White resigns. (*2 Q×f6 R×e5+ 3 Kh4 Rh5+ 4 Kg3 Rh3* mate.)
255. Smyslov–Flohr, Moscow, 1949.
 1 g6+!! h×g6 (or *1 . . . K×g6 2 Rg8+! Kf7 3 Rbg1 R×c6 4 R1g7* mate) 2 Rb7 mate.
256. Kwilezki–Rozlinski, Poznan, 1954.
 1 Qe5+ Kf8 (*1 . . . Kg8* is bad on account of *2 Re8+*, while *1 . . . Kh6* is met by *2 Qf4+!*) 2 Qf6!!, and White wins, since 2 . . . Q×e7 and 2 . . . R×e7 both fail to 3 Qh8 mate.

## Test 33 Positions 257–264

There are two themes in this test, namely 'X-ray', i.e. the penetrating action of pieces (Nos. 257–260), and 'Combinations involving the overloading of pieces' (Nos. 261–264). The test is set for 50 minutes.

257 B

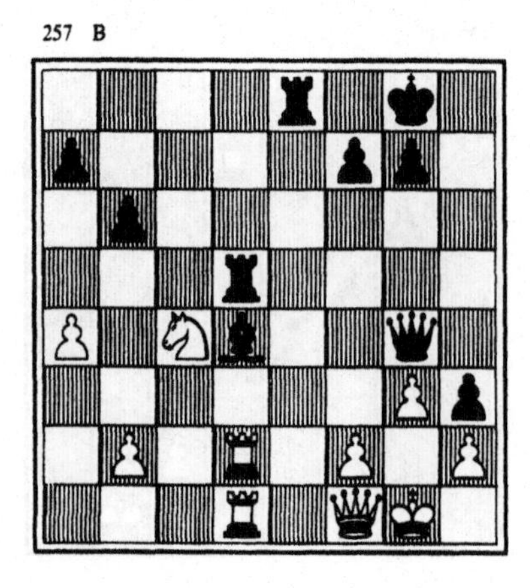

258 W

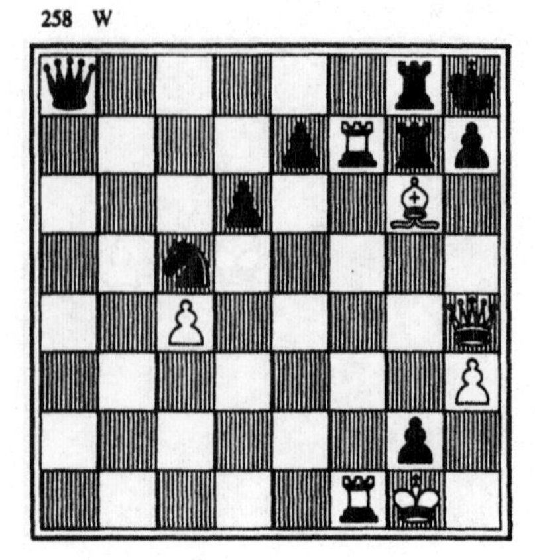

259 B

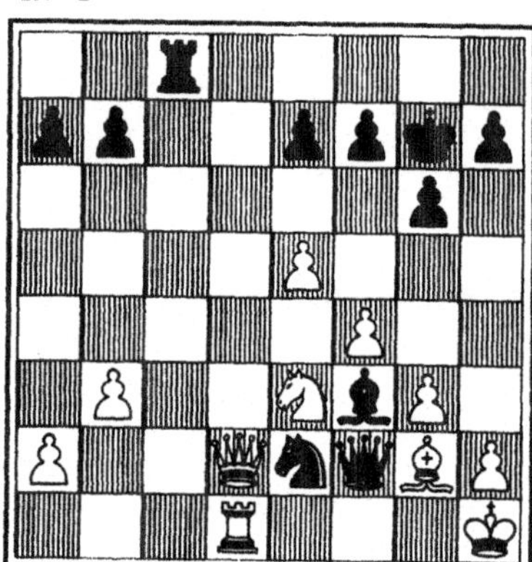

260 W

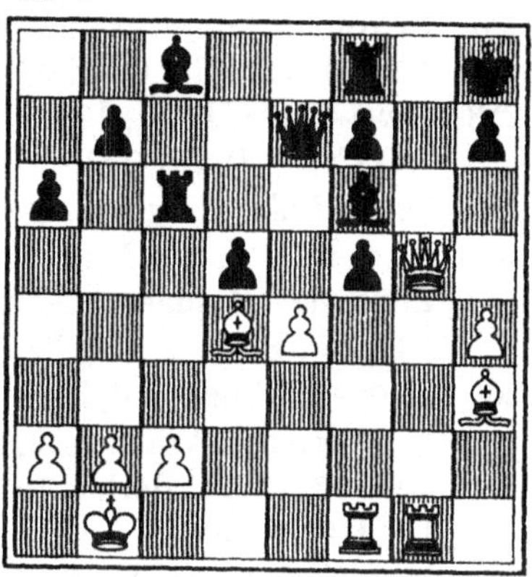

261 B

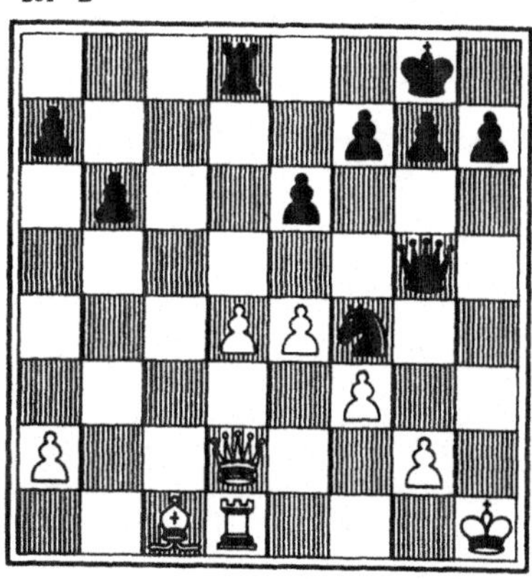

262 W

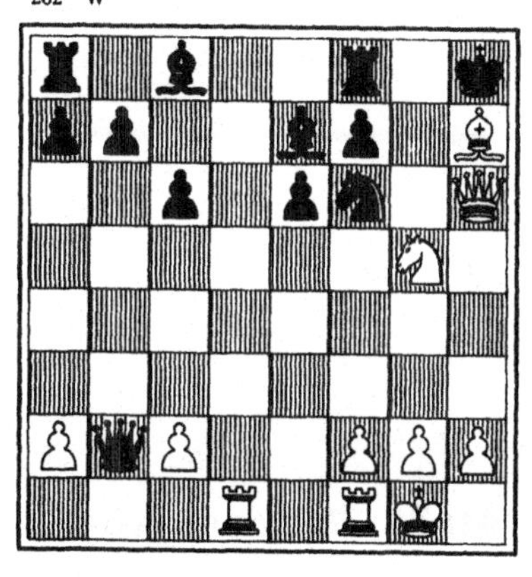

263 B

264 W

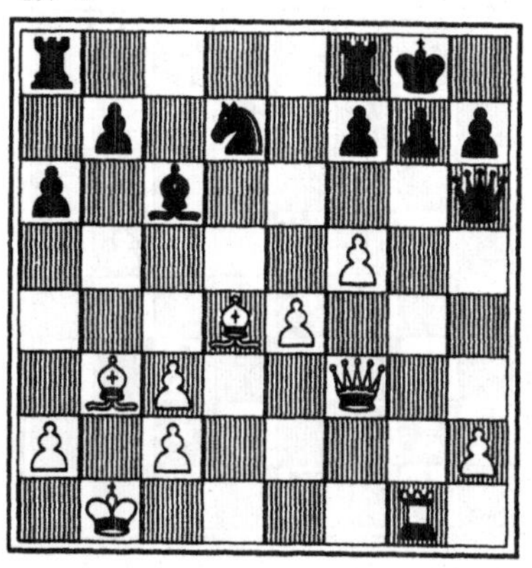

## *Solutions to Test 33*

257. Novotelnov–Averbakh, Moscow, 1951.
 1 . . . B×f2+!! 2 Q×f2 Q×d1+!! White resigns.
258. Sliwa–Doda, Lodz, 1967.
 1 Q×h7+! R×h7 2 R×h7 mate.
259. Dieks–Miles, England, 1973.
 1 . . . Rc1!! 2 B×f3 (or *1 R×c1 N×g3+!*) 2 . . . Qg1+!! White resigns.
260. Zhuravlev–Romanov, Kalinin, 1952.
 1 Qg7+! B×g7 2 B×g7+ Kg8 3 Bf6 mate.
261. Saidy–Marsalek, Reykjavik, 1957.
 1 . . . R×d4!! White resigns.
262. Teschner–Flad, Berlin, 1954.
 1 Rd8!! Resigns.
263. Montell–Serrano, Spain, 1962.
 1 . . . Qh6!! White resigns.
264. Beni–Schwarzbach, Vienna, 1969.
 1 Qh3!! Resigns.

## Test 34 Positions 265–272

The theme 'Combinations based on the overloading of pieces' is continued. The test is not difficult, and is calculated for 50 minutes.

265 B

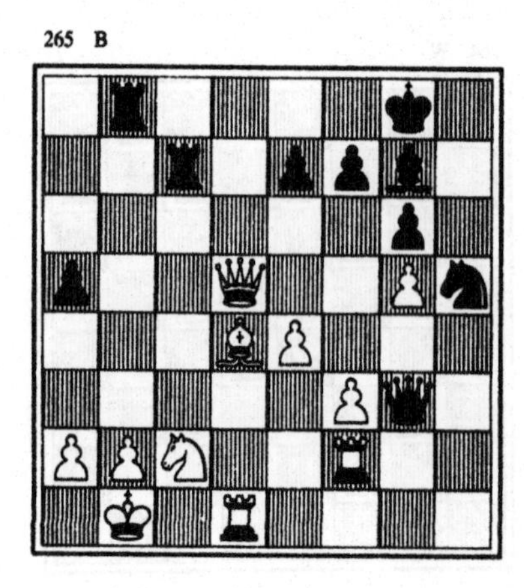

266 W

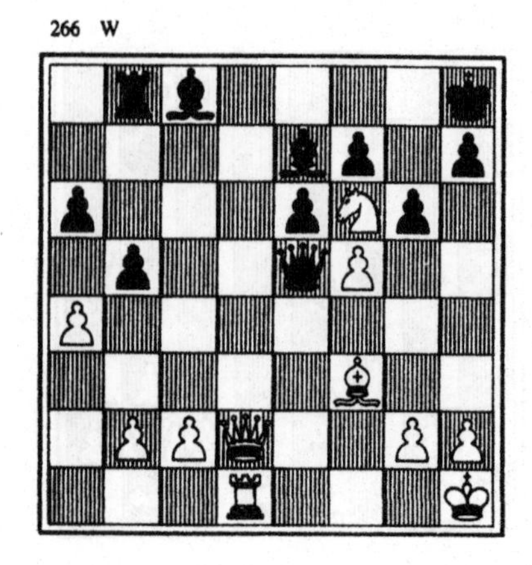

267 W

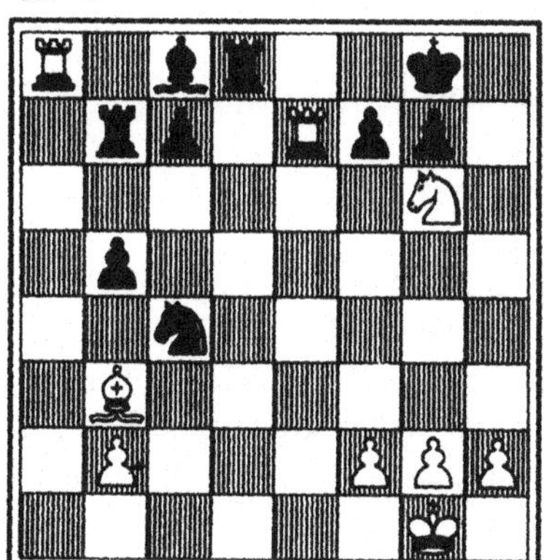

268 W

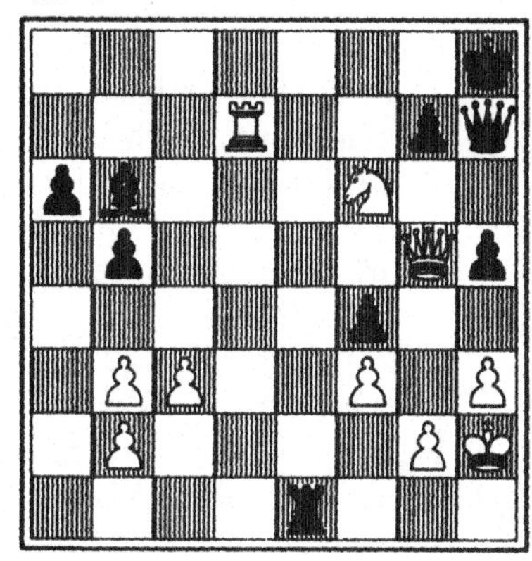

269 W

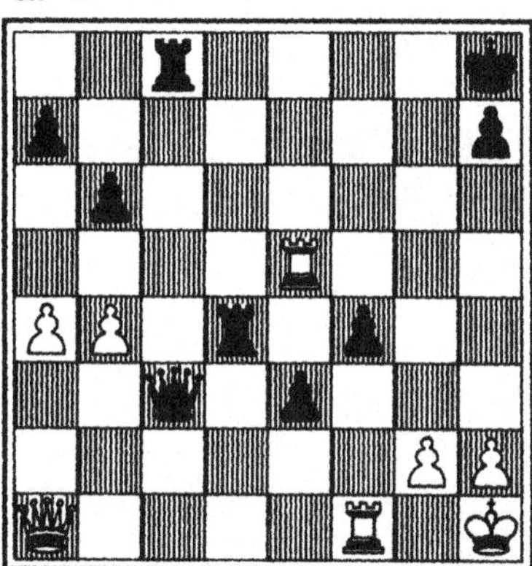

270 W

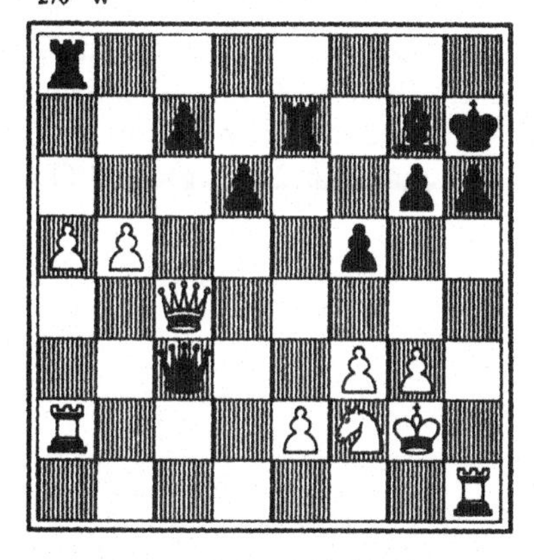

271 W

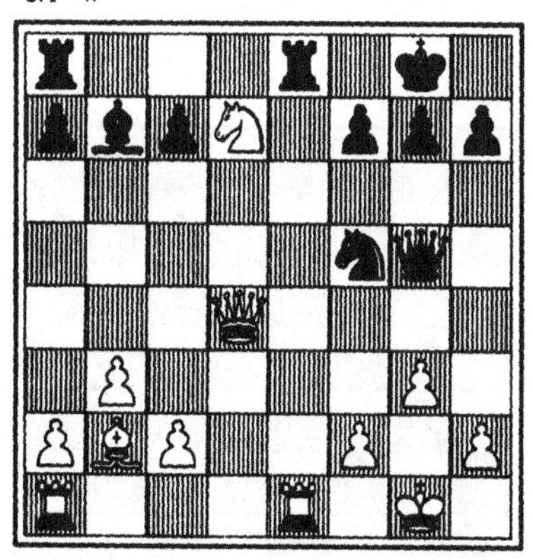

It appears that White can capture on a7, but is this so?

272 W

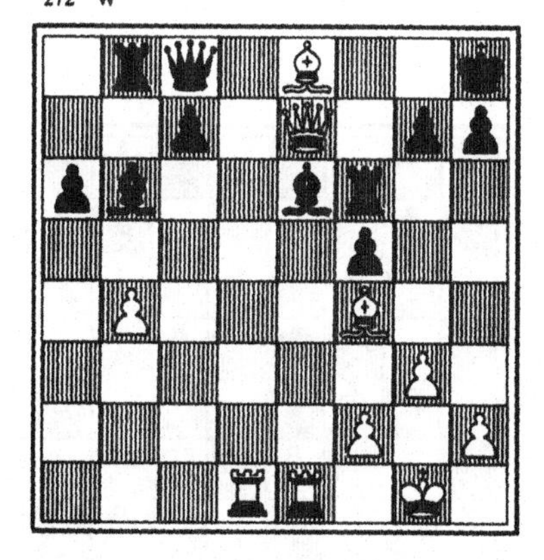

### Solutions to Test 34

265. Bannik–Zaitsev, A., Minsk, 1962.
1 . . . Q×f2!! Resigns. After 2 B×f2 R×b2+ 3 Ka1 Rb5+ Black wins.
266. Aitken–Paine, England, 1962.
1 Qh6 Q×f6 2 Rd8+! Resigns (*2 . . . B×d8 3 Qf8* mate).
267. Tal–N. N., Tbilisi, 1965. (From a simultaneous display.)
1 Rd7!! Resigns (since *1 . . . R×d7* is answered by *2 R×c8+ Kh7 3 Nf8+*).
268. Kreschmer–Laue, Eisenach, 1951.
1 Qc5!! Resigns. 1 h4?? is a mistake on account of 1 . . . Rh1+ 2 K×h1 Qb1+ and 3 . . . Qg1+ followed by mate, while 1 Q×f4 similarly fails to win after 1 . . . Rh1+ 2 Kg3 (*2 K×h1 Qb1+ 3 Kh2 Qg1+* and *4 . . . Bf2* mate) 2 . . . Qg6+ 3 Ng4 h×g4.
269. Simagin–Nikolich, Kislovodsk, 1968.
1 Re8+!! Kg7 2 R×c8 Resigns.
270. Smejkal–Adorján, Vrnjacka Banja, 1972.
1 R×h6+!! Resigns (since if *1 . . . B×h6 2 Q×c3*, or *1 . . . K×h6 2 Qh4* mate).
271. Linek–Mazin, Cologne, 1953.
1 Q×a7?? N×g3!!, and Black wins. If 2 f×g3, then 2 . . . Qd5!, or 2 Q×b7 Ne4+, and mate with the knight at d2 or f2, or 2 f3 Ne2++! 3 Kf2 R×a7.
272. Katalymov–Mnatsakanyan, Tashkent, 1959.
1 Rd7!! B×d7 2 Bh6!! Resigns. Since if 2 . . . Q×e8 3 Q×g7 mate, 2 . . . Rg6 3 Qf8 mate, or 2 . . . g×h6 3 Q×f6+ Kg8 4 Qf7+ and 5 Qf8 mate.

### Test 35 Positions 273–280

We conclude the previous theme. This test is somewhat more difficult. Time for solution—45 minutes.

273 W

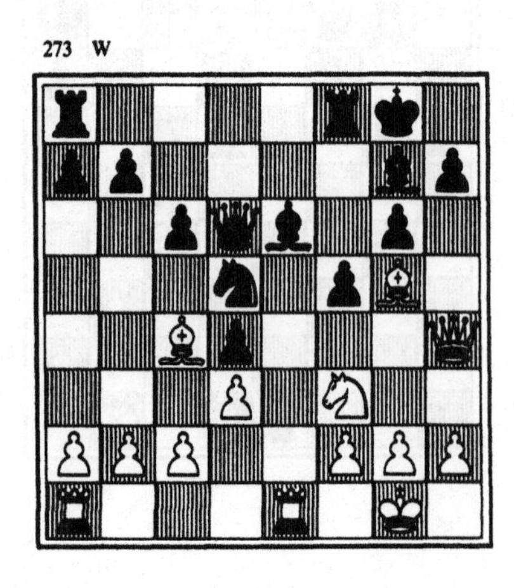

274 W

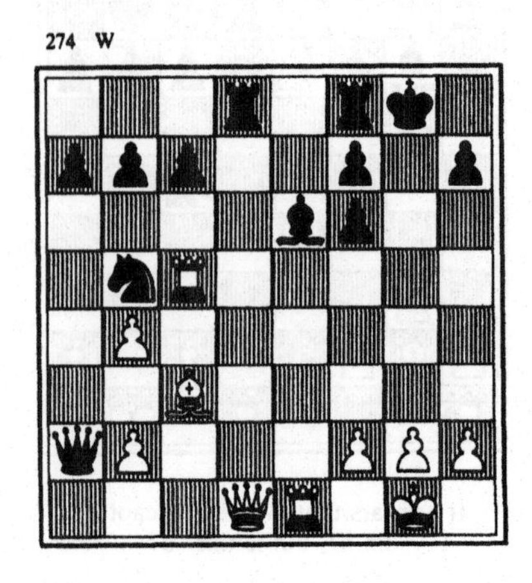

275 W

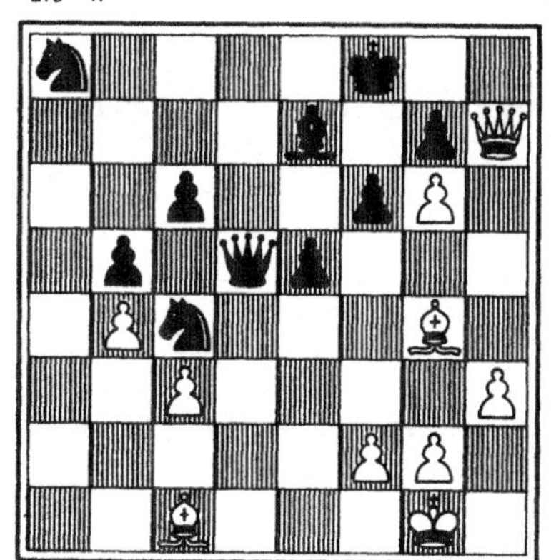

276 W

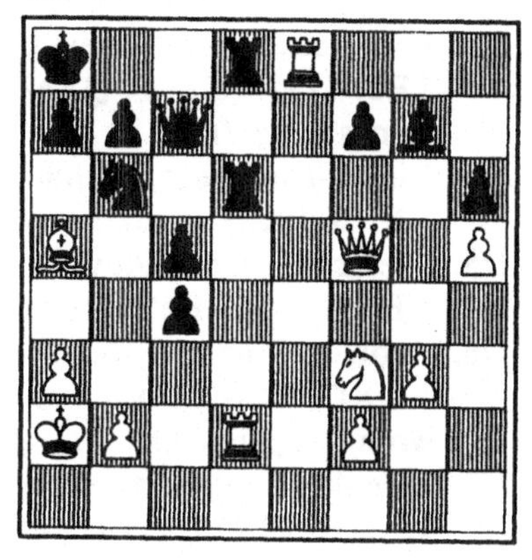

277 B

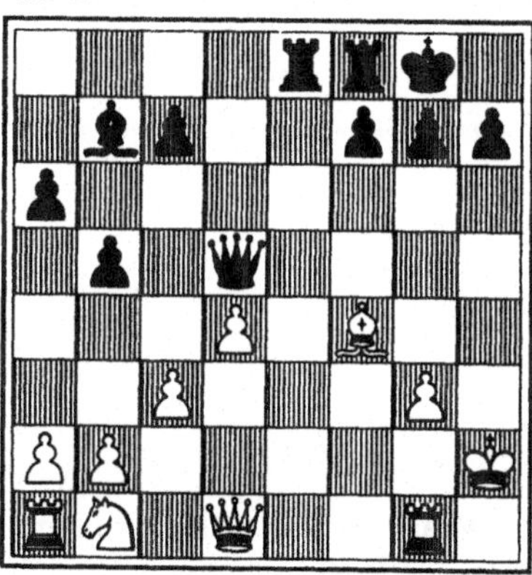

278 W

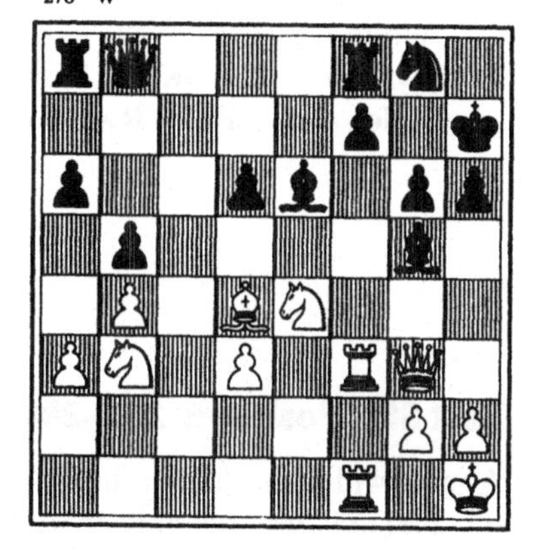

279 W

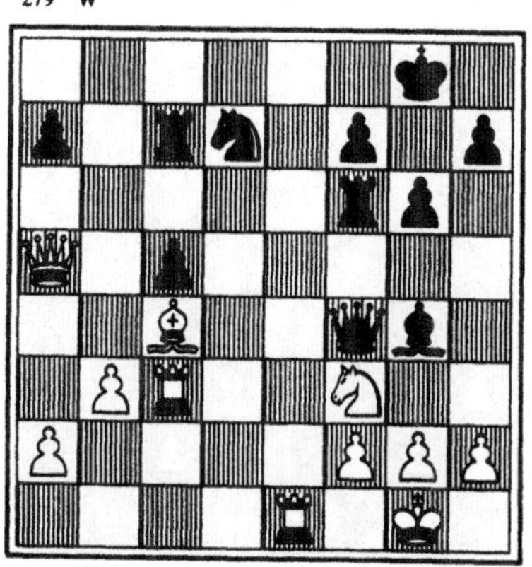

280 W

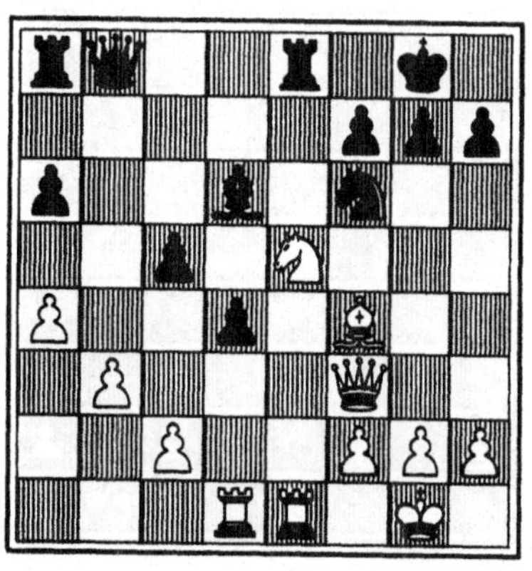

## *Solutions to Test 35*

273. Landstetter–Janos, West Germany, 1972.
1 Be7!! Qd7 (if *1 . . . Q×e7*, then *2 B×d5!!*) 2 R×e6! Resigns (on *2 . . . Q×e6* there comes *3 Ng5!*).
274. Kinzel–Duckstein, Vienna, 1958.
1 B×f6!! Rd5 2 Qd2!! Resigns.
275. Shelochilin–Chernikov, Leningrad, 1950.
1 Bh6!! Qg8 2 Be6!! Resigns.
276. Radulov–Pomar, Nice, 1974.
1 Q×f7!! R×d2 ( or *1 . . . Q×f7 2 R×d8+*) 2 B×d2! Resigns. It would have been wrong to play 2 Q×c7?, on account of 2 . . . R×b2+.
277. Belenky–Pirogov, Moscow, 1957.
1 . . . Re1!! 2 Qg4 (*2 Q×e1 Qh5* mate, or *2 R×e1 Qg2* mate) 2 . . . Qh1+! 3 R×h1 R×h1 mate.
278. Peter–Marcus, Switzerland, 1960.
1 Qh3!! B×h3 2 R×f7+ R×f7 3 R×f7 mate.
279. Flohr–Bivshev, Leningrad, 1951.
1 B×f7+! R×f7 2 Rc4 Qd6 3 R×g4, and with his extra pawn and superior position White won easily.
280. Bykova–Kogan, Kiev, 1954.
1 Nc6 Qc7 2 Re7!! R×e7 3 B×d6 Resigns.

## Test 36 Positions 281–288

A most widely occurring theme—'Exploiting a back rank weakness'. In practical games this theme is met possibly more frequently than any other. To this theme we naturally devote considerable attention. We begin our acquaintance with some fairly simple examples; 35 minutes are allotted to this test.

281 B

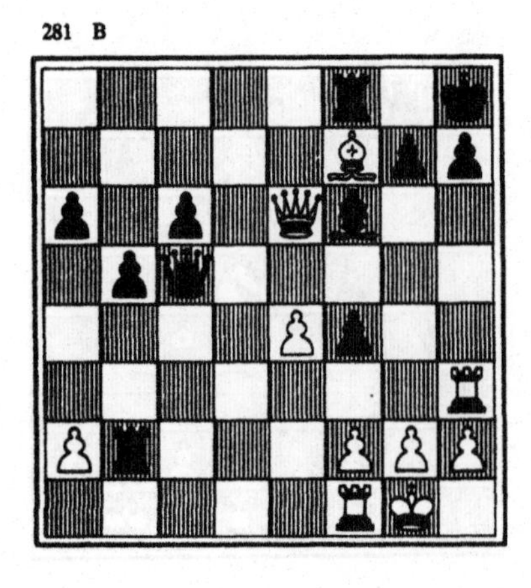

282 B

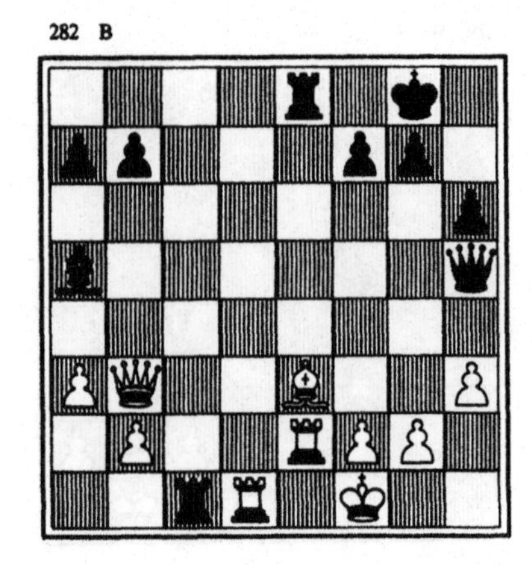

283 W

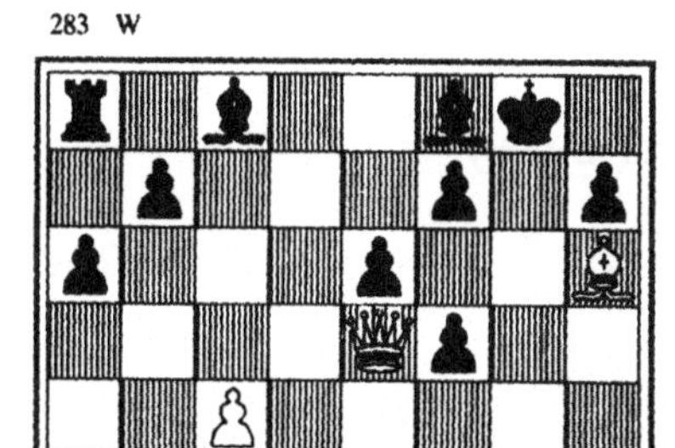

284 W

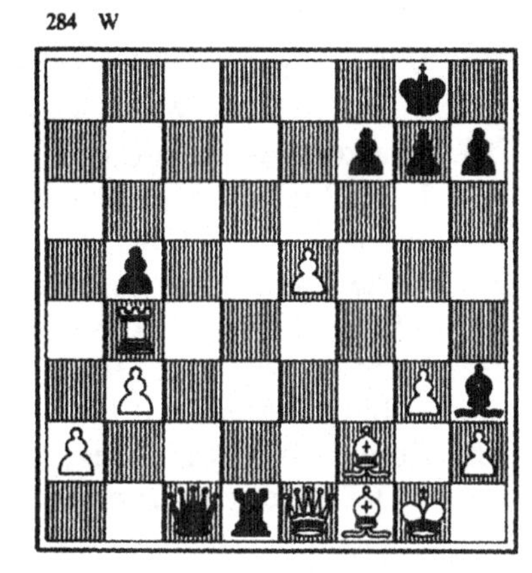

285 W

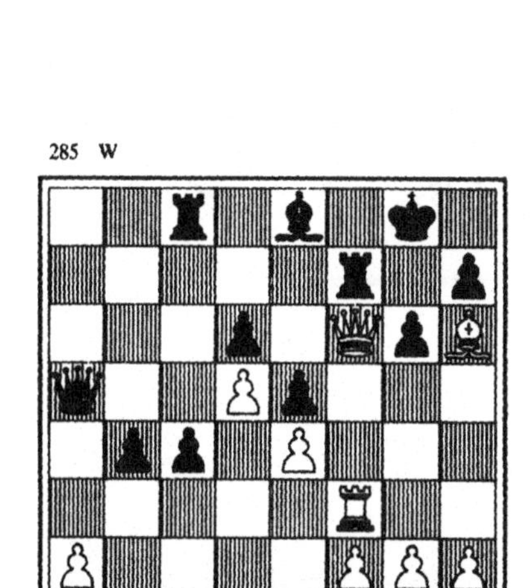

286 W

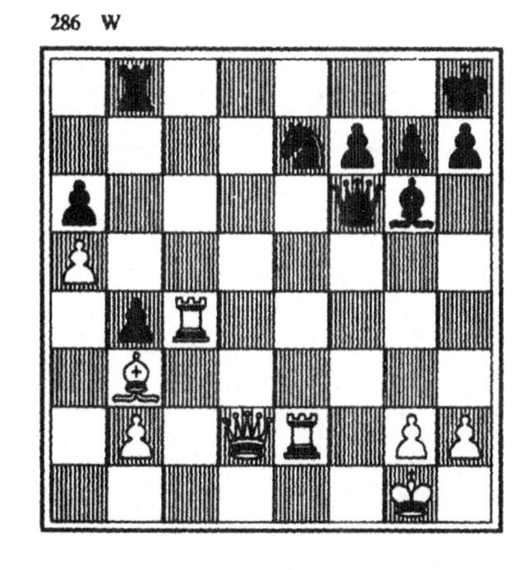

287 W

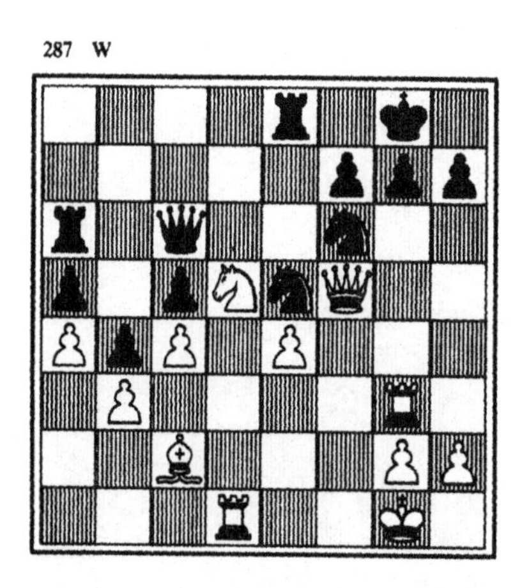

288 B

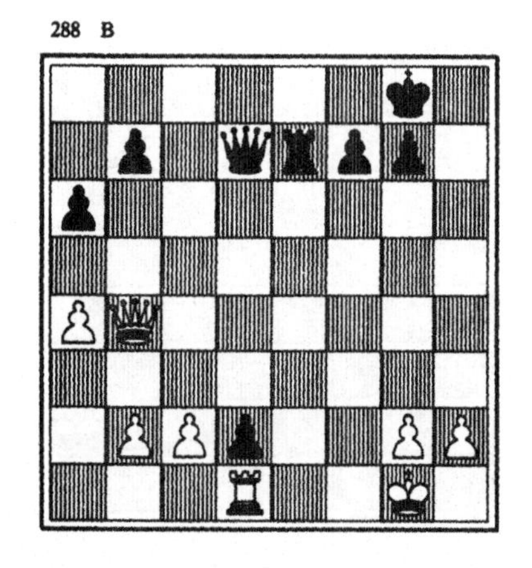

## *Solutions to Test 36*

281. Villup–Pitksaar, Tallinn, 1956.
 1 . . . Q×f2+!! White resigns (*2 R×f2 Rb1+ 3 Rf1 Bd4+*).
282. Chaikovskaya–Dmitrieva, Vilnius, 1972 (variation).
 1 . . . Qb5!!, and Black wins. The game in fact continued 1 . . . R×d1+ 2 Q×d1 Rd8, and ended in a draw.
283. Verle–Laurine, Helmstedt, 1951.
 1 Qg7+!! B×g7 2 Rd8+ Resigns.
284. Petrov–Mirkovich, Moscow, 1970.
 1 Rd4!! Resigns.
285. Zurakhov–Polyak, Kiev, 1952.
 1 Qe7!! Resigns. The threat is 2 Qf8+ and 3 R×f8+, against which there is no defence. If 1 . . . R×f3, then 2 Qg7 mate, or 1 . . . R×e7 2 Rf8 mate, while if the bishop moves from e8 there follows 2 Q×f7+ and 3 Qg7 mate.
286. Keres–Levenfish, Moscow, 1949.
 1 Q×b4!! Resigns. On 1 . . . R×b4 there follows 2 Rc8+ Ng8 3 R×g8+! K×g8 4 Re8 mate, while if 1 . . . Re8, then 2 Q×e7!.
287. Grager–Dorn, Vienna, 1958.
 1 Ne7+!! R×e7 2 Q×f6!! Resigns (*2 . . . Q×f6 3 Rd8+*, or *2 . . . Ng6 3 Q×e7*).
288. Madsen–Napolitano, Italy, 1953.
 1 . . . Re1+! 2 R×e1 Qd4+!! White resigns.

## Test 37 Positions 289–296

A continuation of the previous theme, but slightly more difficult. Time for the solution of this test—40 minutes.

289 W

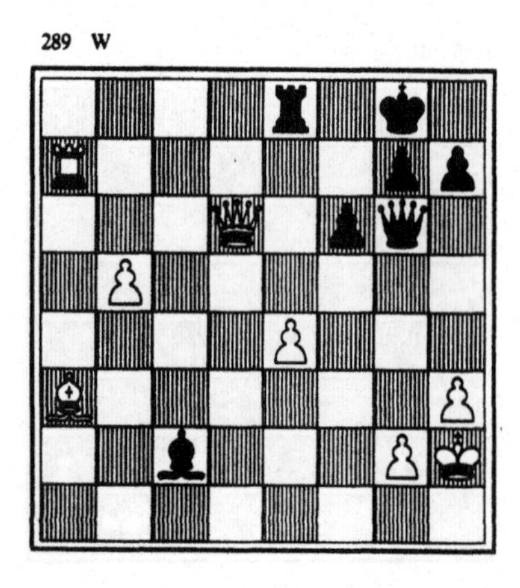

290 W

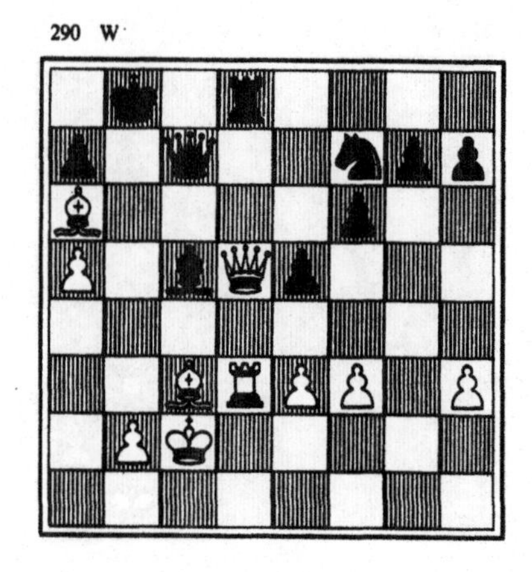

291 W

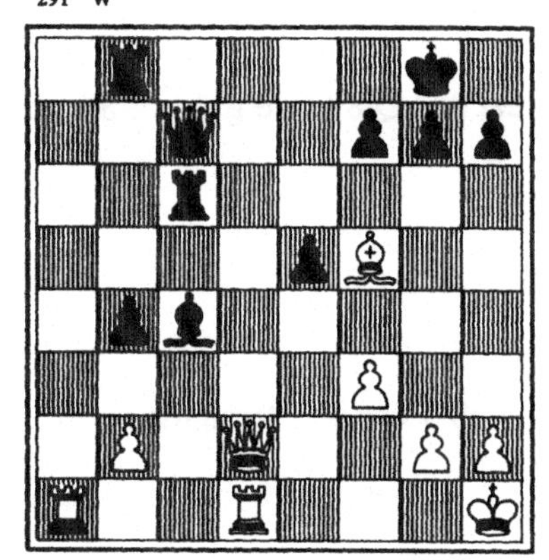

292 W

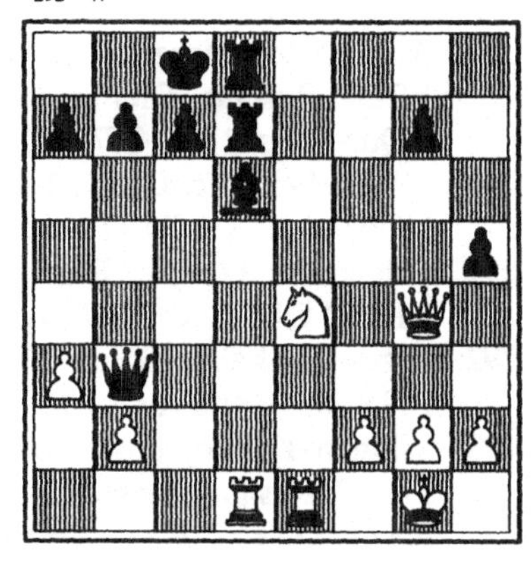

293 W

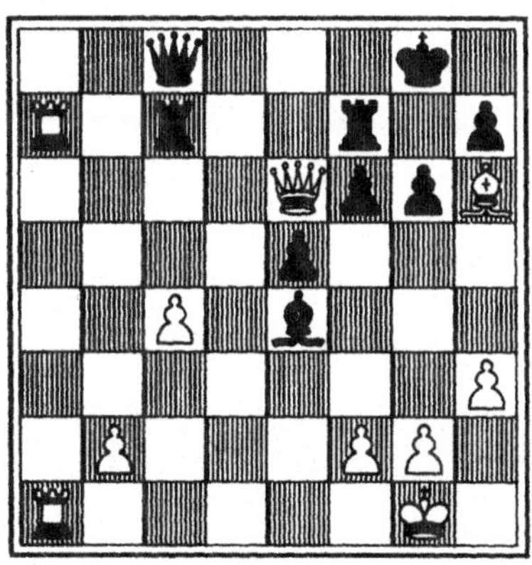

294 B

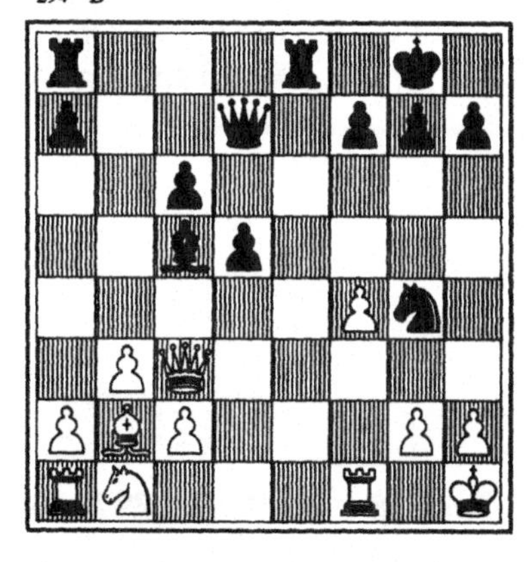

295 W

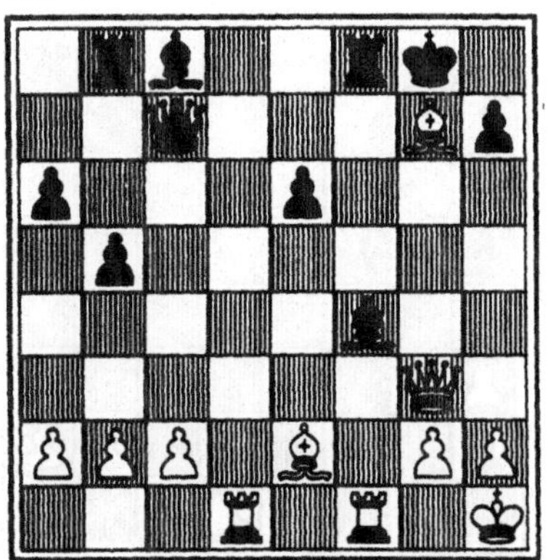

296 W

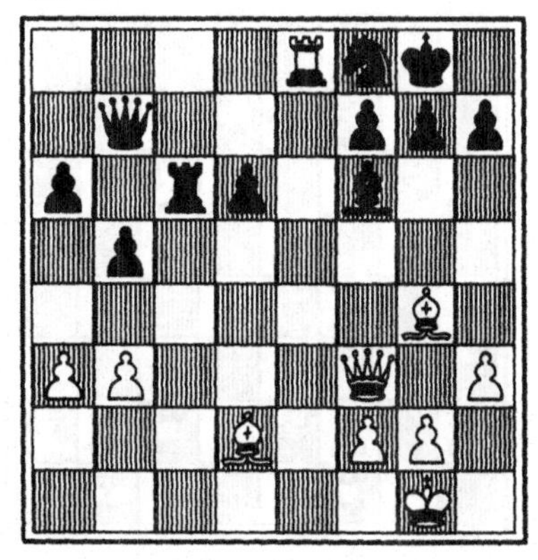

### Solutions to Test 37

289. Aizenshtadt–Margulis, Leningrad, 1957.
1 Ra8!! Resigns. There is no defence against the threat of 2 Qf8+!!, e.g. 1 . . . R×a8 2 Qd5+, or 1 . . . Qf7 2 Qd8!.
290. Paroulek–Kapic, Corr., 1966.
1 Qb3+! Ka8 2 Q×f7!! Resigns.
291. Mileika–Voitkevich, Riga, 1963.
1 Ra7!! Qb6 2 Rb7!! Resigns.
292. Lozev–Daskalov, Sofia, 1958.
1 N×d6+ c×d6 (or *1 . . . Kb8 2 Q×d7!*) 2 Rc1+ Kb8 3 Q×d7!! Resigns.
293. Vikman–Kanko, Corr., 1972–3.
1 Rd1!! Resigns. Since if 1 . . . Q×e6 2 Rd8+, or 1 . . . Bb7 2 R×b7, or 1 . . . Bc6 2 R×c7! Q×e6 3 R×c6 Qe8 4 Rcd6.
294. Marszinjak–Dobosz, Poland, 1973.
1 . . . Nf2+! 2 R×f2 Bd4!! White resigns.
295. Bhend–Lokvenc, Amsterdam, 1954.
1 Bh6+!! Kh8 2 R×f4! Resigns.
296. Dueball–Gereben, Skopje, 1972.
1 Q×f6!! h5 (*1 . . . g×f6 2 Bh6!*) 2 R×f8+! Resigns. Since if 2 . . . K×f8 3 Qd8 mate, or 2 . . . Kh7 3 Bf5+ g6 4 Rh8 mate.

### Test 38 Positions 297–306

A further eight examples on the same theme, but rather more difficult. Time for the solving of this test—50 minutes.

297 B

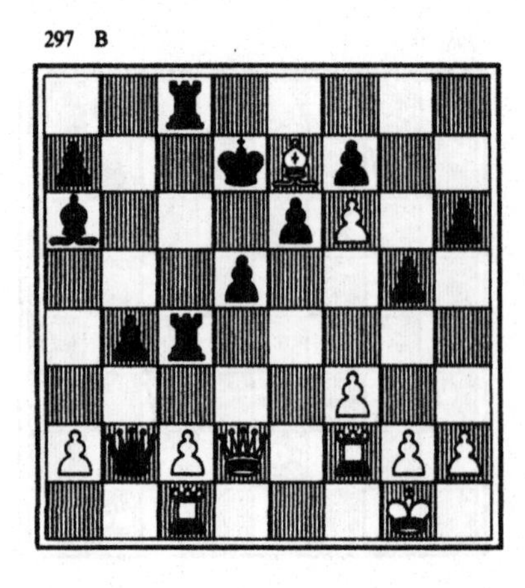

298 B

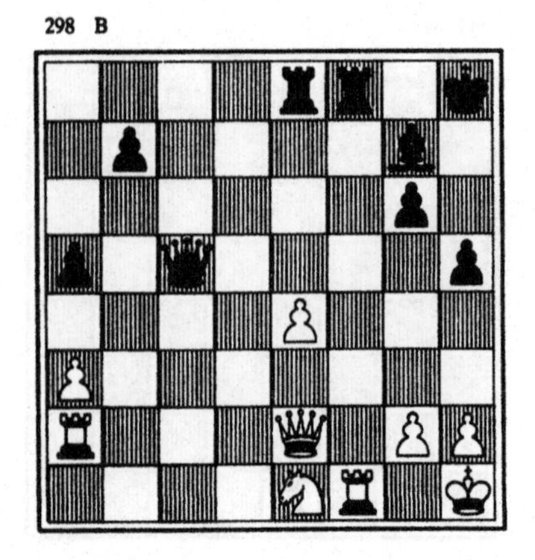

299 B

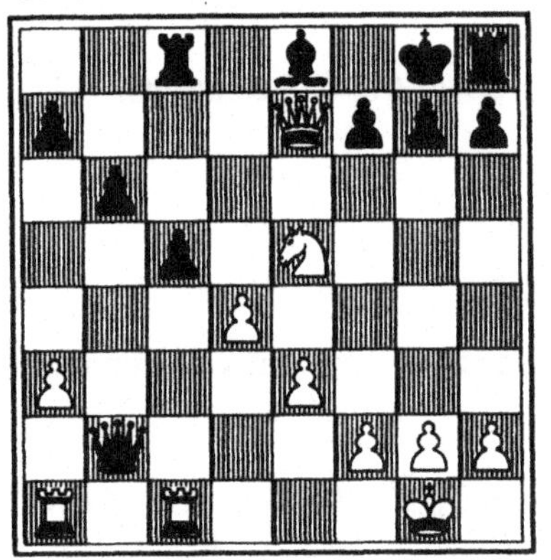

Why is it bad to play 1 . . . c×d4?

300 W

What follows after 1 R×d5?

301 W

302 B

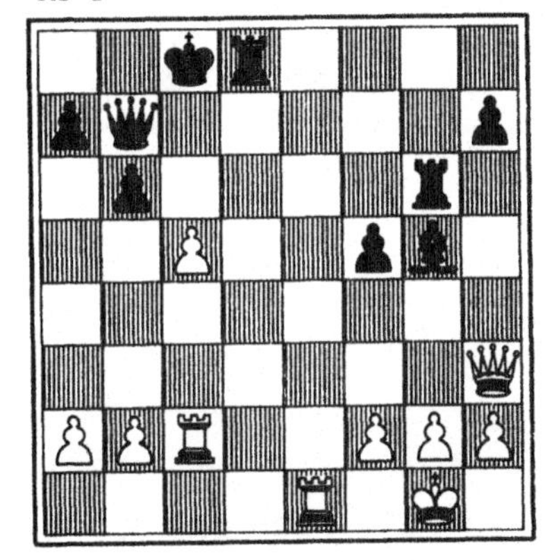

303 B

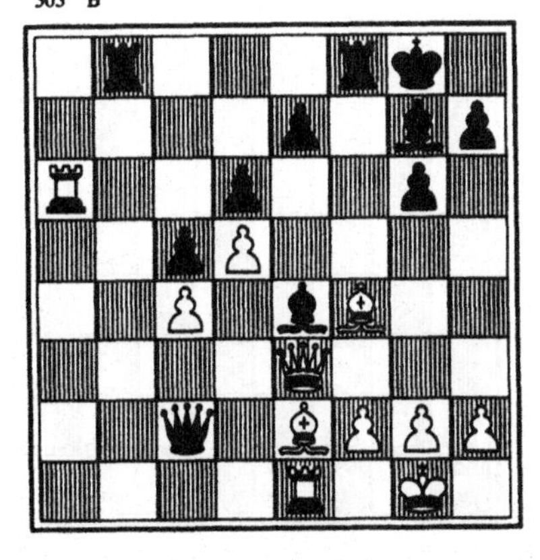

304 W

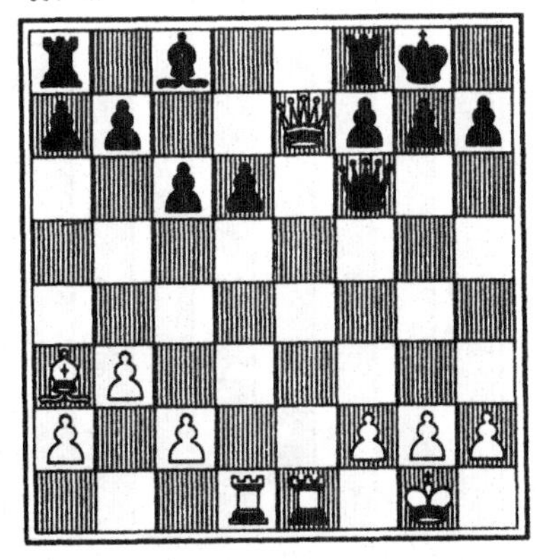

### *Solutions to Test 38*

297. Nilsson–Geller, Stockholm, 1954.
1 . . . R×c2!! 2 Q×c2 (or *2 R×c2 Qb1+!!*) 2 . . . Q×c1+!! White resigns.
298. Hegloff–Andersson, B., Corr., 1968–9.
1 . . . R×e4! 2 Qd3 (*2 R×f8+ Q×f8* is no better) 2 . . . Qf5!! White resigns.
299. Gior–Olafsson, Reykjavik, 1953.
1 . . . c×d4?? 2 Q×f7+!! B×f7 3 R×c8+ Resigns.
300. Teschner–Portisch, Monaco, 1969 (Variation).
1 R×d5?? Qf2!! (Black actually played *1 . . . Qa6*, and after *2 Ng3* the game ended in a draw) 2 Ng3 Qe1+, and Black wins.
301. Flórián–Köberl, Budapest, 1961.
1 Q×c6 Re8 (on *1 . . . Rb8* there would have followed *2 Qb7!! Re8 3 Q×e7+!! R×e7 4 Rb8+*) 2 R×e7!! Resigns. Since if 2 . . . R×e7 3 Rd8+, or 2 . . . Rb8 Qd6!
302. Ivarsson–Ljungquist, Eksjö, 1973.
1 . . . Qe4!! 2 Qc3 Bd2! White resigns. After 3 R×e4 B×c3 he comes out a rook down.
303. Schmid–Bilek, Varna, 1962.
1 . . . R×f4! 2 Q×f4 Q×e2! White resigns.
304. Gusev–Arakelov, Leningrad, 1970.
1 Q×f8+!! K×f8 2 R×d6! Resigns.

## Test 39 Positions 305–312

The final test on the theme 'Exploiting a back rank weakness'. A more difficult test. Time for solution 60 minutes.

305 W

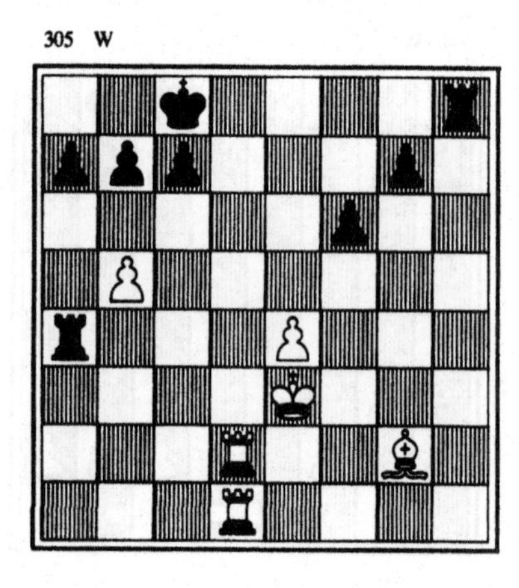

306 B

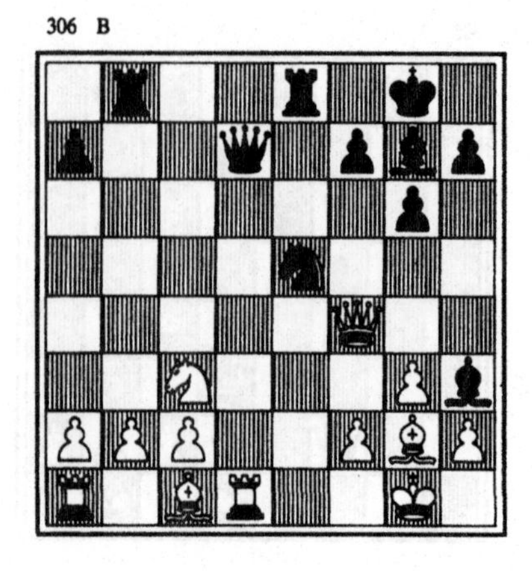

307 B

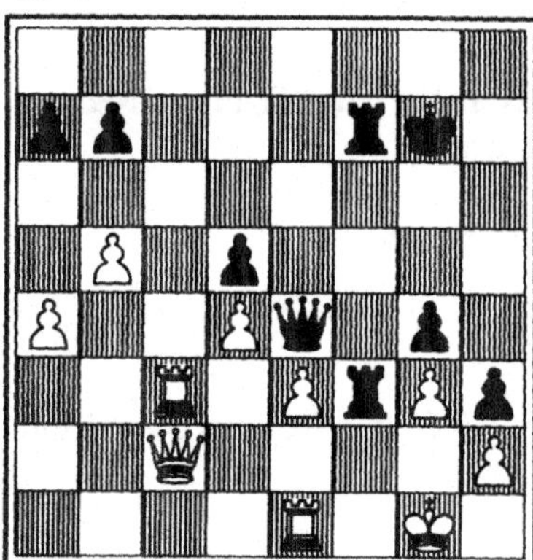

308 B

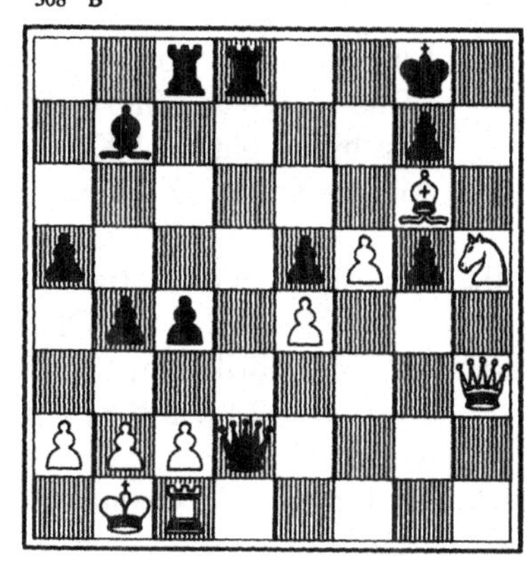

309 W

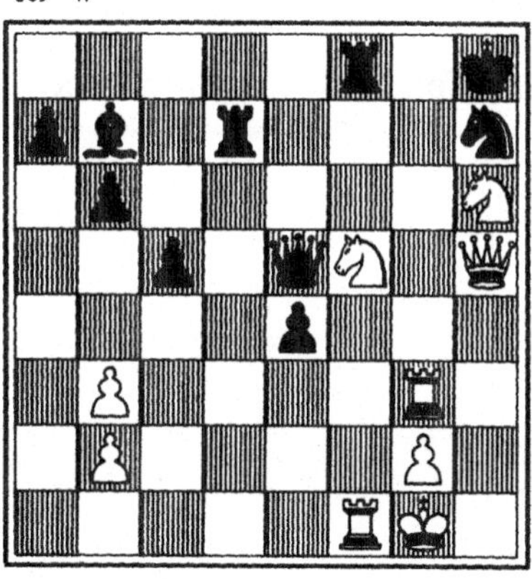

310 B

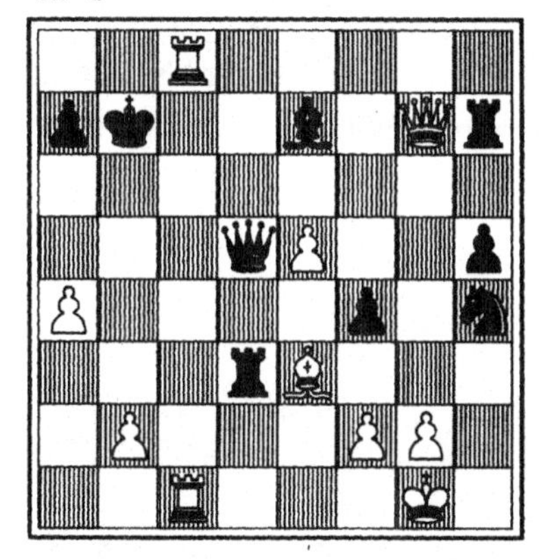

311 W

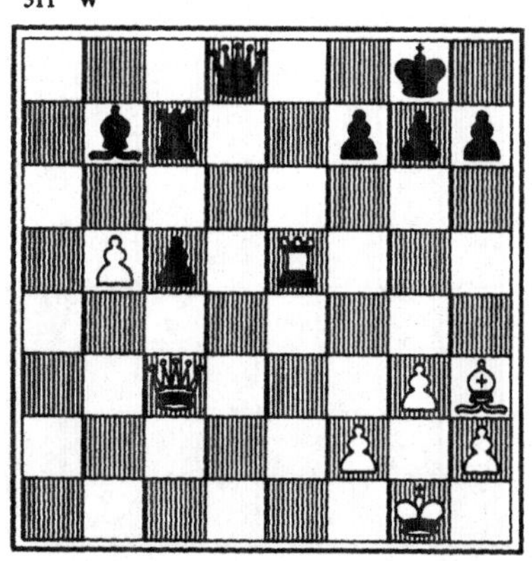

312 B

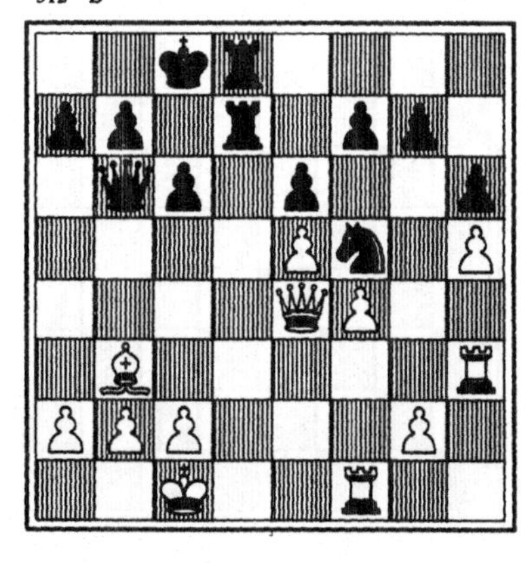

## *Solutions to Test 39*

305. Kan–Simagin, Moscow, 1952.
1 Rd8+!! R×d8 2 Bh3+ Rd7 3 R×d7, and White wins. In the game White missed this possibility, played 1 Kf2, and the game ended in a draw.
306. Aitken–Keffler, Edinburgh, 1954.
1 . . . Q×d1+!! 2 N×d1 Nf3+ 3 Q×f3 Re1+ White resigns.
307. Borsyak–Kizilov, Mogilev, 1962.
1 . . . Rf1+!! 2 R×f1 Qh1+!! 3 K×h1 R×f1 mate.
308. Westin–Fridriksson, Sweden, 1973.
1 . . . Q×c2+!! 2 R×c2 (or *2 K×c2 B×e4+*) 2 . . . Rd1+ 3 Rc1 B×e4+ White resigns.
309. Muller–Kinzel, Vienna, 1961.
1 Qf7!! Qd5 (if *1 . . . Rd×f7*, then *2 Rg8+ R×g8 3 N×f7* mate, or *1 . . . Q×g3 2 Q×d7*, or *1 . . . Qe8 2 Q×e8 R×e8 3 Nd6!*) 2 Nd6! Rd×f7 3 Nd×f7+ Resigns.
310. Kurajica–Planinc, Umag, 1972.
1 . . . Nf3+!! 2 Kf1 (or *2 g×f3 R×g7+*) 2 . . . Rd1+ 3 Ke2 Ng1 mate.
311. Ivkov–Eliskases, Munich, 1958.
1 Qd2!! Qa8 (if *1 . . . Qf8*, then *2 Qe3!!*) 2 Qa5! Qb8 3 Q×c7! Resigns.
312. Boiser–Vogt, Corr., 1962.
1 . . . Qf2!! 2 Qe1 Ne3! White resigns. On 3 R×e3 there follows 3 . . . Rd1+! 4 Q×d1 Q×e3+.

## **Test 40 Positions 313–320**

Theme: 'Weakness of the second rank'. A relatively simple test. Time—35 minutes.

313 B

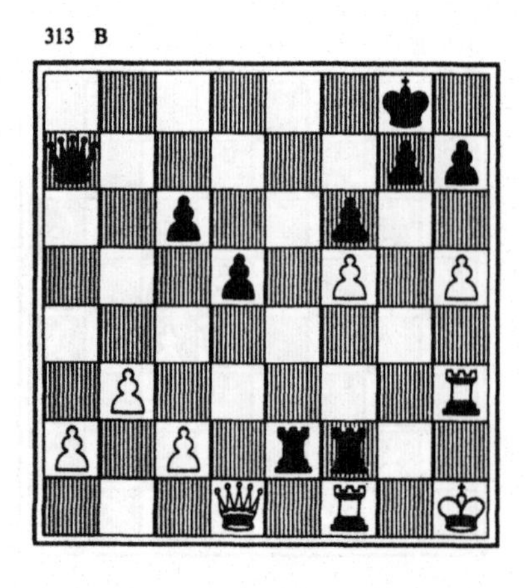

314 B

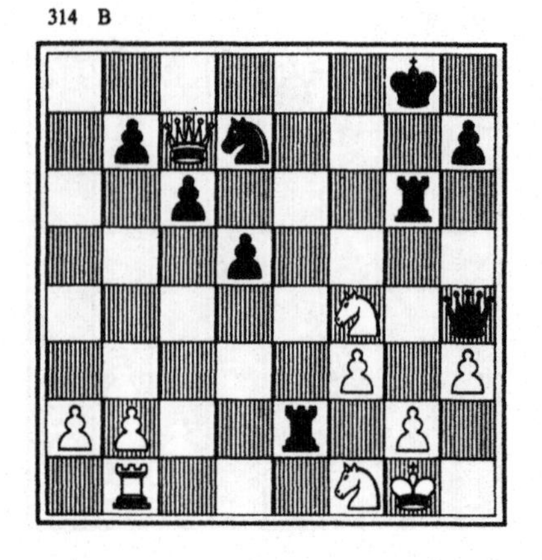

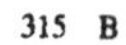

315 B

316 W

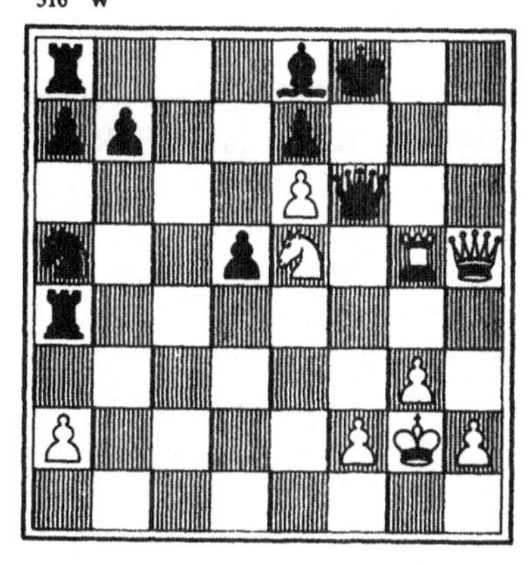

317 W

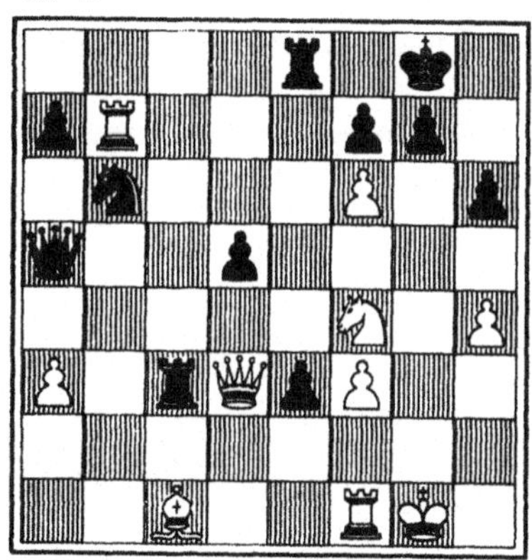

318 B

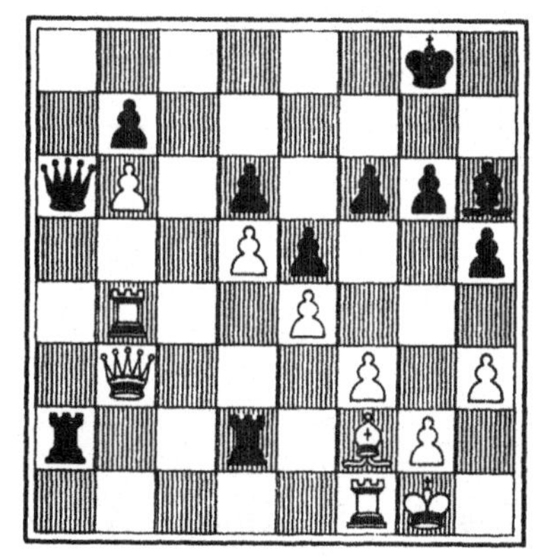

319 W

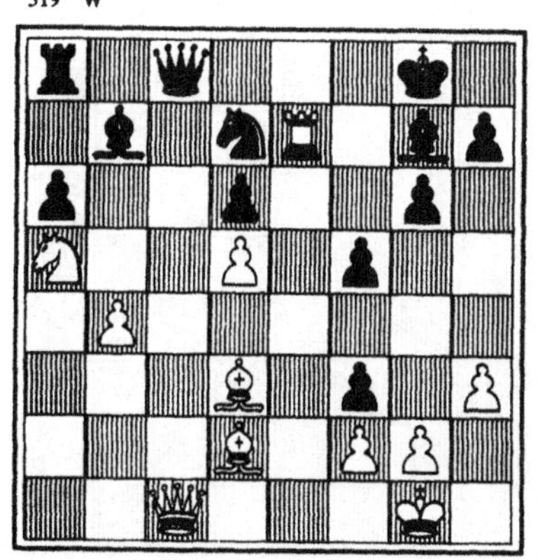

320 W

## *Solutions to Test 40*

313. Hjorth–Lundin, Motala, 1946.
1 . . . Qe3!! White resigns.
314. Ryzhkov–Faas, USSR, 1978.
1 . . . Q×f4! White resigns: 2 Q×f4 Re×g2+ 3 Kh1 Rg1+ 4 Kh2 R6g2 mate.
315. Lundin–Smyslov, Groningen, 1946.
1 . . . Rf2!! and wins. In the game Black missed this possibility, and only drew after 1 . . . Nf2+.
316. Lieb–Kunstoviz, West Germany, 1974.
1 Qh7! Resigns. On 1 . . . Q×g5 there follows 2 Nd7+ B×d7 3 Qf7 mate.
317. Bronstein–Geller, Moscow, 1961.
1 Qg6!! Resigns.
318. Gheorghiu–Diez del Corral, Las Palmas, 1973.
1 . . . Q×f1+!! 2 K×f1 R×f2+ 3 Kg1 (or *3 Ke1 R×g2 4 Kf1 Raf2+ 5 Ke1 Bd2+*) 3 . . . R×g2+ 4 Kh1 Rgc2 White resigns.
319. Ciocaltea–Ungureanu, Bucharest, 1971.
1 N×b7! Q×b7 2 B×f5!! g×f5 3 Bc3! Resigns (if *3 . . . Be5*, then *4 Qh6!*).
320. Kuzmin–Krivonosov, Daugavpils, 1974.
1 B×b7! Rb8 (*1 . . . B×b7 2 Rd7*, or *1 . . . Q×b7 2 Rd8* mate) 2 B×c8 R×c8 3 Rd7! Resigns.

## Test 41 Positions 321–328

We conclude the theme 'Weakness of the second rank' with a rather more difficult test. Solving time—45 minutes.

321 B

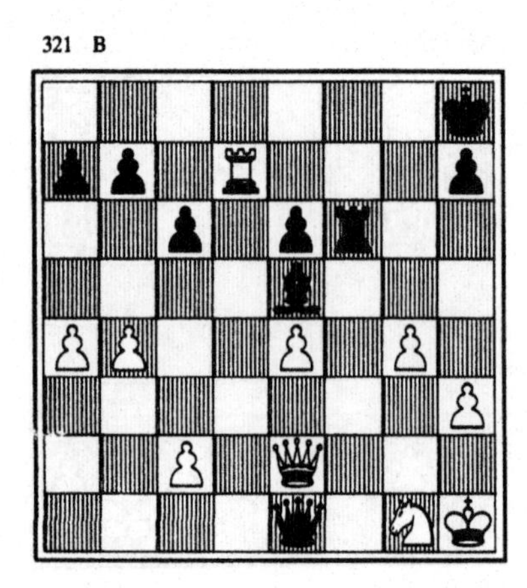

322 W

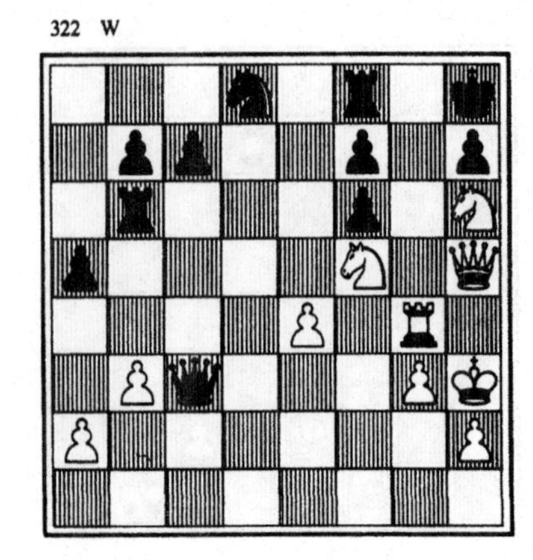

323 B

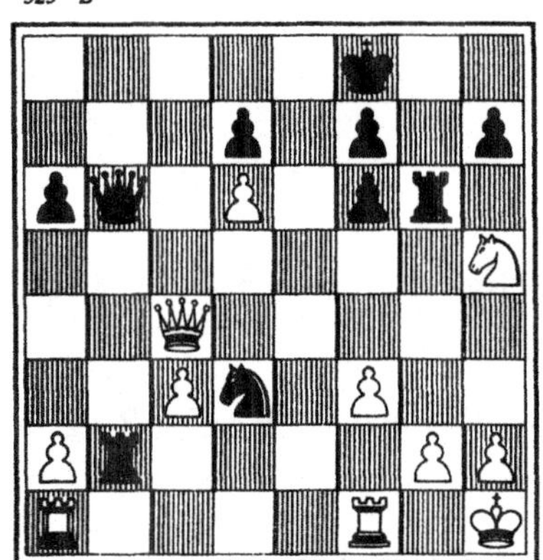

324 W

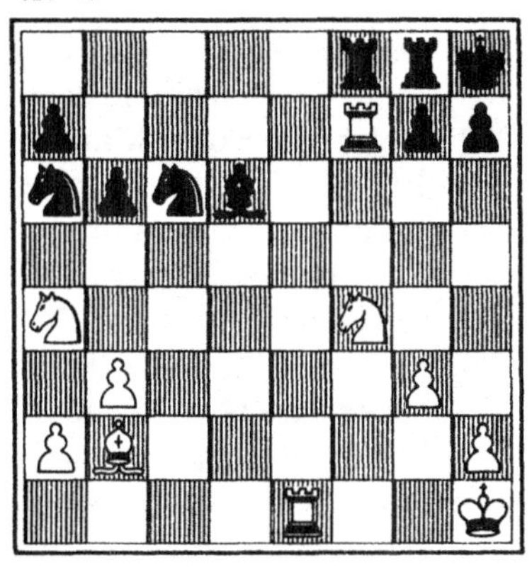

325 W

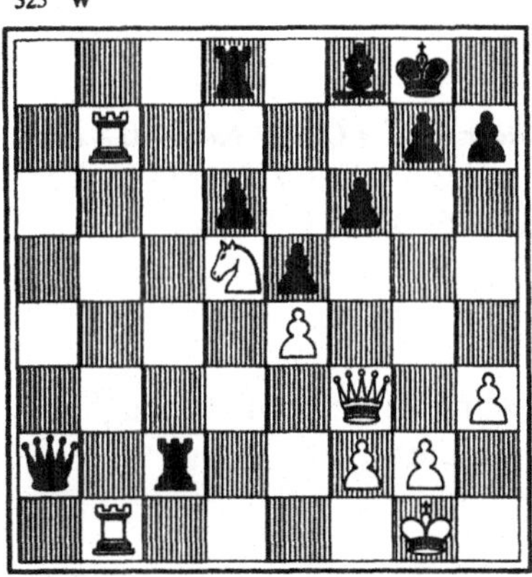

326 W

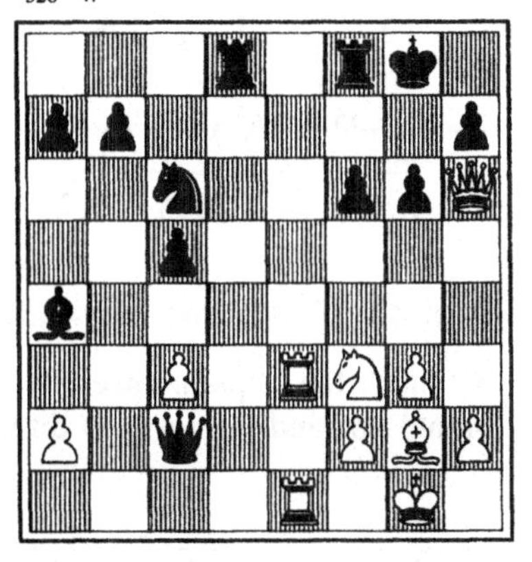

327 W

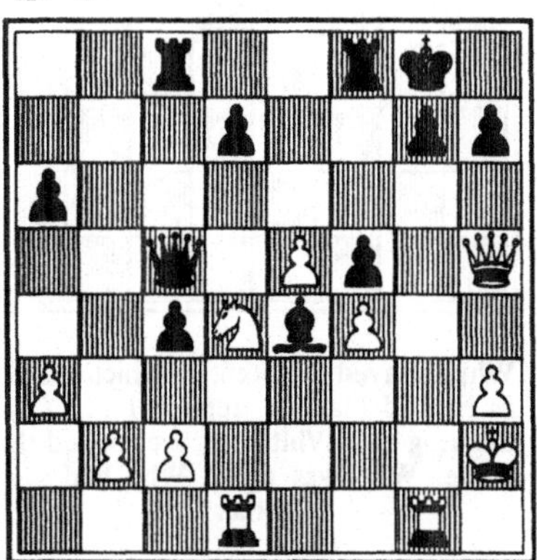

328 W

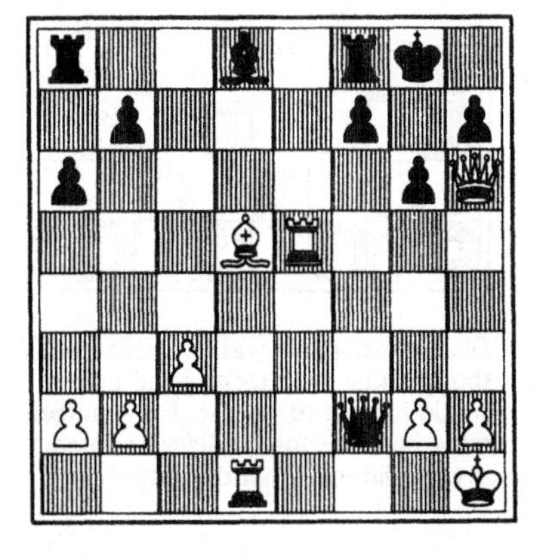

## *Solutions to Test 41*

321. Dantes–Wexler, Mar del Plata, 1951.
1 . . . Rf2!! White resigns.
322. Doler–Haywood, Manchester, 1950.
1 Q×f7+!! N×f7 2 Rg8+!! R×g8 3 N×f7 mate.
323. Ilchenko–Sozina, Voronezh, 1971.
1 . . . Qg1+!! 2 K×g1 (or *2 R×g1 Nf2* mate) 2 . . . Rg×g2+ 3 Kh1 R×h2+ 4 Kg1 Rbg2 mate.
324. Furman–Witkowski, Polanica Zdroj, 1967.
1 Re4!! B×f4 (*1 . . . R×f7* fails to *2 Ng6+!! h×g6 3 Rh4* mate) 2 B×g7+ R×g7 3 R×f8+ Resigns.
325. Stoma–Chekhlov, Riga Ch., 1975.
1 N×f6+! g×f6 (*1 . . . Kh8 2 Qf5*) 2 Qg4+ Kh8 3 R×h7+! Resigns.
326. Botvinnik–Smyslov, Moscow, 1958 (variation).
1 Nd4!! N×d4 (on *1 . . . c×d4* there follows *2 Bd5+! R×d5 3 Re8!!*) 2 Bd5+! R×d5 3 Re7!, and White wins. In the game there followed 1 Bh3 Ne5 2 N×e5 f×e5 3 f4 Bc6, and White's tactical chances were eliminated.
327. Kislov–Beribesov, USSR, 1971.
1 R×g7+! K×g7 2 Ne6+! Resigns.
328. Shaudis–Grigorevsky, USSR, 1977.
1 Rh5! g×h5 (if *1 . . . Re8*, then *2 Q×h7+ Kf8 3 Qh8+ Ke7 4 Qe5+ Kd7 5 B×b7+*, mating) 2 Be4 f5 (or *2 . . . Re8 3 B×h7+ Kh8 4 Bf5+ Kg8 5 Qh7+ Kf8 6 Qh8+ Ke7 7 Rd7* mate) 3 Bd5+ Rf7 4 B×f7+ K×f7 5 Rd7+ Be7 6 Q×h7+ Resigns.

## Test 42 Positions 329–336

We make the acquaintance of a new theme, 'Intermediate move' or 'Zwischenzug'. You should not find the test too difficult. Solving time—45 minutes.

329 W

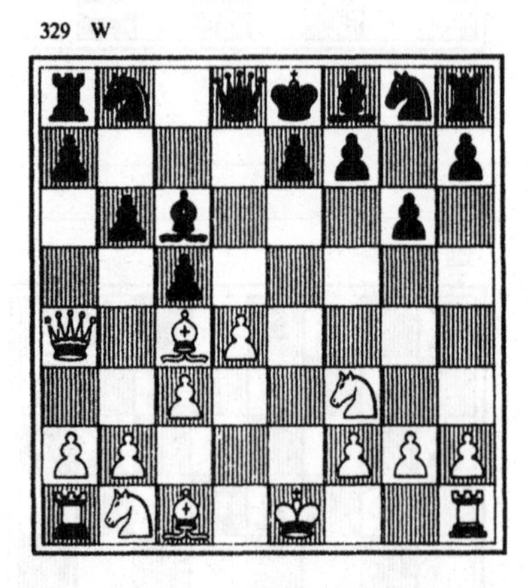

Black's last move was . . . Bd5–c6. He thought that by attacking the queen he would force it to retreat. But a surprise move by White forced Black's immediate capitulation. What did White play?

330 W

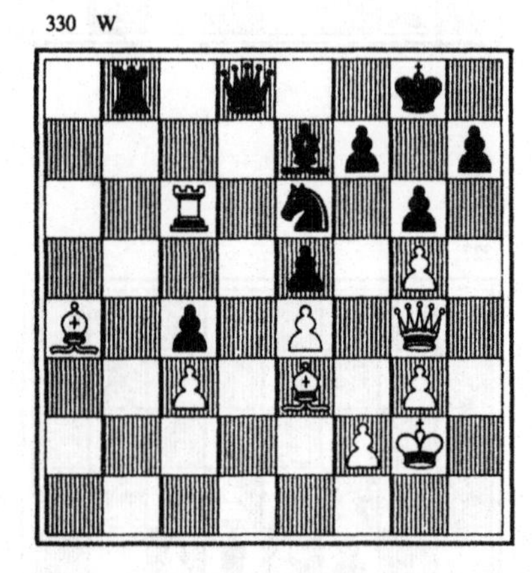

White played 1 R×e6, to which Black, as he had planned, replied 1 . . . Qc8, thinking that White had overlooked this move. Who was right? Who had seen further?

331 W

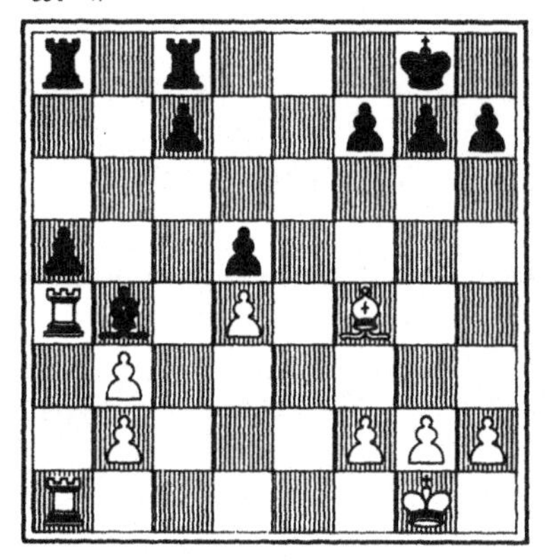

Why shouldn't White capture the pawn at c7? After 1 B×c7 R×c7 2 R×b4 everything appears to be in order. But is this so?

332 W

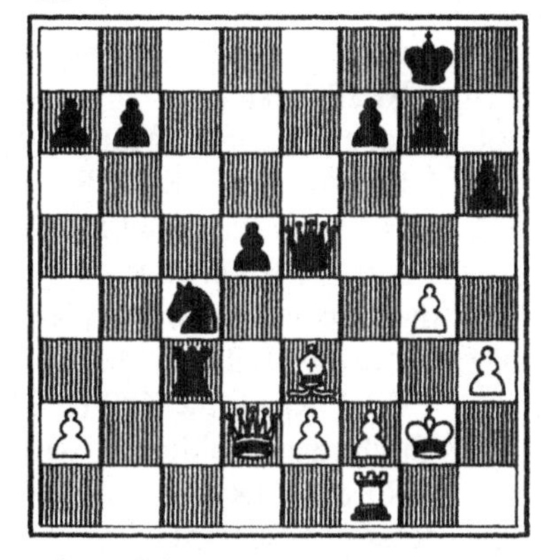

After 1 Bd4 it appears that the worst is over. But nevertheless White had overlooked something. What?

333 W

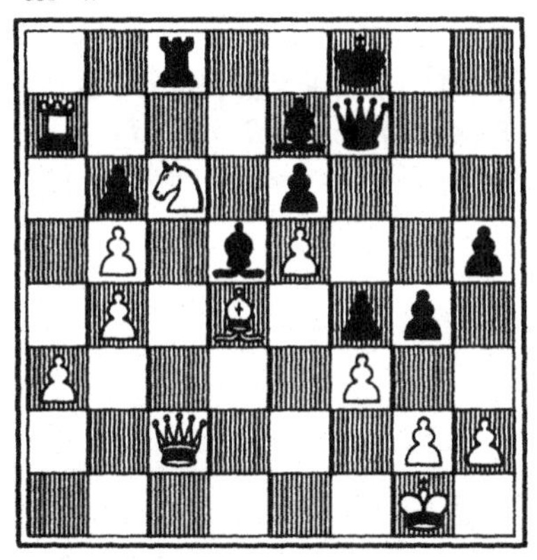

White to play. How does he win most quickly?

334 W

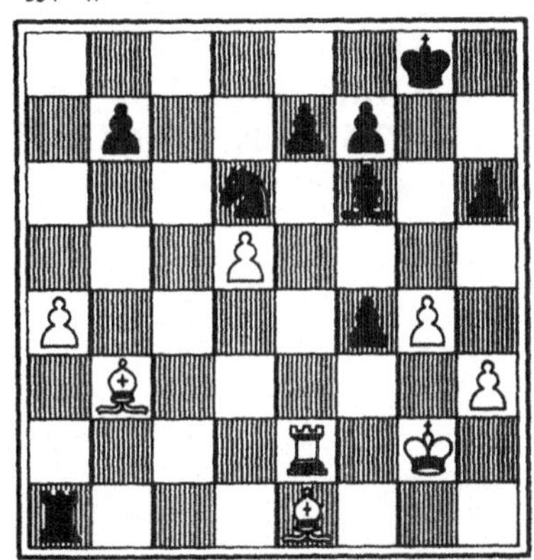

White to play decided to simplify the position by 1 Bb4 Rb1 2 B×d6, hoping thereby to gain a draw, but he overlooked his opponent's reply, after which he was immediately forced to lay down his arms. What was it that White missed?

335 B

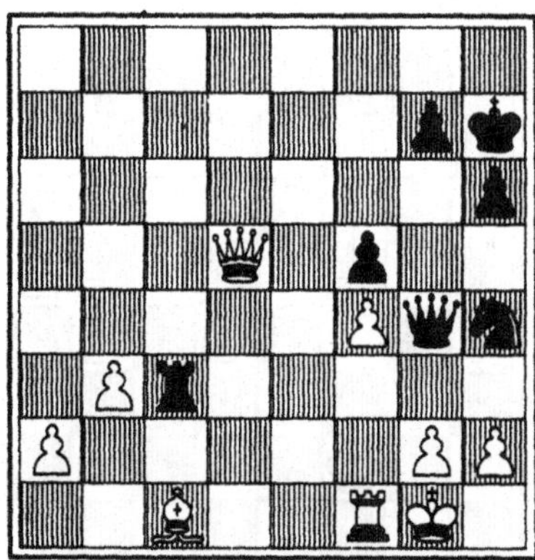

White had considered only 1 . . . Rc2, on which 2 Bd2 is perfectly adequate. But Black had another way to win. What was it?

336 W

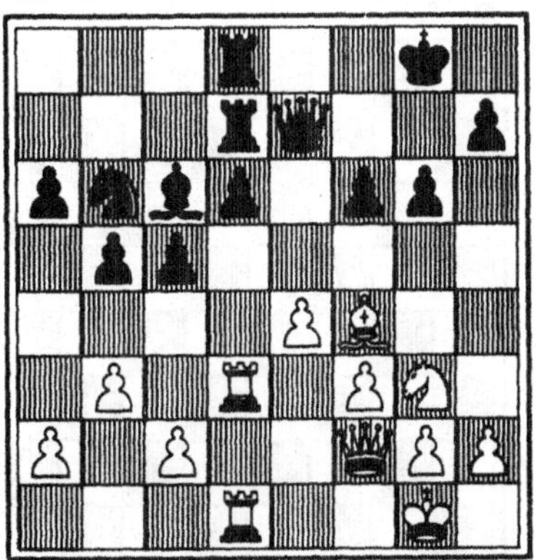

Of course, in their preliminary calculations both players considered the capture on d6, but assessed it differently. Which of them was right?

## *Solutions to Test 42*

329. Aronin–Kantorovich, Moscow, 1960.
1 Ne5!! Resigns.
330. Fischer–Shocron, Mar del Plata, 1959.
1 R×e6!! Qc8 2 Bd7! Resigns. On 2 . . . Q×d7 there follows 3 R×g6+!.
331. Tuk–Assenova, Lublin, 1969.
1 B×c7?? R×c7! 2 R×b4 Rac8!! White resigns. There is no defence against both of the threats—mate at c1 and the capture on b4.
332. Letunov–Ubilava, Tbilisi, 1973.
1 Bd4? Rg3+!! 2 Kh2 (if *2 f×g3*, then *2 . . . Qe4+!*) 2 . . . N×d2! White resigns.
333. Yukhtman–Goldenov, Kirovograd, 1952.
1 R×e7!! Q×e7 2 Bc5! Resigns.
334. Rossetto–Sherwin, Portoroz, 1958.
1 Bb4? Rb1! 2 B×d6 f3+!! White resigns.
335. Euwe–Keres, The Hague, 1948.
1 . . . Rc5!! 2 Qd2 (*2 Qb7* loses to *2 . . . Rc2!*) 2 . . . R×c1!! 3 Qf2 (on *3 h3* there follows *3 . . . Nf3+!*) 3 . . . Rc3 White resigns.
336. Taimanov–Serebrisky, Leningrad, 1951.
1 B×d6! R×d6 2 Nf5!! g×f5 3 R×d6, and White won. If 3 . . . R×d6, then 4 Qg3+ Kf7 5 Q×d6 Qb7 6 Q×c5 Nc8 7 Q×f5, or 3 . . . Rc8 4 Q×c5 Qc7 5 Q×f5.

## Test 43 Positions 337–344

We meet a theme which will occupy the next three tests: 'Creation and utilization of passed pawns'. The solving time is 40 minutes.

337 B

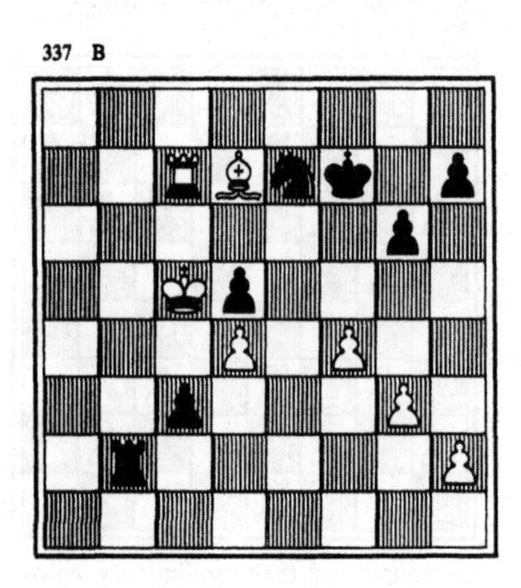

338 W

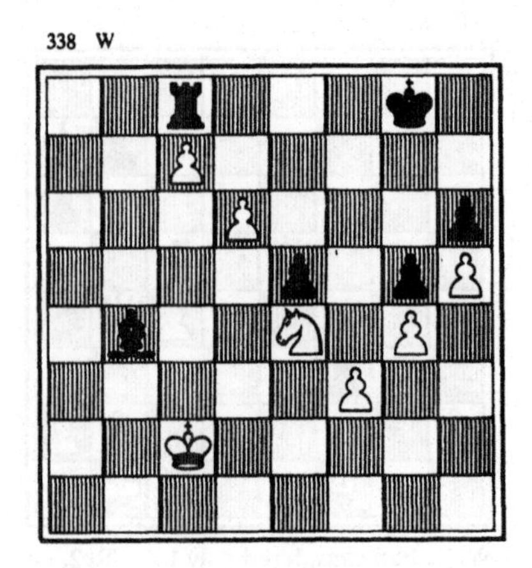

339 B

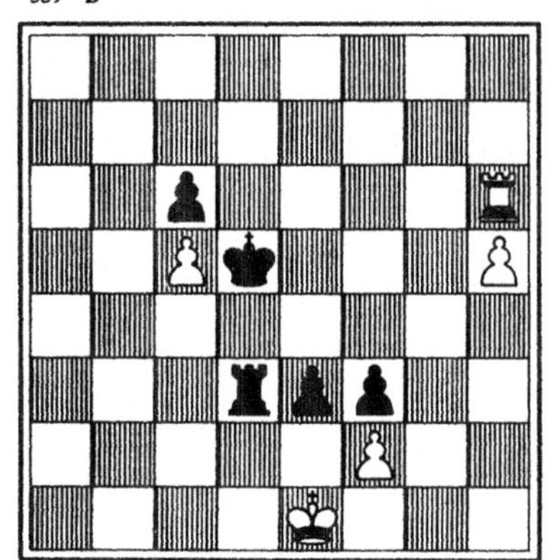

340 B

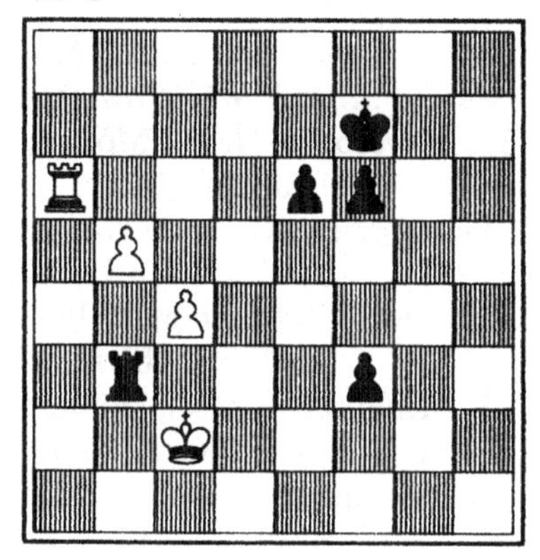

341 B

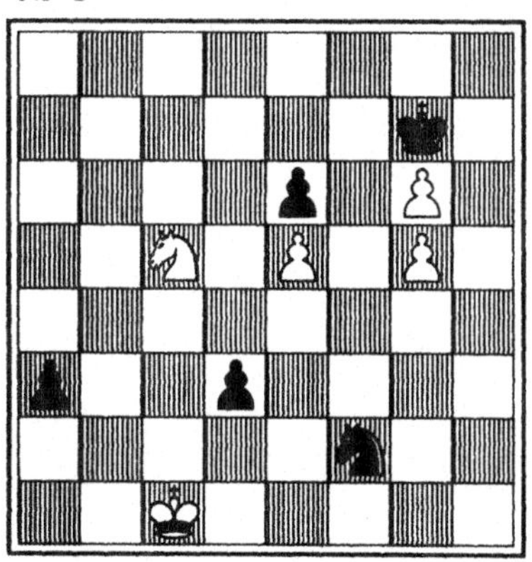

342 B

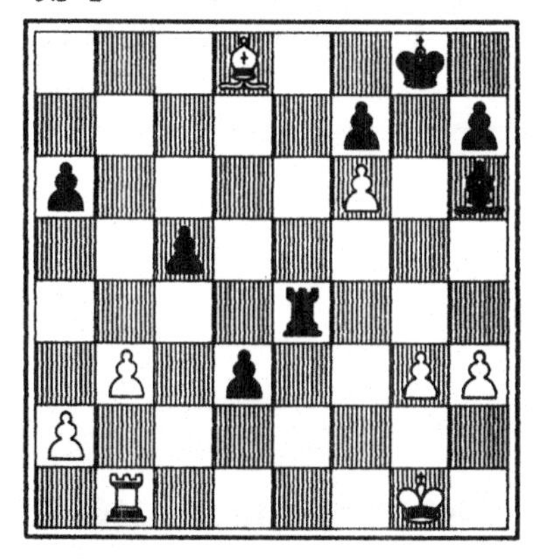

343 W

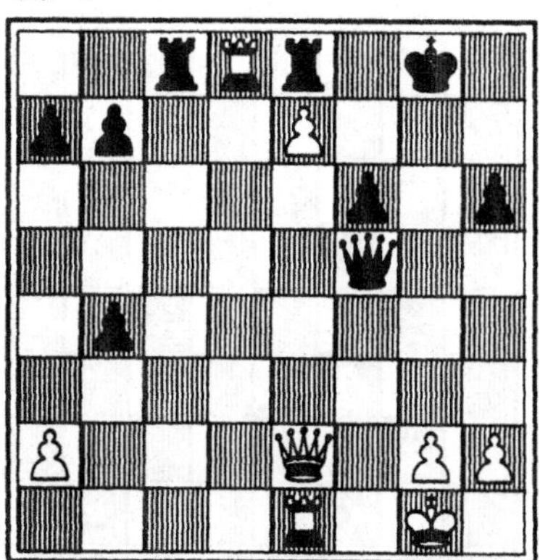

344 B

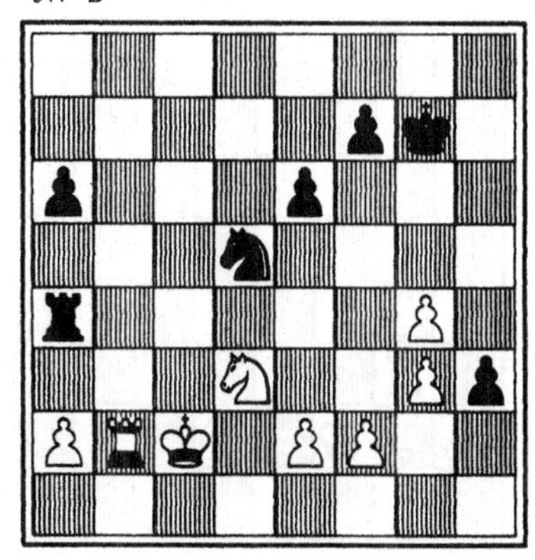

## *Solutions to Test 43*

337. Stolle–Just, Corr., 1976.
1 . . . Rb7! White resigns (*2 R×b7 c2*, and wins).
338. Averbakh–N. N., Moscow, 1960. (From a simultaneous display.)
1 Nc5!! Resigns (on *1 . . . B×c5* there comes *2 d7!*).
339. Filippov–Kaikamadzhozov, Sofia, 1958.
1 . . . Rd1+!! 2 K×d1 e×f2 White resigns.
340. Oms–Karls, Bremen, 1949.
1 . . . Rb1!! 2 K×b1 f2 White resigns.
341. Knudsen–Bichsel, Winterthur, 1976.
1 . . . d2+! 2 K×d2 Ne4+! 3 N×e4 a2 White resigns.
342. Seredenko–Belousov, Maikop, 1972 (variation).
1 . . . Bc1!!, and Black wins, since 2 R×c1 is met by 2 . . . d2!. The game in fact continued 1 . . . Be3+? 2 Kg2 Bd4 3 Rd1 Re8? 4 Be7, and White won.
343. Flórián–Koska, Brno, 1950.
1 Qc4+!! R×c4 (on *1 . . . Kg7* there follows *2 Q×c8 Q×c8 3 R×c8 R×c8 4 e8=Q*) 2 R×e8+ Resigns (*2 . . . Kg7 3 Rg8+!*).
344. Averbakh–Korchnoi, Yerevan, 1965.
1 . . . Rc4+! 2 Kd2 Rc1!! White resigns (on *3 K×c1* comes *3 . . . h2*).

## Test 44 Positions 345–352

A continuation of the previous theme. Difficulty roughly the same as in the preceding test. Solving time—40 minutes.

345 B

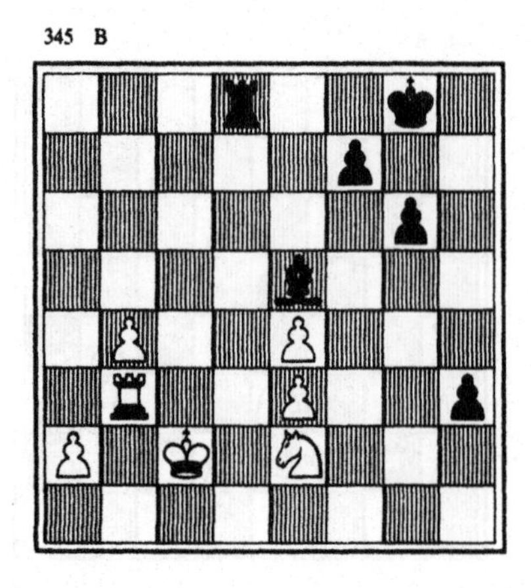

346 W

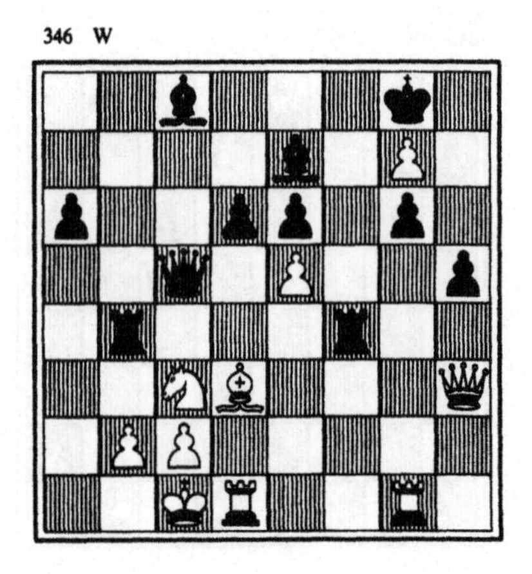

347 B

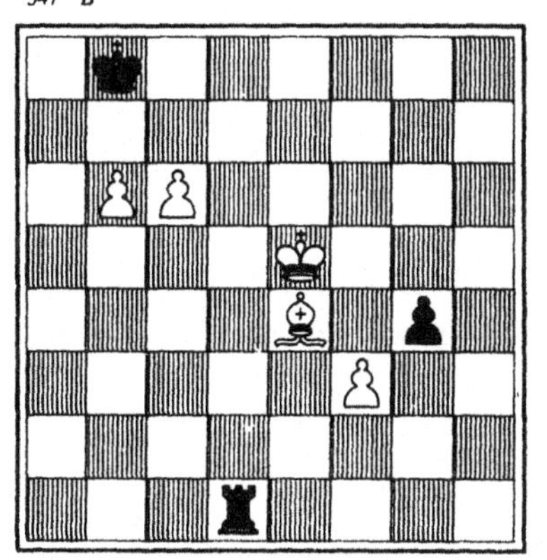

Black to play and draw

348 W

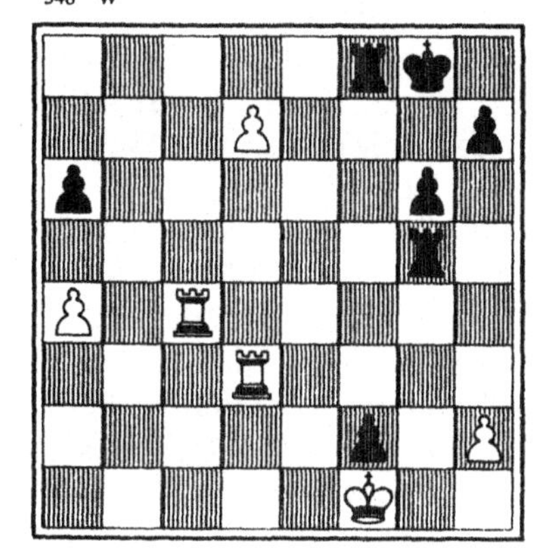

349 W

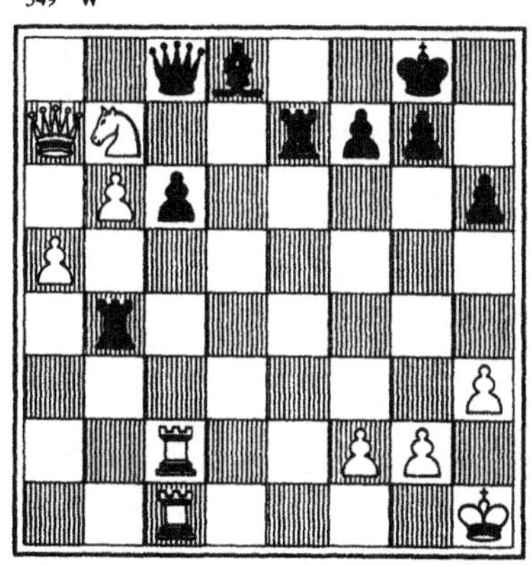

350 W

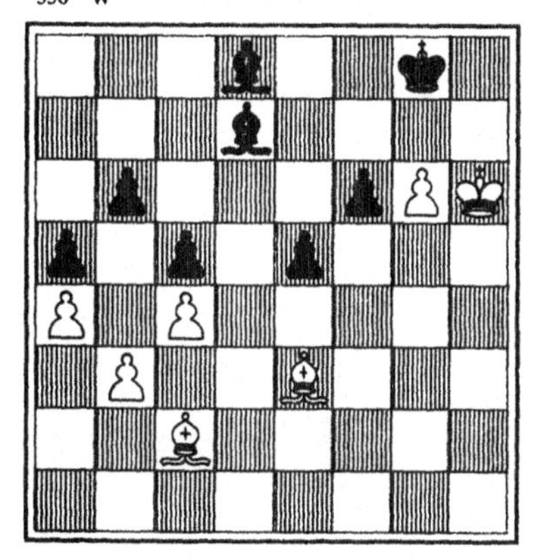

351 W

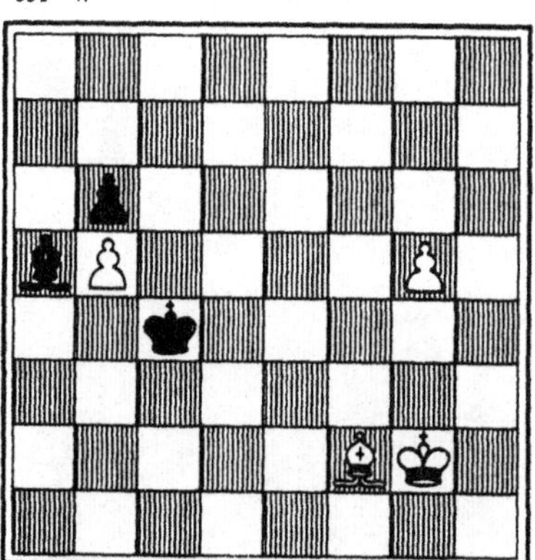

352 W

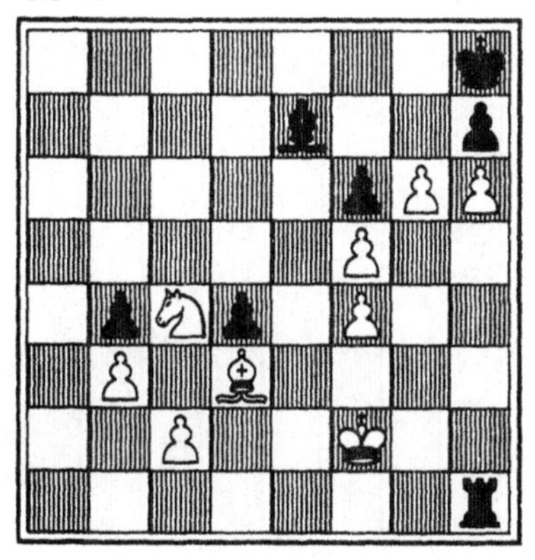

## Solutions to Test 44

345. Zhavel–Dubaya, Corr., 1961.
1 . . . Rd1!! 2 K×d1 h2 White resigns.
346. Lobigas–Mitchell, Skopje, 1972.
1 Q×h5!! g×h5 2 Bh7+! Resigns.
347. Goldstein–Shakhnovich, Moscow, 1946.
1 . . . g×f3 2 B×f3 (*2 c7+* fails to win after *2 . . . Kc8 3 Bf5+ Rd7 4 Bh3 f2 5 Ke6 f1=Q 6 B×f1 R×c7*) 2 . . . Rd7!!, and draws. 3 c×d7 gives stalemate, while if 3 Bd5, then 3 . . . Rb7!.
348. Rossolimo–Monson, Paris, 1945.
1 Rf3!! Rd5 2 Rc8! Resigns.
349. Radev–Neikirch, Sofia, 1970.
1 N×d8!! R×a7 2 N×c6!! Resigns. On 2 . . . Q×c6 there follows 3 b×a7!.
350. Hennings–Walther, Leipzig, 1964.
1 Bg5!! Be7 (if *1 . . . f×g5*, then *2 g7* and *3 Bh7+*) 2 g7! Resigns.
351. Bannik–Nikolayevsky, Odessa, 1958.
1 B×b6!! Bc3 2 Ba5!! Resigns.
352. Rogul–Syomkov, Varna, 1977.
1 g7+ (not *1 Ne5 R×h6*) 1 . . . Kg8 2 Nd6! R×h6 3 Ne8!, and there is no defence against 4 Bc4+.

## Test 45 Positions 353–360

We conclude the section on 'Passed pawns'. Solving time—40 minutes.

353 B

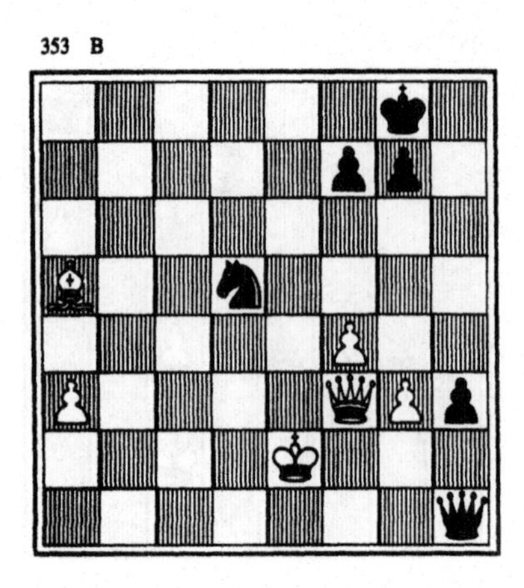

354 B

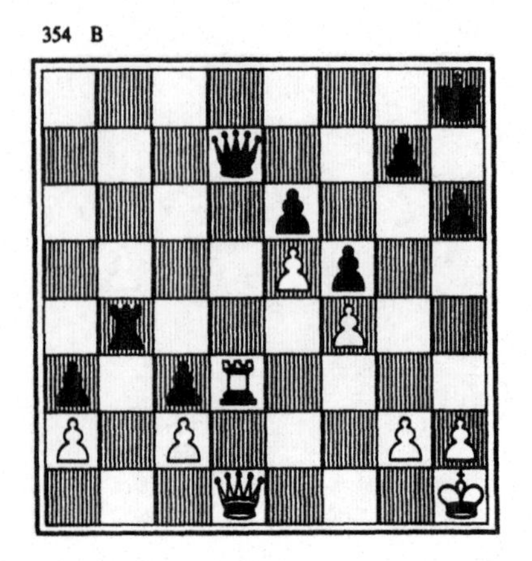

355 W

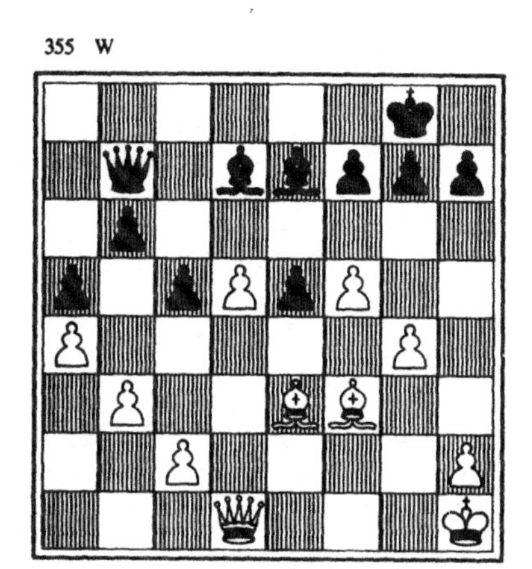

356 W

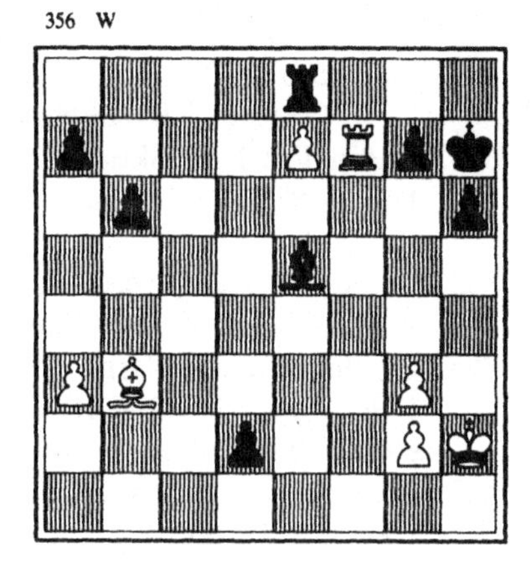

357 W

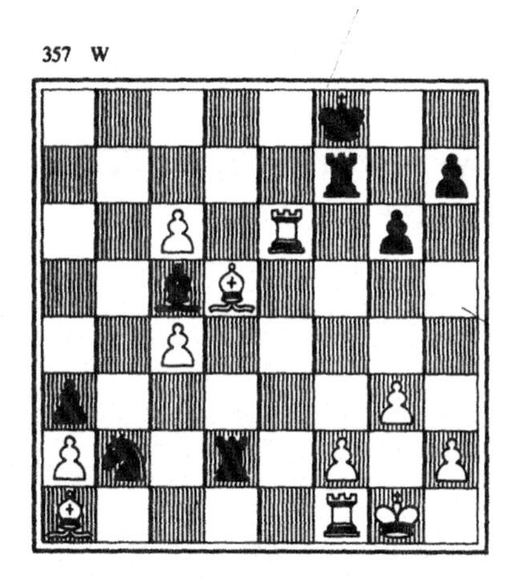

358 B

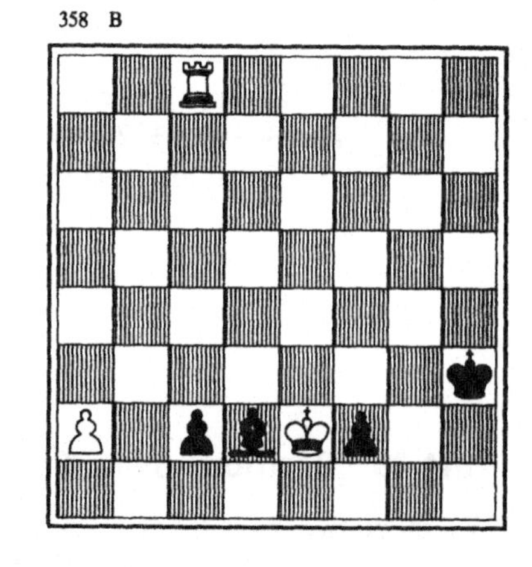

359 W

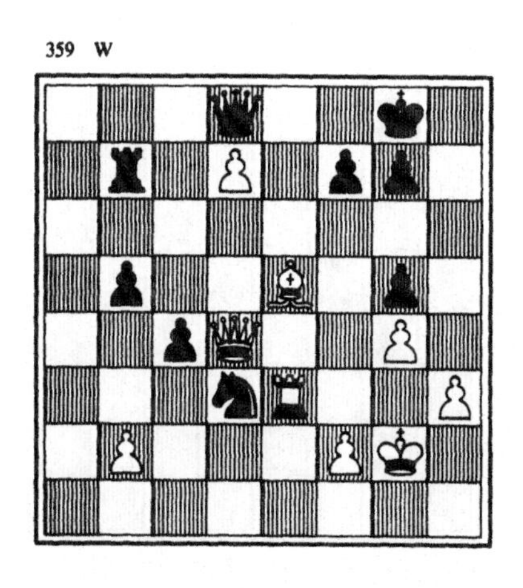

360 B

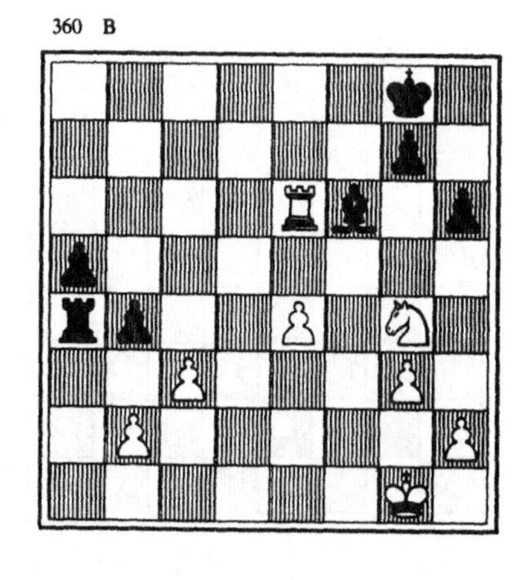

## Solutions to Test 45

353. Medina–Tal, Palma de Mallorca, 1966.
1 . . . Q×f3+! 2 K×f3 Ne3!! White resigns.
354. Kadiri–Pritchett, Skopje, 1972.
1 . . . Q×d3! 2 c×d3 Rb2! White resigns. There is no defence against 3 . . . c2 and 4 . . . Rb1.
355. Baikov–Bitman, Moscow, 1972.
1 d6! Bc6 2 d×e7 B×f3+ 3 Kg1 Resigns.
356. Dikshit–Kaluanasdarm, Dely, 1961.
1 Bc2+ Kg8 2 Rf8+! R×f8 3 Bb3+! Resigns. If 3 . . . Kh8 or 3 . . . Kh7, then 4 e×f8=Q(+), or 3 . . . Rf7 4 e8=Q+.
357. Gufeld–Etruk, Krasnodar, 1966.
1 Rf6!! R×f6 2 c7 Kg7 3 c8=Q, and White wins. The game concluded 3 . . . Bd4 4 Qb7+ Kh6 5 Bg8, and Black resigned.
358. Ksandi–Forintos, Budapest, 1963.
1 . . . Bc3!! 2 R×c3+ Kg2! White resigns.
359. Fischer–Attilo di Kapilo, Colombia, 1956.
1 Bc7!! Nf4+ 2 Kf1 Resigns. It would have been wrong to play 2 B×f4, on account of 2 . . . R×d7.
360. Rokhlin–Lomaya, Rostov-on-Don v. Tbilisi, 1957.
1 . . . B×c3! 2 b×c3 (2 *b3 Ra1+ 3 Kg2 a4* is no better) 2 . . . b3 3 Rb6 Rb4!! 4 c×b4 a4 5 Rb8+ Kh7 White resigns (if *6 Ra8 b2 7 R×a4 b1=Q+ 8 Kg2 Qc2+*).

## Test 46 Positions 361–368

We meet two new themes: 'Simplifying combinations' (Nos. 361–364) and 'Drawing combinations by perpetual check' (Nos. 365–368). Since in both sections there are difficulties which we have not yet met, the time allowed is 55 minutes.

361 B

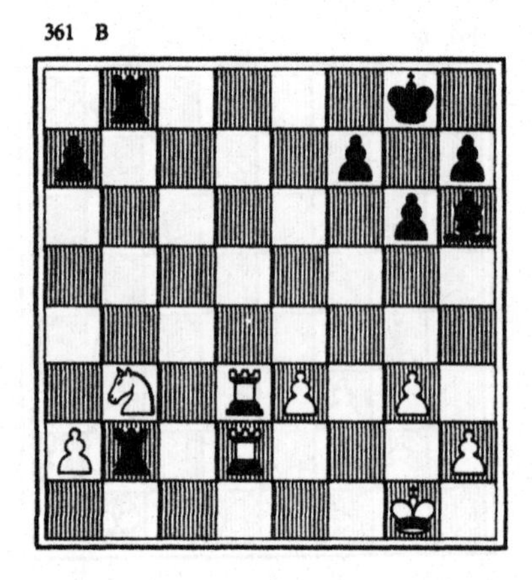

362 B

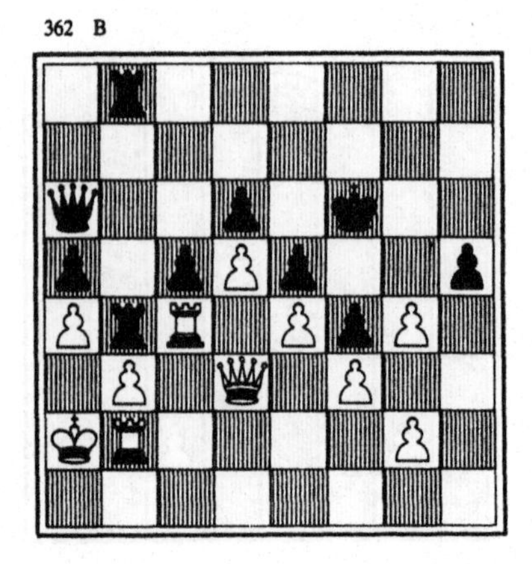

363 W

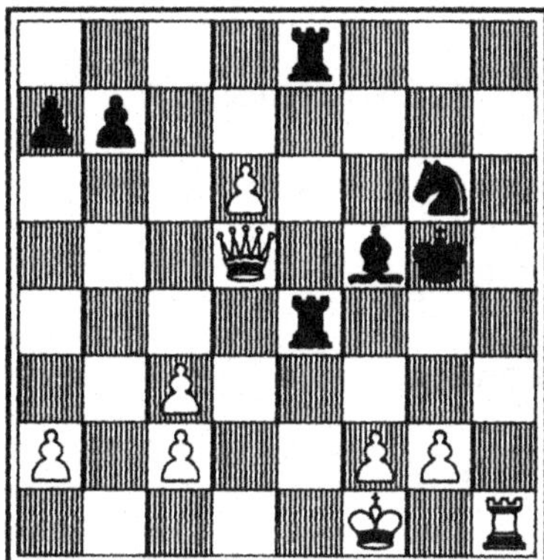

364 W

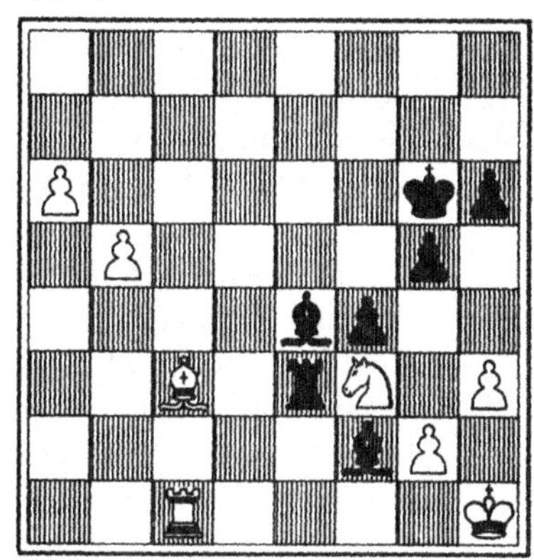

365 W =

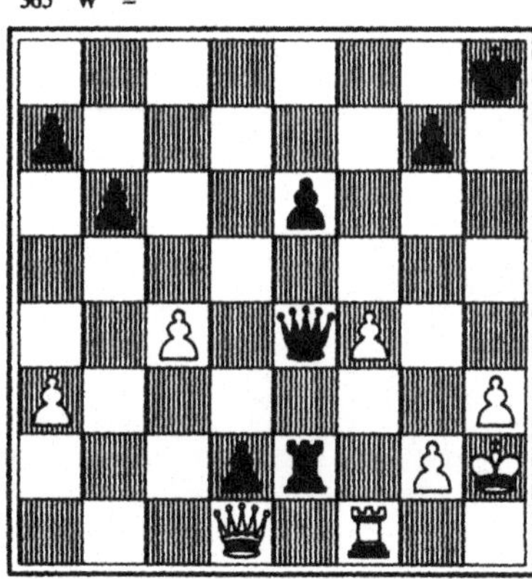

366 W =

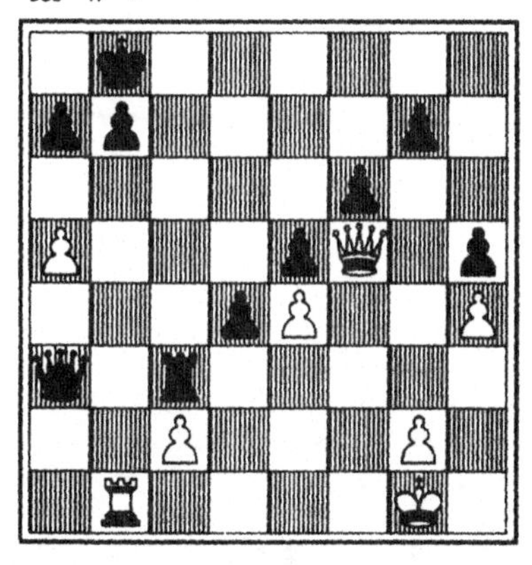

367 B =

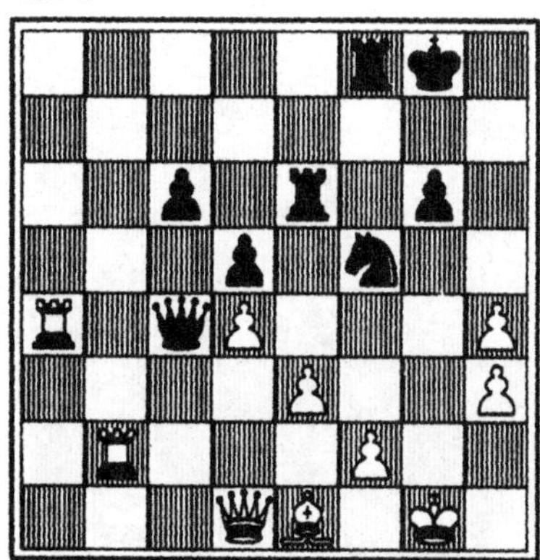

368 W =

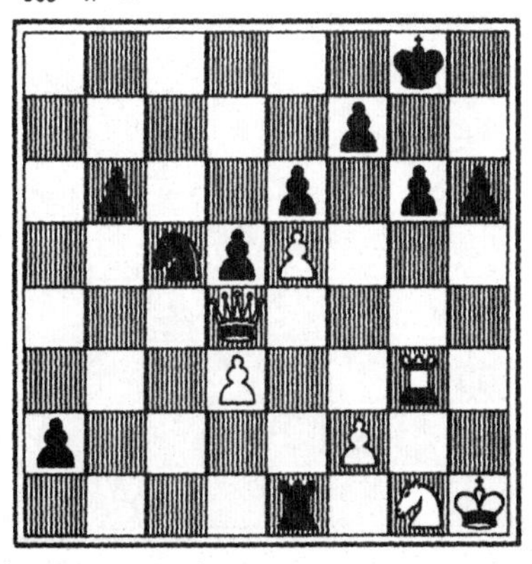

## Solutions to Test 46

361. Porat–Barcza, Moscow, 1956.
 1 . . . R8×b3!! 2 a×b3 R×d2 3 R×d2 B×e3+ 4 Rf2 Kg7 White resigns.
362. Rytov–Taimanov, Tallinn, 1975.
 1 . . . Q×c4! White resigns: Black forcibly transposes into a won pawn ending.
363. Abrahams–Winter, London, 1946.
 1 Rh5+! K×h5 2 Q×f5+ Kh6 3 Q×e4! R×e4 4 d7 Resigns.
364. Averbakh–Chistyakov, Moscow, 1951.
 1 Be1! B×e1 2 R×e1 B×f3 3 R×e3 f×e3 4 Kg1 Resigns.
365. Nedwezki–Kampen, Augsburg, 1955.
 1 Rf2!! R×f2 2 Qh5+, with a draw by perpetual check.
366. Kuznetsov–Zaikin, Ryazan, 1952.
 1 Qd7 Rc7 2 R×b7+!!—draw. If 2 . . . K×b7, then 3 Qb5+ Kc8 4 Qe8+, with perpetual check. 2 . . . R×b7? loses to 3 Qd8 mate.
367. Kopayev–Vistanetskis, Vilnius, 1949.
 1 . . . Qf1+!! 2 K×f1 N×e3+ 3 Ke2 Nc4+, with perpetual check (*4 Kf1 Ne3+ 5 Ke2*, etc.).
368. Vitolinsh–Bukhman, Riga, 1976 (variation).
 1 Qh4! a1=Q 2 Qd8+ Kh7 3 R×g6! with perpetual check.

## Test 47 Positions 369–376

A new theme: 'Stalemating combinations'. The time for this test is 50 minutes.

369 W =

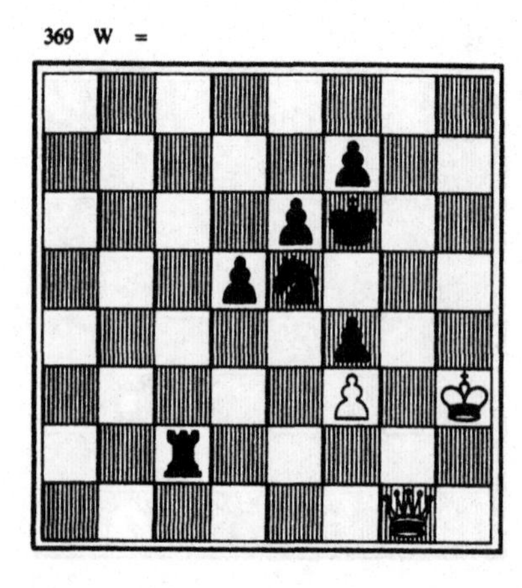

370 B =

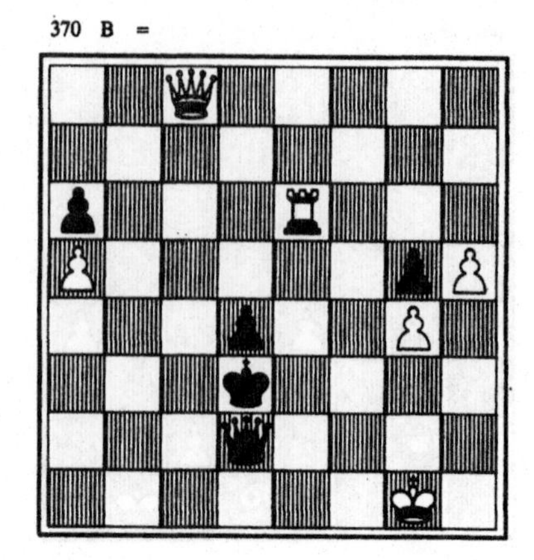

371 **W** =

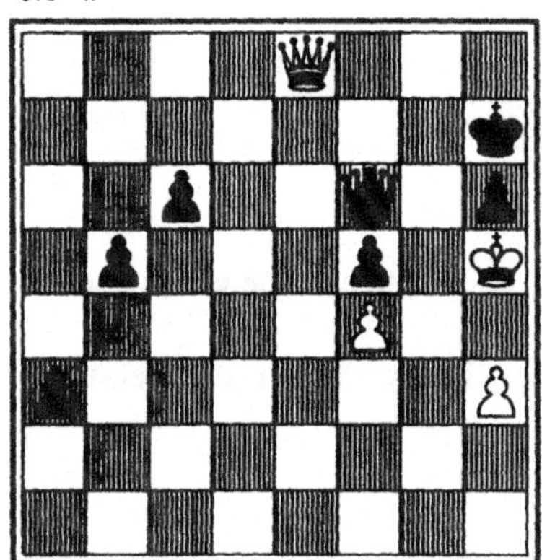

372 **W** =

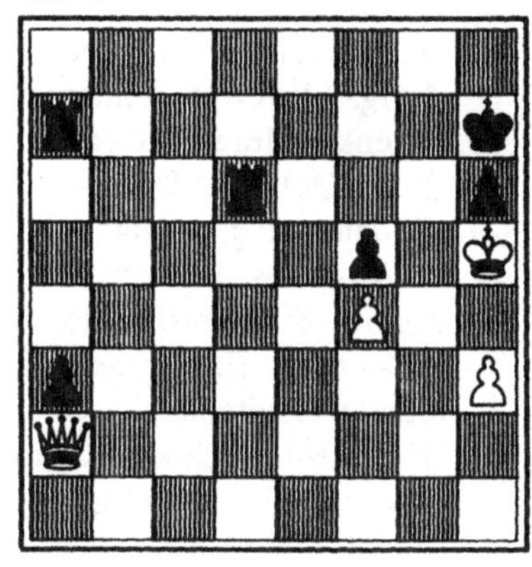

373 **B** =

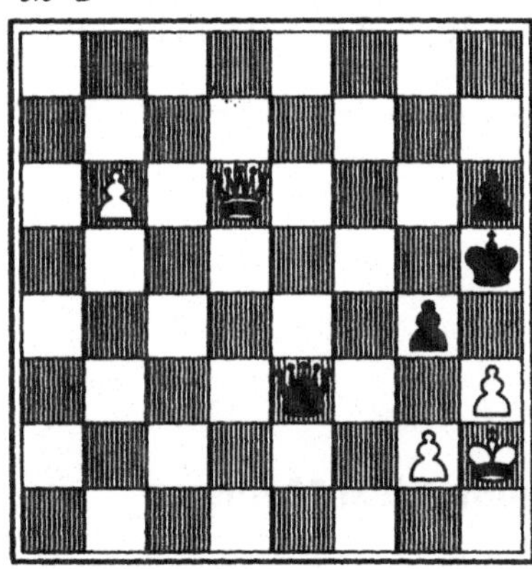

374 **W** =

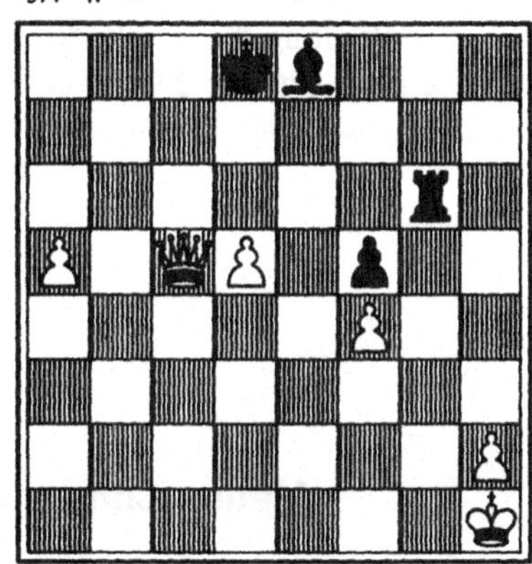

Thinking that he could win as he pleased, White played 1 d6??, which allowed Black to draw. How?

375 **W** =

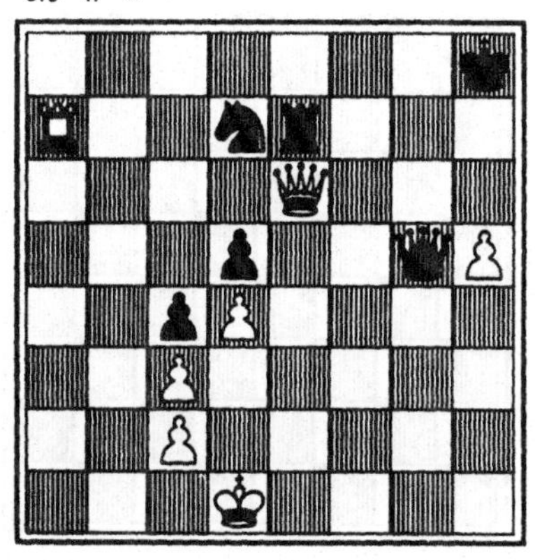

376 **B** =

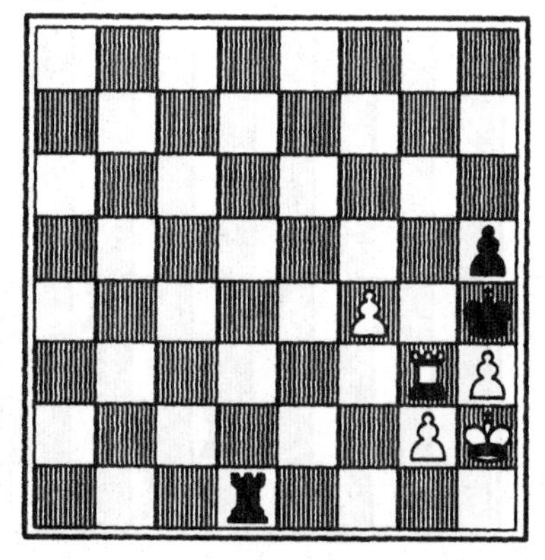

## *Solutions to Test 47*

369. Köberl–Tipary, Budapest, 1955.
 1 Qg5+!! K×g5—stalemate.
370. Titenko–Murey, Moscow, 1963.
 1 . . . Qc1+!! 2 Q×c1—stalemate.
371. Zhdanov–Pigits, Riga, 1953.
 1 h4!—draw. Black cannot prevent stalemate after the sacrifice of the white queen.
372 Biglova–Strandström, Rostov, 1953.
 1 h4—draw. Exactly as in the previous example; after the sacrifice of the queen, the draw is inevitable.
373. Heintze–Kruschwitz, Grunbach, 1951.
 1 . . . g3+! 2 Q×g3 Qg1+!! 3 K×g1—stalemate.
374. Fichtl–Blatny, Bratislava, 1956.
 1 d6?? Bc6+!! 2 Q×c6 Rg1+!! 3 K×g1—stalemate.
375. Kestler–Pesch, East Germany, 1956.
 1 Ra8+! Kh7 2 Rh8+!! K×h8 3 Qh6+!! Q×h6—stalemate.
376. Kondratiev–Lapigin, Moscow, 1975.
 1 . . . Rd3!! 2 Rg7 (after *2 Rf3 R×f3 3 g×f3* it is stalemate, while other moves by the rook along the ‘g’ file do not achieve anything) 2 . . . Rg3!! 3 Rg5 R×g2+!—draw. Either capture gives stalemate!

## Mating Combinations Based on Geometrical Motifs
## Schematic Diagrams

Before tackling Tests 48 and 49 in Book 1, and certain Tests in Book 2, you should refer to the appropriate schematic diagrams.

377

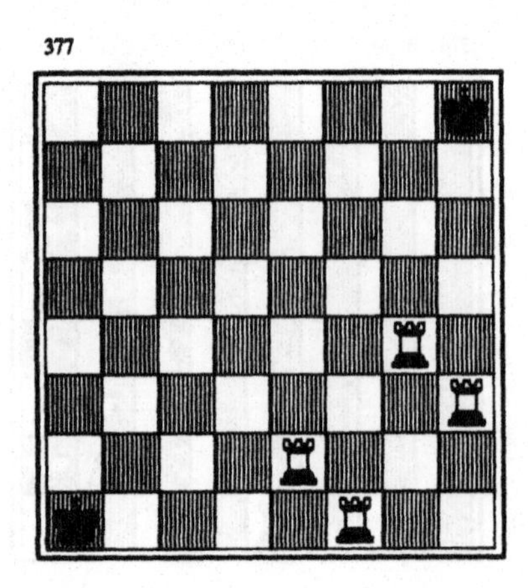

378

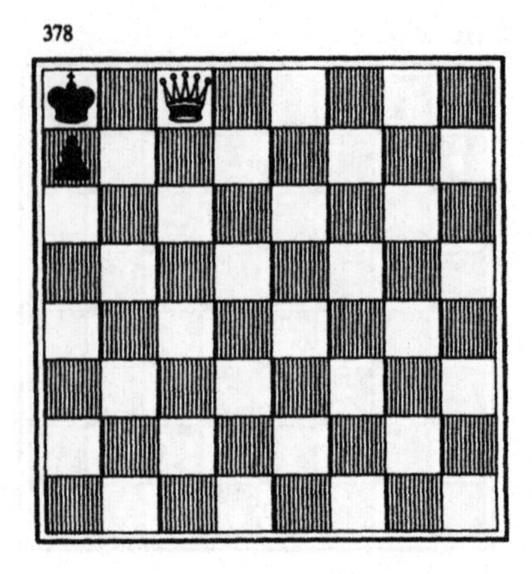

379

380

381

382

383

384

385

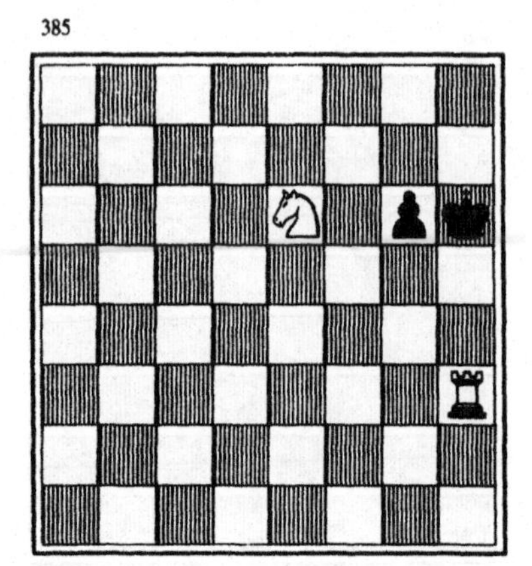

386

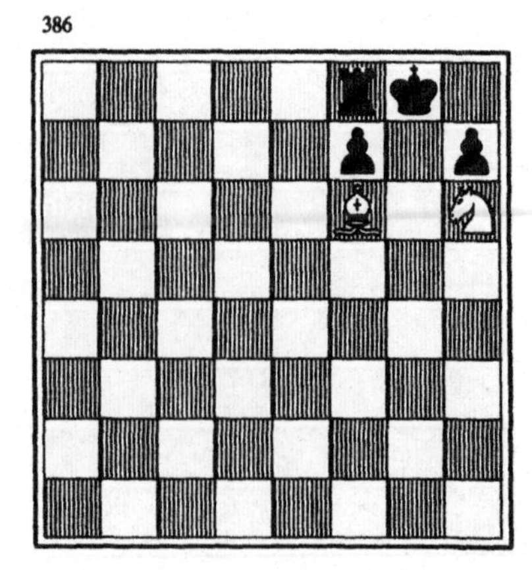

## Test 48 Positions 387–394

The first test on the theme 'Mating combinations based on geometrical motifs'; cf. schematic diagrams 377 (the so-called 'linear mate'), 378 and 381. The time allowed is 40 minutes.

387 W

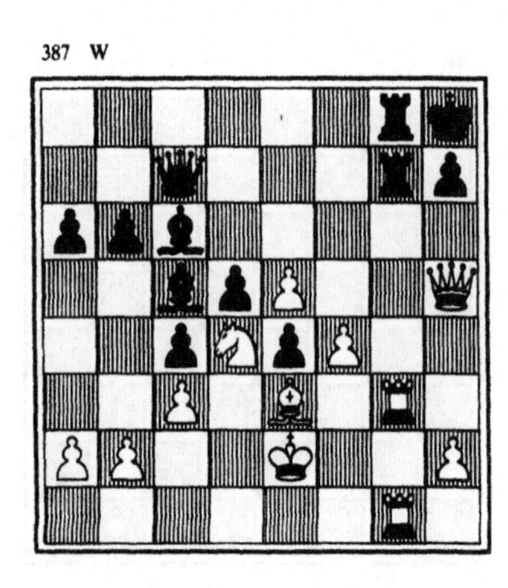

388 W

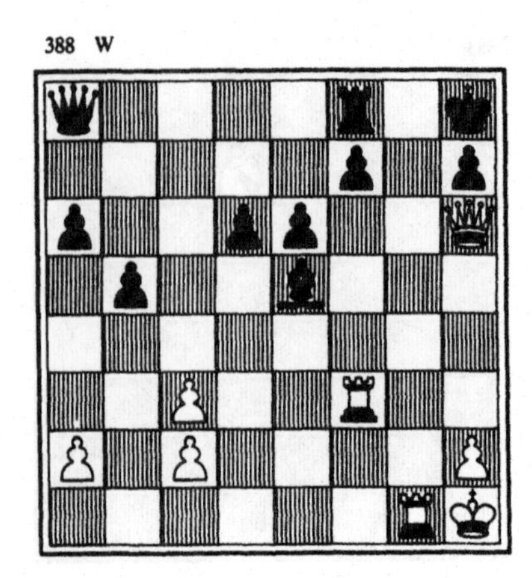

389 W

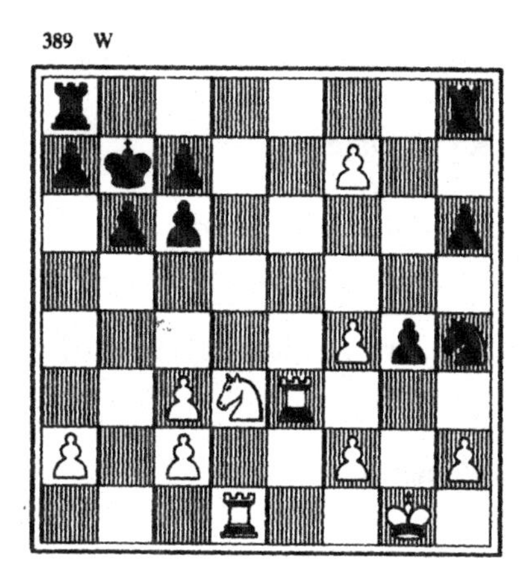

390 W

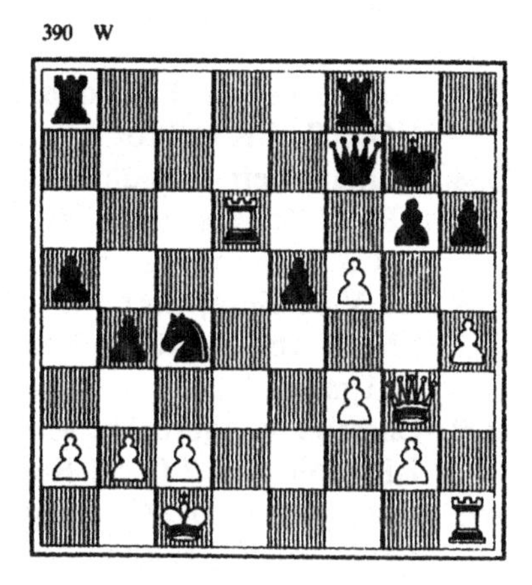

391 W

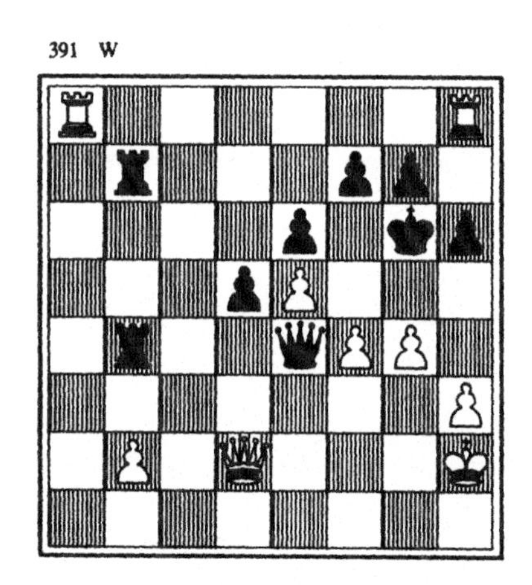

392 W

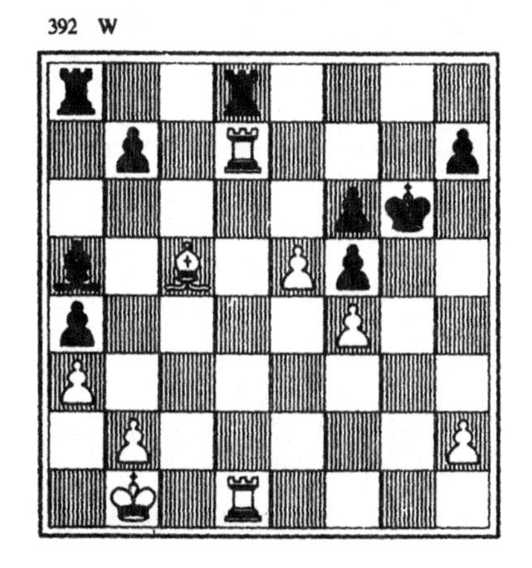

393 W

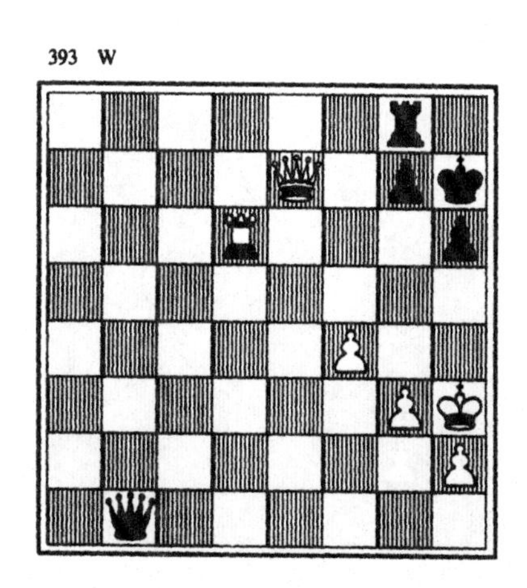

394 W

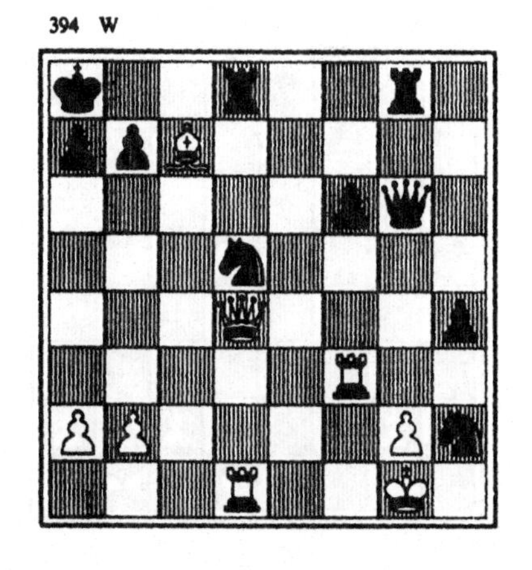

### Solutions to Test 48

387. Segylacek–Balogh, Budapest, 1953.
1 Q×h7+! R×h7 (or *1 . . . K×h7 2 Rh3* mate) 2 R×g8 mate.
388. Soultanbeieff–Borodin, Brussels, 1946.
1 Rg2!! Resigns. There is no defence against 2 Q×h7+ K×h7 3 Rh3 mate; on 1 . . . Q×f3 there follows 3 Q×f8 mate.
389. De Vine–Buse, Corr., 1966.
1 Nc5+!! b×c5 2 Rb1+ Resigns. If 2 . . . Ka6, then 3 c4!, or 2 . . . Kc8 3 Re8+ Kd7 4 Rd1 mate.
390. Cherepkov–Averbakh, Moscow, 1960.
1 R×g6+ Kh7 2 Qg5!! Resigns (*2 . . . h×g5 3 h×g5* mate).
391. Bernstein–Kotov, Groningen, 1946.
1 f5+!! e×f5 2 Q×h6+!! g×h6 3 Rag8 mate.
392. Polugayevsky–Szilágyi, Moscow, 1960.
1 Rg1+! Kh6 2 Bf8+!! R×f8 3 Rd3! Resigns. Against 4 Rh3 mate there is no defence.
393. Vilenkin–Zavada, Corr., 1971.
1 R×h6+!! K×h6 2 Qg5+ Kh7 3 Qh5 mate.
394. Tartakover–Falk, Paris, 1954.
1 Q×a7+!! K×a7 2 Ra3 mate.

### Test 49 Positions 395–402

We conclude the theme 'Mating combinations based on geometrical motifs'; cf. schematic positions 381, 382 and 383. The time for the test is 40 minutes.

395 W

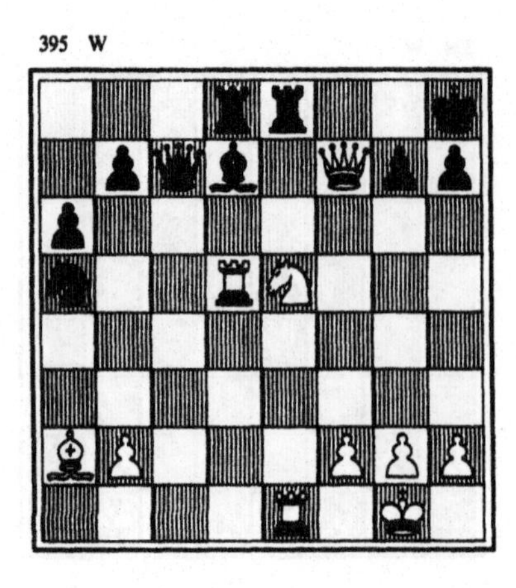

396 W

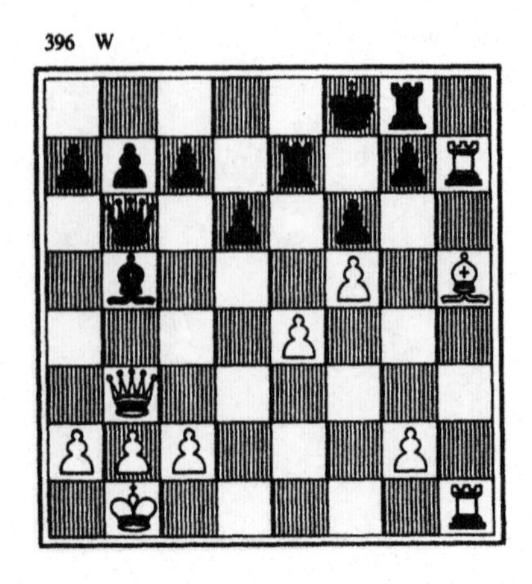

397 B

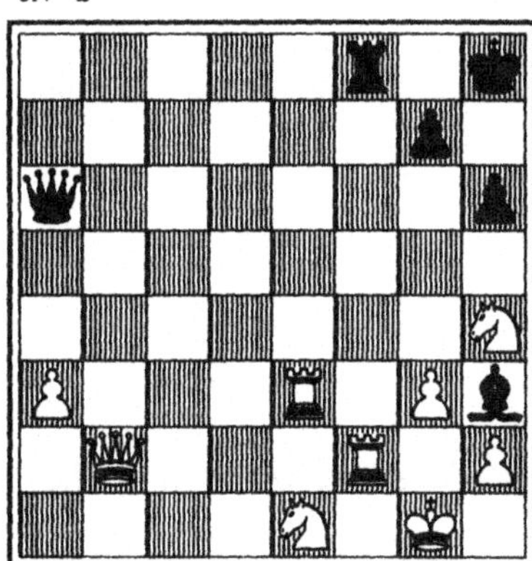

398 W

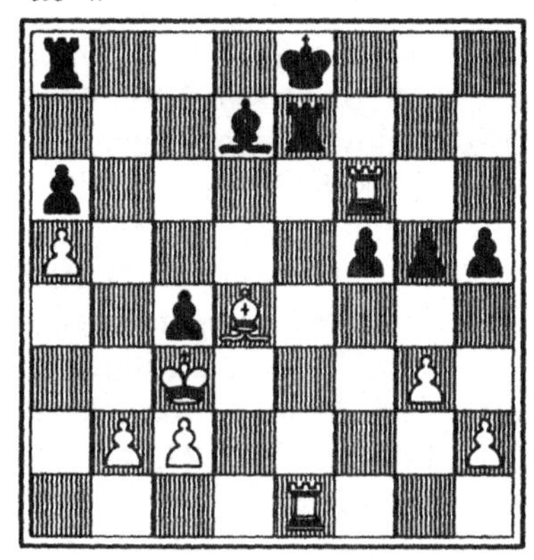

399 W

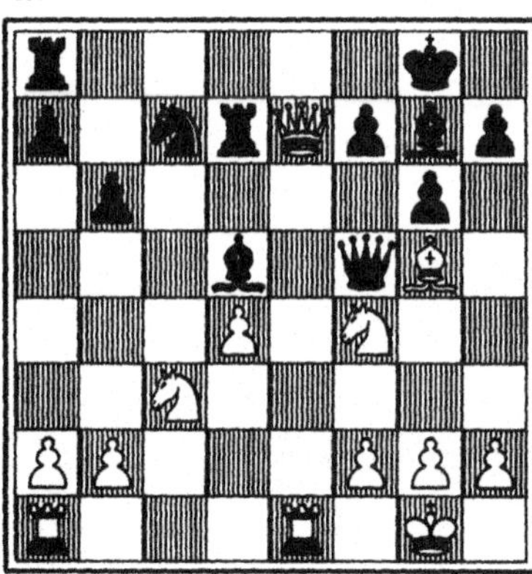

400 W

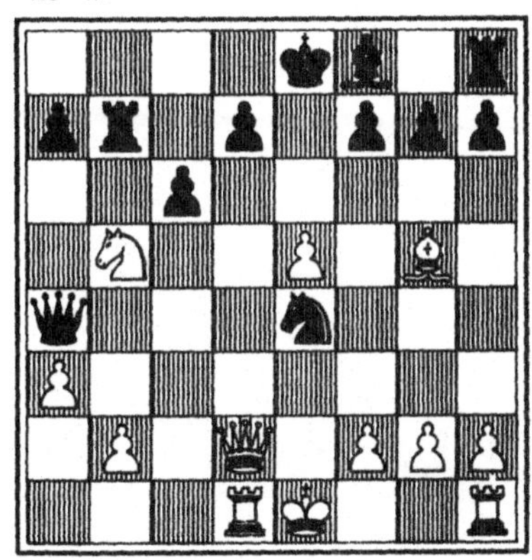

401 W

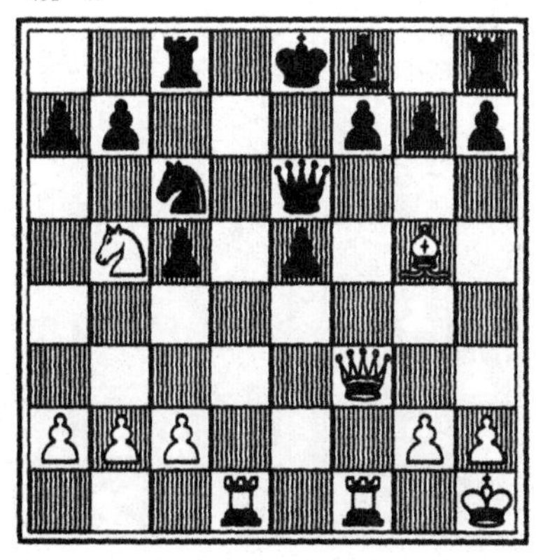

402 W

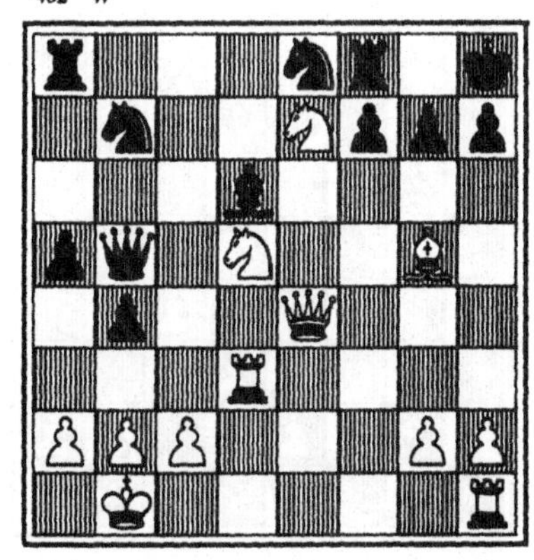

### Solutions to Test 49

395. Udovcic–Szabados, Zurich, 1952.
1 Ng6+! h×g6 2 Rh5+! g×h5 3 Q×h5 mate.
396. Krilov–Tarasov, Tula, 1960.
1 Q×g8+!! K×g8 2 Rh8+!! K×h8 3 Bf7 mate.
397. Schultz–Laurens, Prenzlau, 1954.
1 . . . Qf1+!! 2 R×f1 R×f1 mate.
398. Ciocaltea–Kupper, Lugano, 1968.
1 Bc5!! R×e1 2 Rf8 mate.
399. Zinn–Brumel, Magdeburg, 1964.
1 N×d5! N×d5 2 Qe8+! Resigns (on *2 . . . R×e8 3 R×e8+ Bf8* there follows *4 Bh6*).
400. Ostropolsky–Ivanovsky, Tyumen, 1949.
1 Q×d7+!! R×d7 2 Nc7+ R×c7 3 Rd8 mate.
401. Onderka–N. N., Graz, 1958.
1 Nc7+!! R×c7 2 Q×c6+!! R×c6 3 Rd8 mate.
402. Uzman–Soler, Lugano, 1968.
1 Q×h7+!! K×h7 2 Rh3 mate.

### Test 50 Positions 403–410

A new theme: 'Attack on the K-side castled position'. The time for the test is 40 minutes.

403 W

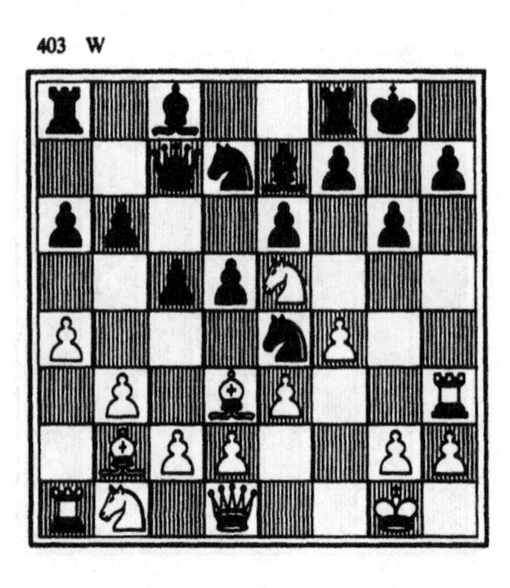

404 B

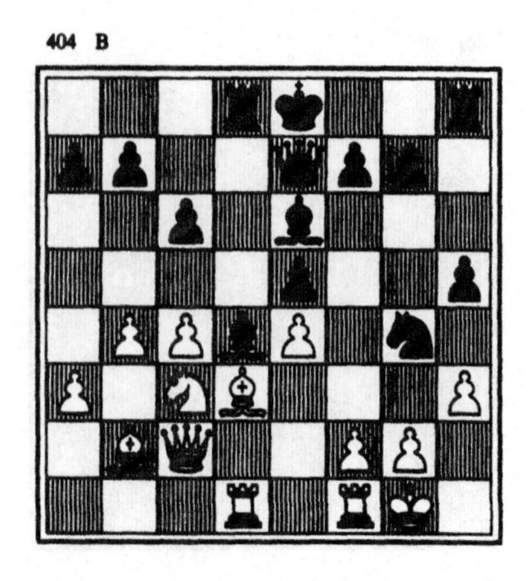

405 W

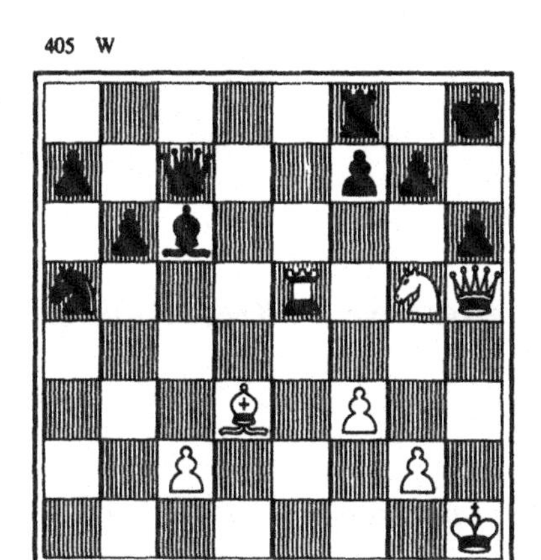

406 W

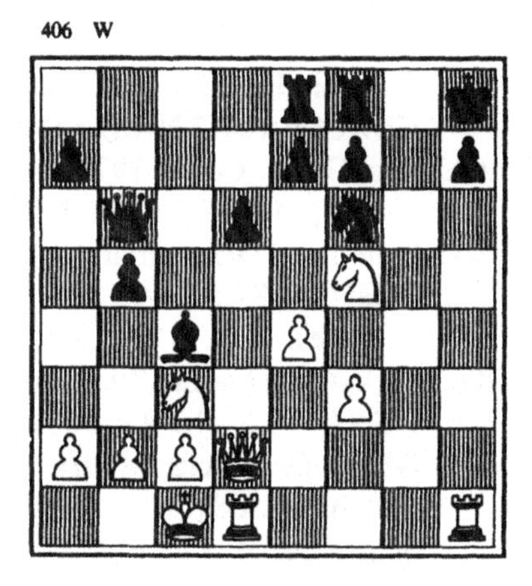

407 W

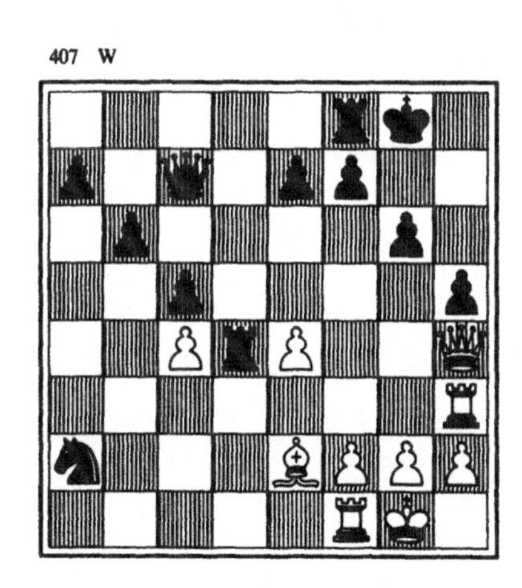

408 B

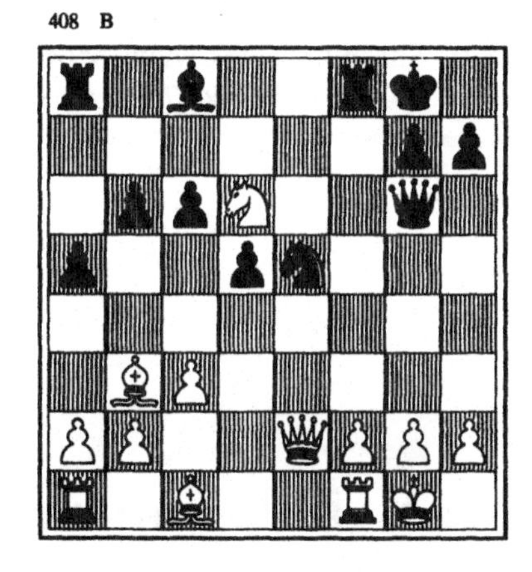

409 B

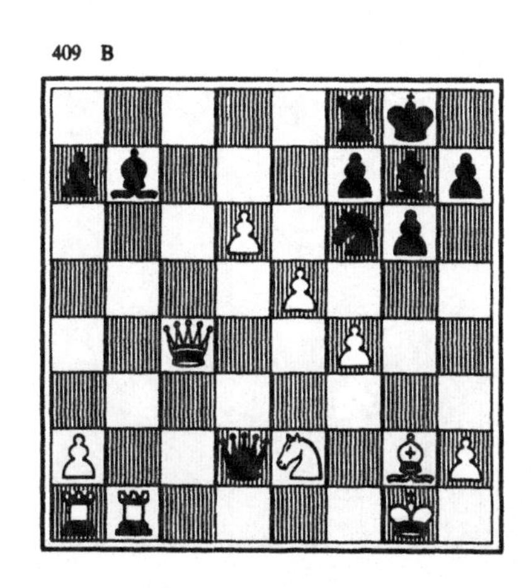

410 W

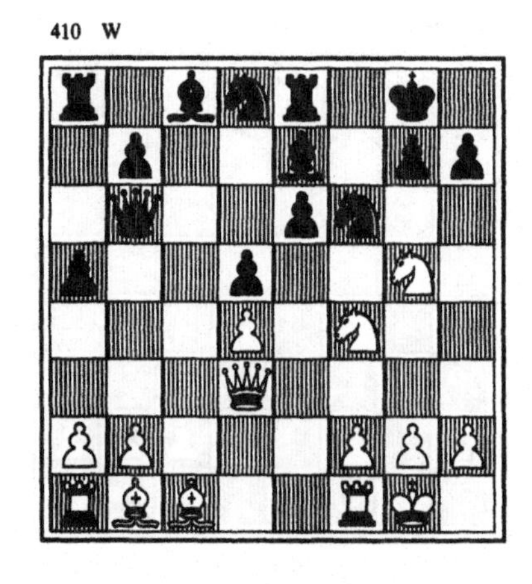

## *Solutions to Test 50*

403. Kubicek–Privara, Czech Ch., 1976.
 1 B×e4 d×e4 2 N×d7 Q×d7 3 Qh5! Resigns.
404. Kas–Gross, Corr., 1976.
 1 . . . Qh4 2 Nb1 Qg3! 3 h×g4 h×g4 4 Re1 Rh2 White resigns.
405. Quinones–Miagmarsuren, Skopje, 1972.
 1 Re6!! Kg8 (if *1 . . . f×e6*, then *2 Qg6!*) 2 Bh7+ Resigns (on *2 . . . Kh8, 3 R×h6!!* is decisive).
406. Mekai–Racasanu, Bucharest, 1950.
 1 R×h7+! N×h7 2 Qh6! Rg8 3 Rh1 Resigns.
407. Uhlmann–Garcia, Madrid, 1973.
 1 B×h5!! Rfd8 (on *1 . . . Kg7* there follows *2 B×g6!*) 2 B×g6! Resigns (if *2 . . . f×g6*, then *3 Qh7+ Kf8 4 Q×g6*).
408. Sonbauer–Despatovic, Yugoslavia, 1974.
 1 . . . Nf3+! 2 Kh1 Bh3!! White resigns (*3 g×h3*) is answered by *3 . . . Q×d6!*).
409. Pokern–Hübner, Bamberg, 1966.
 1 . . . Qe3+ 2 Kh1 (or *2 Kf1 Ng4!*) 2 . . . Qh3!! White resigns. On 3 B×b7 or 3 Rg1, 3 . . . Ng4!! is decisive.
410. Shashin–Dashkevich, Moscow, 1954.
 1 Q×h7+!! N×h7 2 B×h7+ Kf8 3 Ng6 mate.

## Test 51 Positions 411–418

Theme: 'Attack on the king caught in the centre'. The positions are not too difficult, and the time for the test is 45 minutes.

411 W

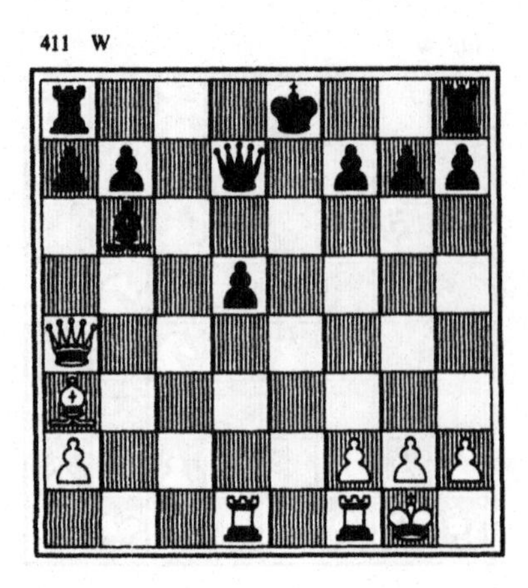

412 W

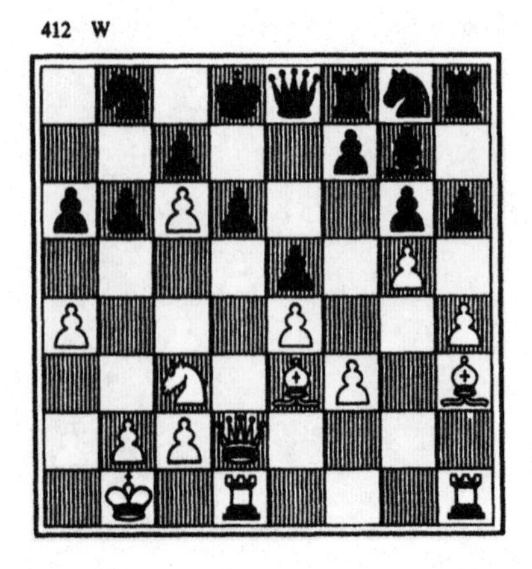

413 W

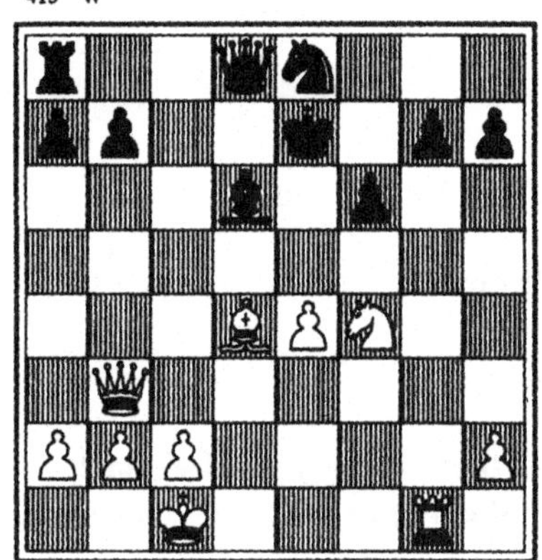

414 W

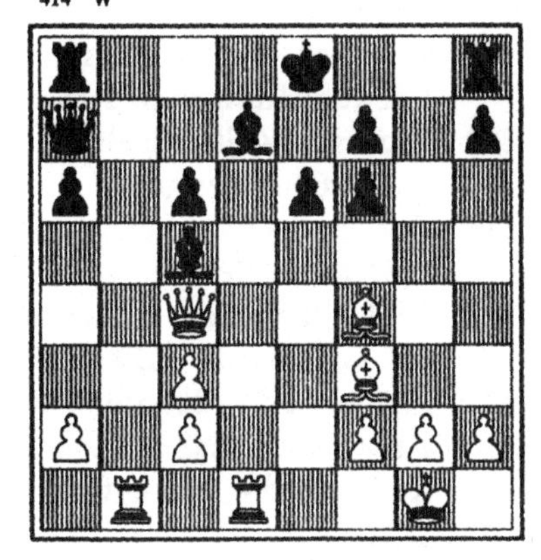

415 W

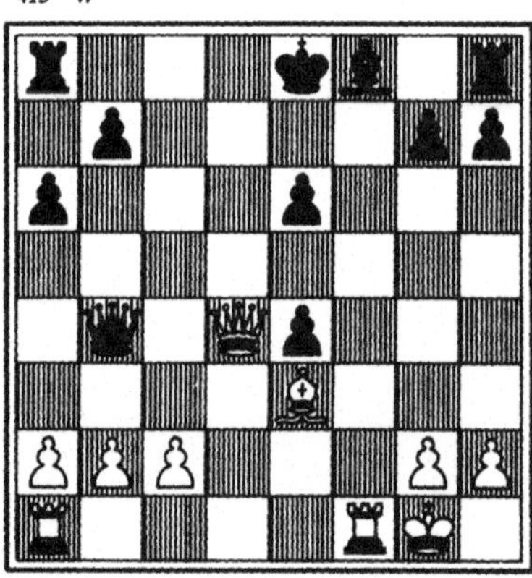

416 B

417 W

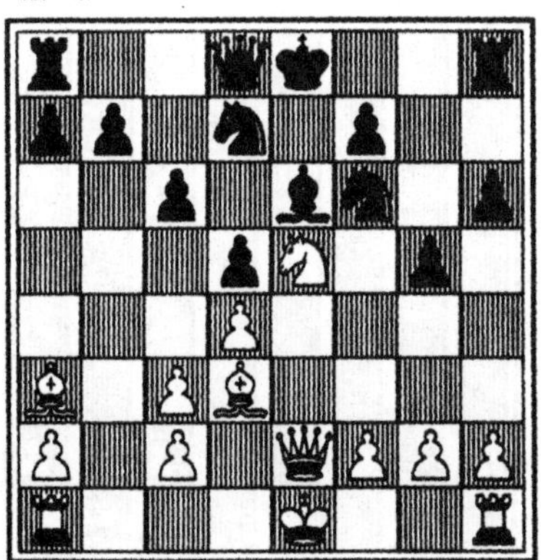

418 W

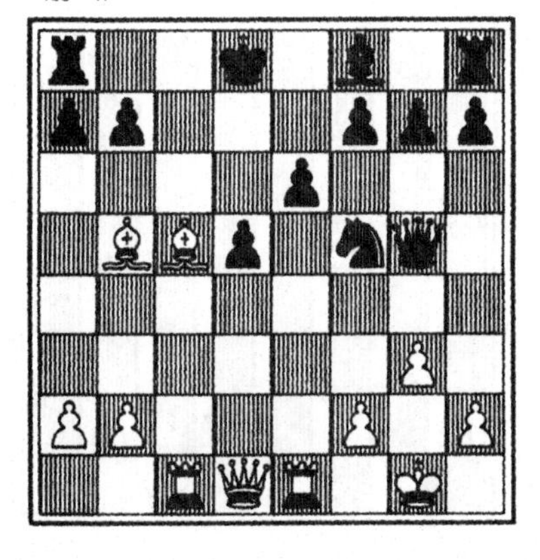

## *Solutions to Test 51*

411. Lehmann–Blau, Lucerne, 1952.
 1 R×d5! Resigns (if *1 . . . Q×a4*, then *2 Re1+*).
412. Pedersen–Keller, Helsinki, 1952.
 1 Q×d6+!! Resigns (*1 . . . c×d6* is met by *2 B×b6+ Ke7 Nd5* mate).
413. Korchnoi–Geller, Kiev, 1954.
 1 B×f6+!! Resigns (*1 . . . g×f6 2 Qe6+ Kf8 3 Rg8* mate).
414. Olafsson–Quinteros, Las Palmas, 1974.
 1 R×d7! K×d7 2 B×c6+! K×c6 3 Qa4+ Resigns.
415. Fischer–Dely, Skopje, 1967.
 1 R×f8+!! Q×f8 2 Qa4+ Resigns. After 2 . . . Kf7 there follows 3 Rf1+, on 2 . . . Ke7–3 Bc5+, while if 2 . . . b5, then 3 Q×e4, with the threats of Q×a8, Qc6+ and Q×e6+.
416. Balashov–Stean, Teesside, 1974.
 1 . . . N×e3!! White resigns. On 2 f×e3 comes 2 . . . B×e3+ 3 K×e3 Q×c3+, while if 3 Kc2, then 3 . . . B×d4 4 Bb2 B×c3 5 B×c3 d4, and wins.
417. Kofman–Filatov, Kiev, 1962.
 1 N×c6!! b×c6 2 Q×e6+!! f×e6 3 Bg6 mate.
418. Fould–Lang, New Zealand, 1956.
 1 Q×d5+!! e×d5 2 Bb6+! a×b6 3 Re8 mate.

## Test 52 Positions 419–426

The first test of our concluding theme 'Destructive combinations', i.e. combinations whose aim is to destroy the opposing king's pawn cover. The solving time allowed is 40 minutes.

419 W

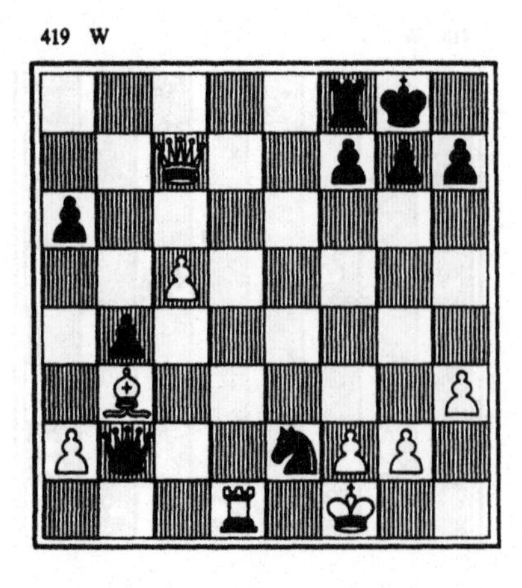

420 W

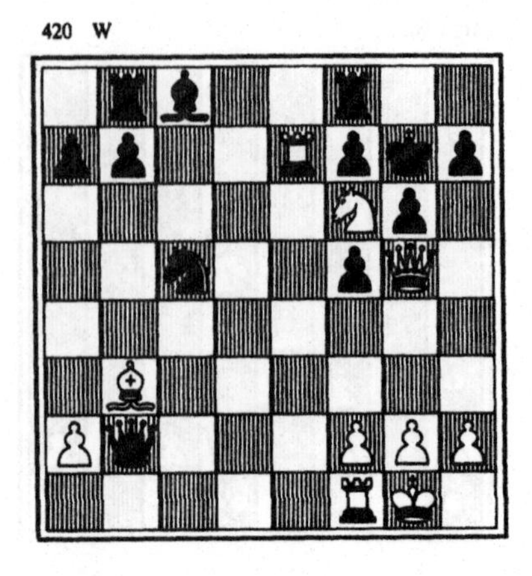

421 W

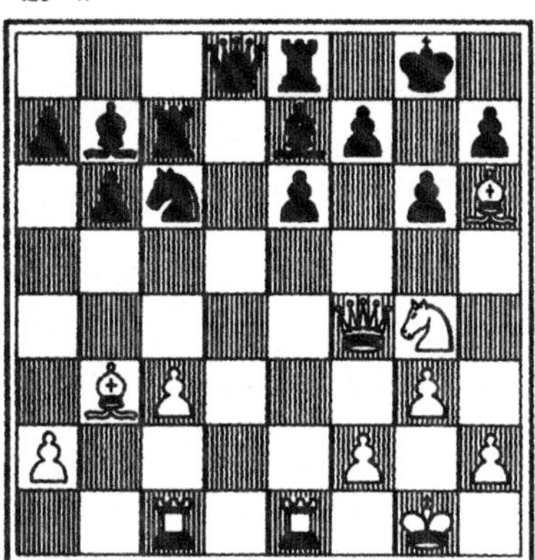

422 W

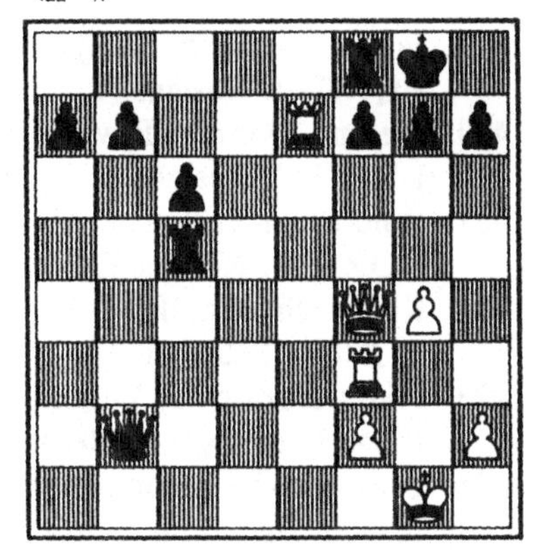

423 W

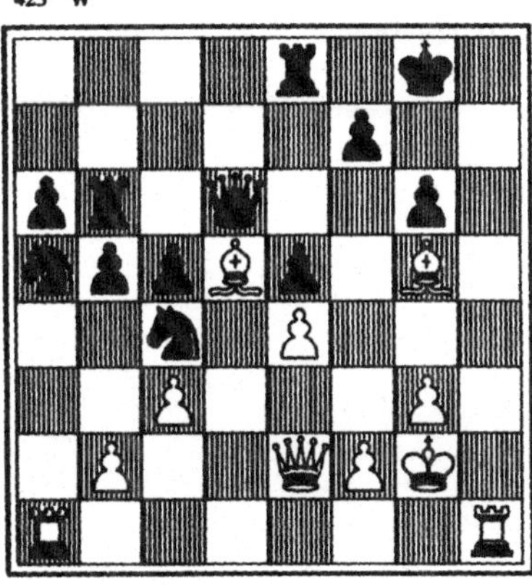

424 W

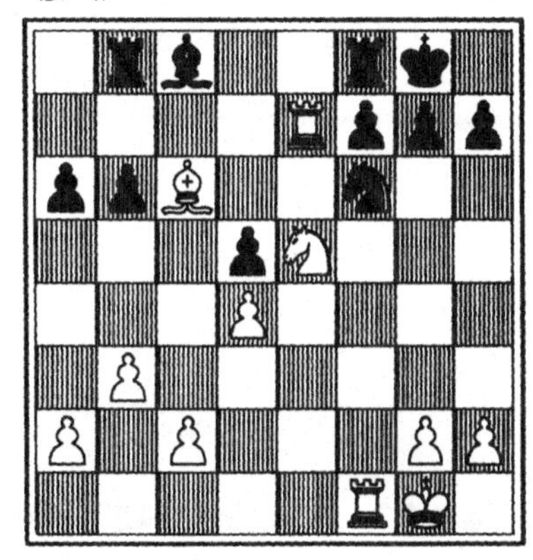

425 W

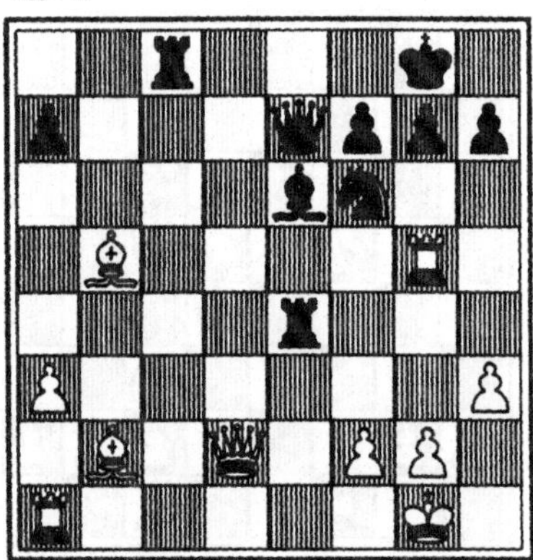

426 W

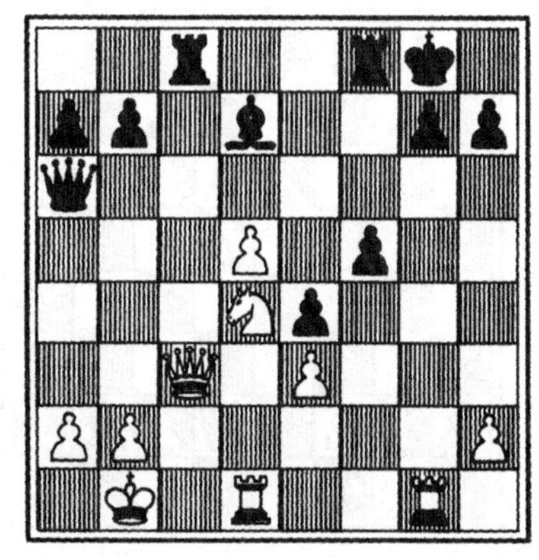

## *Solutions to Test 52*

419. Janosevic–Honfi, Sarajevo, 1966.
 1 Q×f7+!! Resigns (*1 . . . R×f7 2 Rd8* mate).
420. Medina–Donner, Beverwijk, 1965.
 1 R×f7+!! Resigns (*1 . . . R×f7 2 Nh5+ Kg8 3 Qd8* mate).
421. Bolbochan–Pachman, Moscow, 1956.
 1 Q×f7+!! Resigns (*1 . . . K×f7 2 B×e6* mate).
422. Kirby–Oliveira, Tel Aviv, 1964.
 1 Q×f7+!! Resigns (*1 . . . R×f7 2 Re8+*).
423. Ivkov–Durasevic, Yugoslavia, 1956.
 1 B×f7+!! K×f7 2 Rh7+ Kg8 3 Rah1! Resigns.
424. Bronstein–Lehmann, Munich, 1958.
 1 N×f7! Bg4 (on *1 . . . R×f7* White had prepared *2 B×d5! N×d5 3 Rg8+!*) 2 R×f6!! Resigns. If 2 . . . g×f6, then 3 Nh6+, while 3 B×d5 also wins.
425. Boleslavsky–Goldenov, Leningrad, 1947.
 1 R×g7+! Resigns (since if *1 . . . K×g7 2 Qg5+ Kf8 3 B×f6*, or *1 . . . Kf8 2 Qg5*, or *1 . . . Kh8 2 Qh6*).
426. Padevsky–Tsankov, Sofia, 1955.
 1 R×g7+!! Kh8 (or *1 . . . K×g7 2 Ne6++*) 2 Nc6!! Resigns.

## Test 53 Positions 427–434

Continuation of the theme 'Destructive combinations'. In comparison with the previous test, the examples are more difficult. Solving time—50 minutes.

427 W

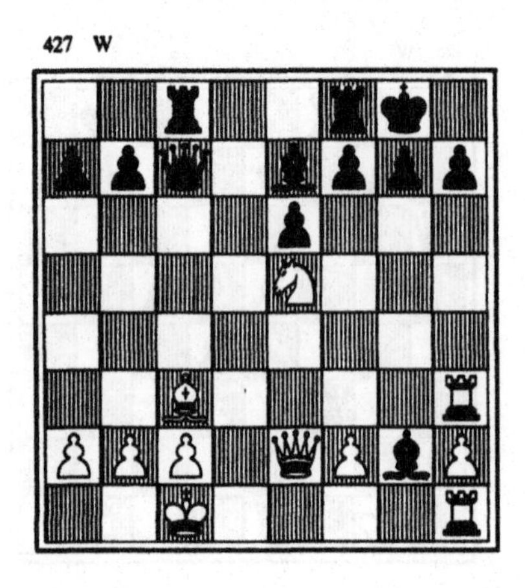

428 B

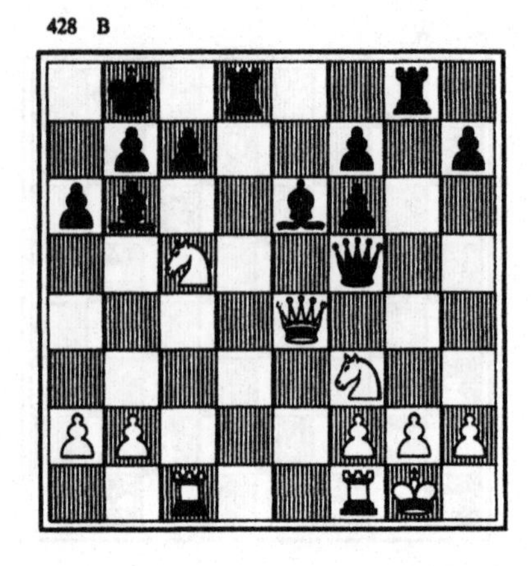

429 W

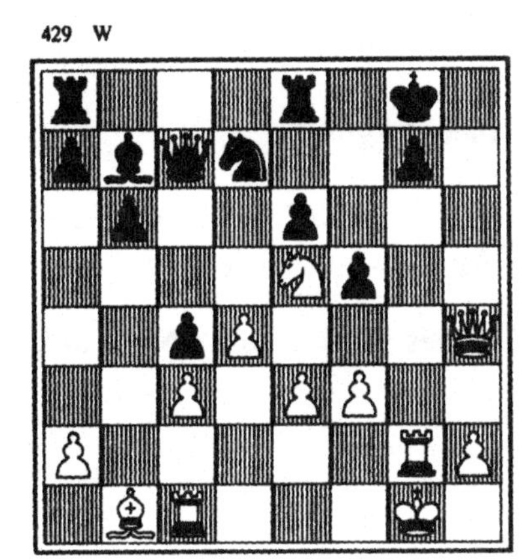

430 W

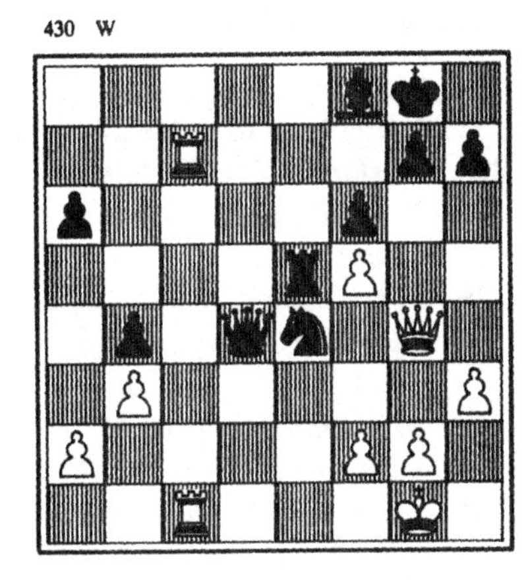

431 W

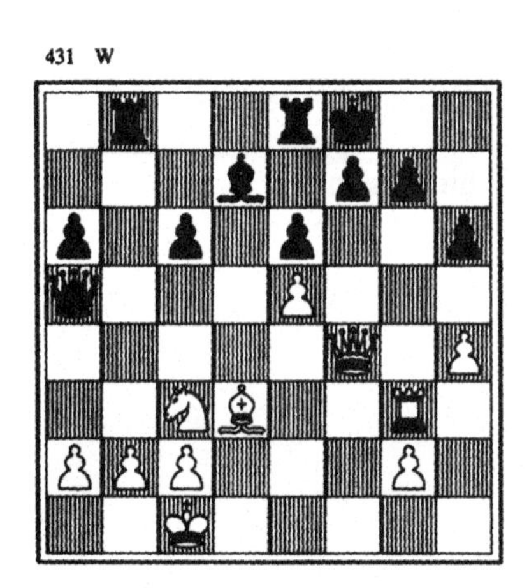

432 B

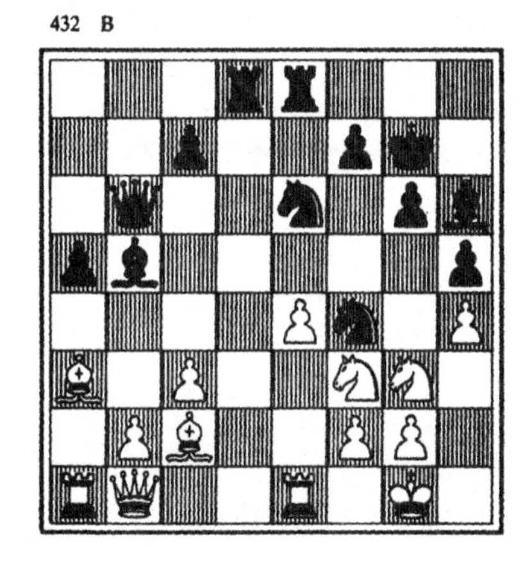

433 W

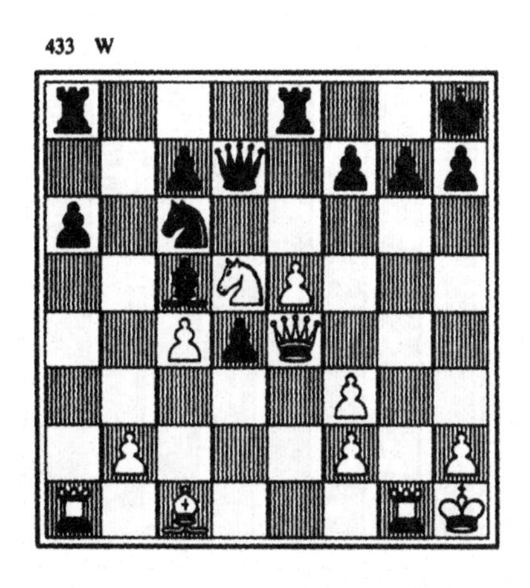

434 B

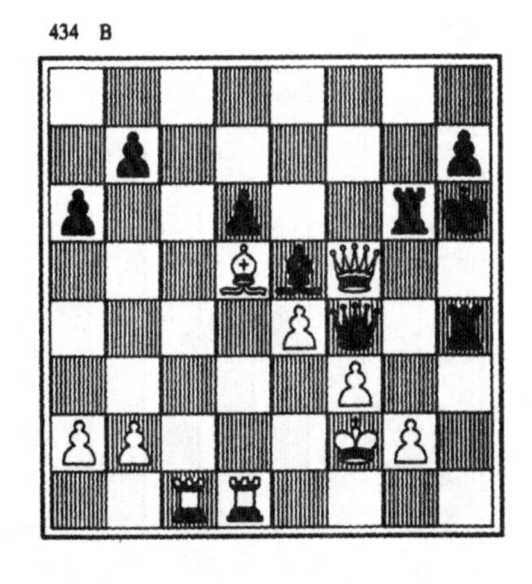

### Solutions to Test 53

427. Martsius–Darga, Munich, 1958.
1 Rg3!! B×h1 2 R×g7+!! Resigns (if *2 . . . Kh8*, then *3 Rg8+!*).
428. Koskinen–Skold, Helsinki, 1957.
1 . . . R×g2+!! 2 Kh1 (or *2 K×g2 Qh3+ 3 Kg1 Bd5!*) 2 . . . R×h2+!! 3 K×h2 (or *3 N×h2 Bd5*) 3 . . . Qh3+ White resigns (since if *4 Kg1*, then *4 . . . Rg8+*).
429. Foguelman–Oliveira, Leipzig, 1960.
1 R×g7+!! K×g7 2 Qg3+! Resigns. On 2 . . . Kh7 comes 3 Qg6+ Kh8 4 Nf7 mate, while if 2 . . . Kf8 or 2 . . . Kh8, then 3 Ng6+.
430. Bronstein–Gligoric, Moscow, 1967.
1 R×g7+!! B×g7 2 Rc8+ Resigns.
431. Keres–Szabó, Moscow, 1955.
1 R×g7! K×g7 2 Qf6+ Kf8 3 Bg6! Resigns.
432. Boleslavsky–Nezhmetdinov, Vilnius, 1958.
1 . . . N×g2!! 2 K×g2 Nf4+ 3 Kh1 (on *3 Kg1* Black wins by *3 . . . Nh3+ 4 Kg2 Q×f2+! 5 K×h3 Bc8+ 6 Nf5 B×f5+ 7 e×f5 Q×f3+ 8 Kh2 Rd2!!*) 3 . . . Q×f2 White resigns.
433. Rang–Winkel, Sweden, 1955.
1 R×g7!! K×g7 2 Bh6+! Kh8 (or *2 . . . K×h6 3 Nf6!*) 3 Nf6! Resigns.
434. Hajtun–Fabian, Budapest, 1953.
1 . . . Bd4+!! 2 R×d4 R×g2+!! 3 K×g2 Rh2+ White resigns.

### Test 54 Positions 435–442

Continuation of the theme 'Destructive combinations'. Here again, in comparison with the previous test, the examples are somewhat more difficult. Time for solution 50 minutes.

435 B

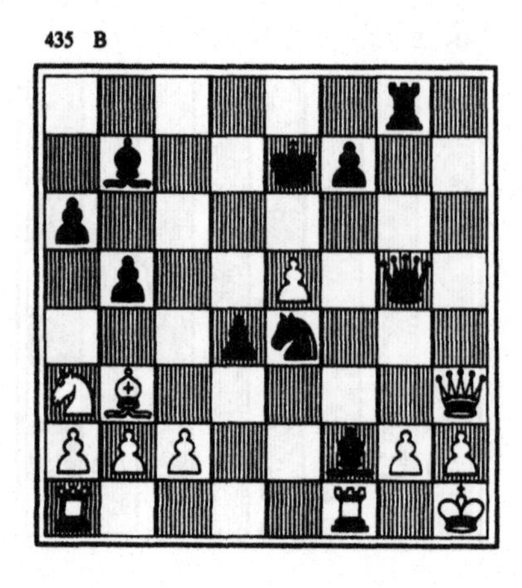

436 B

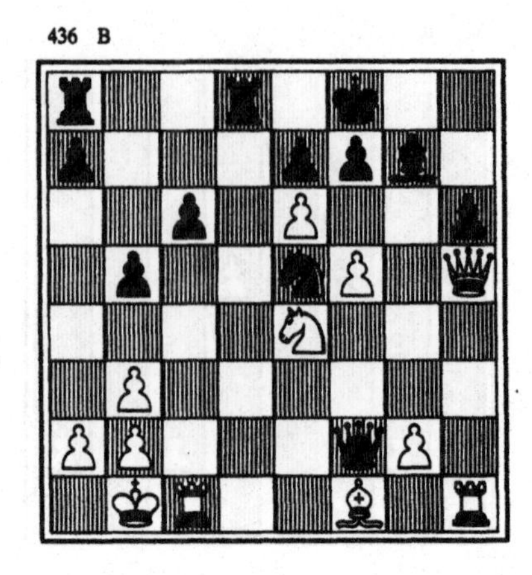

437 B

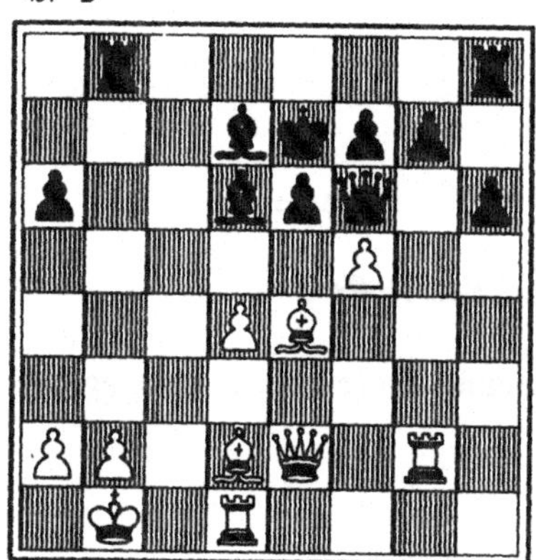

438 B

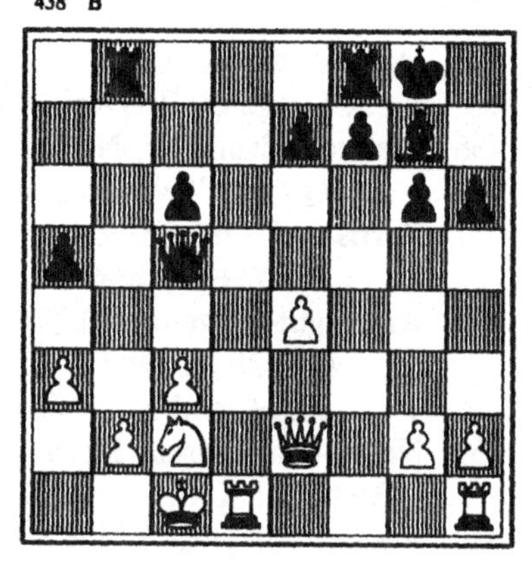

439 W

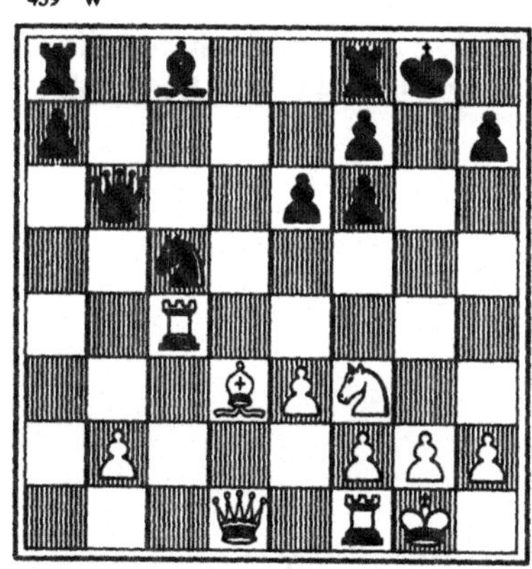

440 W

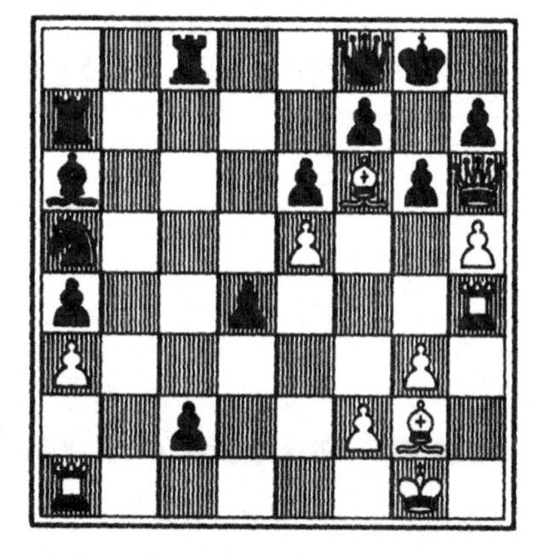

441 W

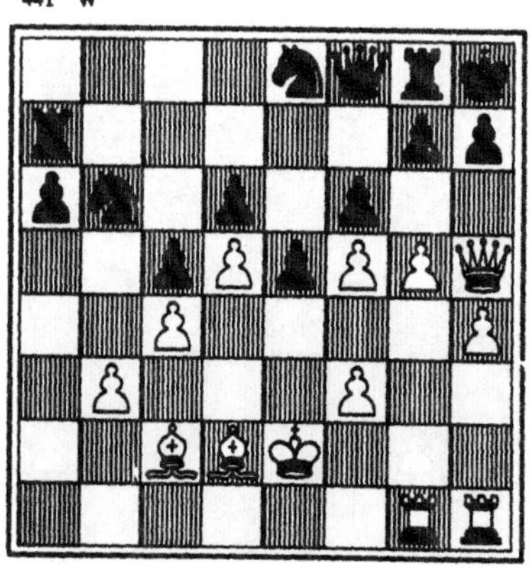

442 W

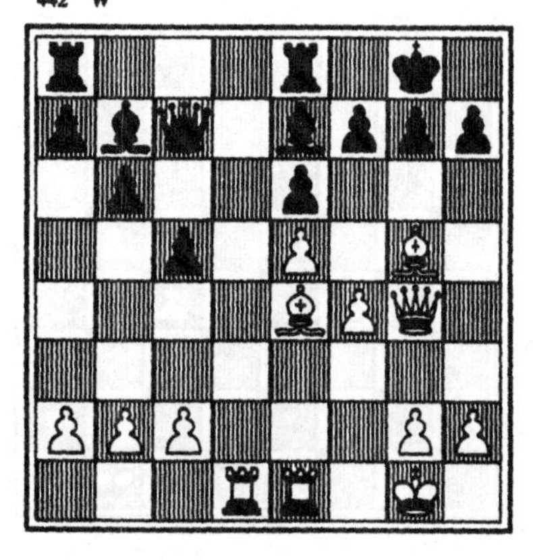

### *Solutions to Test 54*

435. Honan–Mardle, Corr., 1959.
1 . . . Q×g2+!! 2 Q×g2 Ng3+ 3 h×g3 Rh8 mate.
436. Elsukov–Ermakov, Novosibirsk, 1969.
1 . . . Q×b2+!! White resigns (*2 K×b2 Nc4++ 3 Kc2 Na3* mate).
437. Portisch–Flórián, Budapest, 1955.
1 . . . R×b2+!! 2 K×b2 Q×d4+, White resigns (*3 Bc3 Rb8+*).
438. Kapengut–Vaganian, 1970.
1 . . . R×b2!! 2 K×b2 Q×c3+ 3 Kc1 Rb8 White resigns. There is no defence against 4 . . . Rb1+ and 5 . . . Qb2 mate.
439. Negra–Kreculescu, Bucharest, 1957.
1 B×h7+!! K×h7 2 Ne5!! Resigns.
440. Fischer–Miagmarsuren, Sousse, 1967.
1 Q×h7+!! K×h7 2 h×g6++ Resigns (*2 . . . K×g6 3 Be4* mate, or *2 . . . Kg8 3 Rh8* mate).
441. Borisenko–Hakhimovskaya, Riga, 1968.
1 Q×h7+!! K×h7 2 g6+ Kh8 3 Rg5!! Resigns.
442. Batuyev–Abdusamatov, Leningrad, 1951.
1 B×h7+ K×h7 (or *1 . . . Kf8 2 Bh6!!*) 2 Bf6!! B×f6 (on *2 . . . g×f6* there follows *3 Rd3 Bf8 4 Rh3+ Bh6 5 Qh4!*) 3 e×f6 Resigns. If 3 . . . g6, then 4 Qh4+ Kg8 5 Qh6.

## Test 55 Positions 443–450

Continuation of the theme 'Destructive combinations', showing different types of these combinations. In difficulty the test is similar to the previous one. Time for solution 50 minutes.

443 W

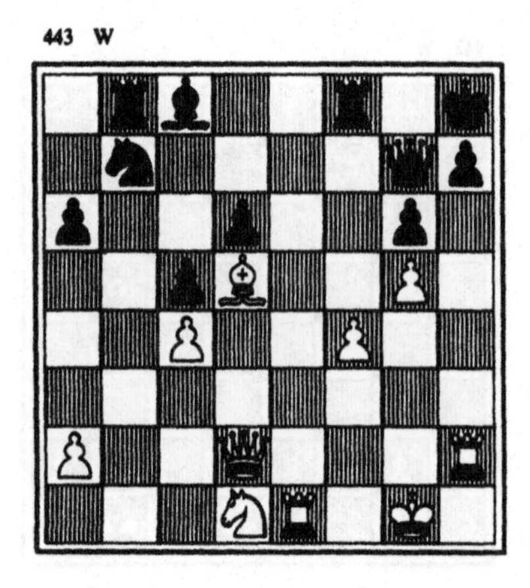

444 B

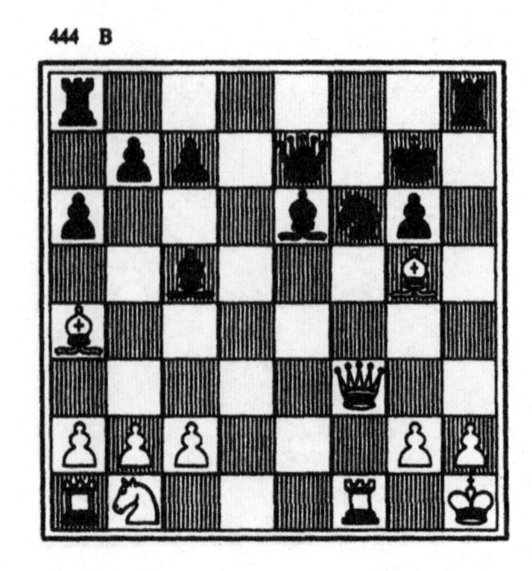

445 W

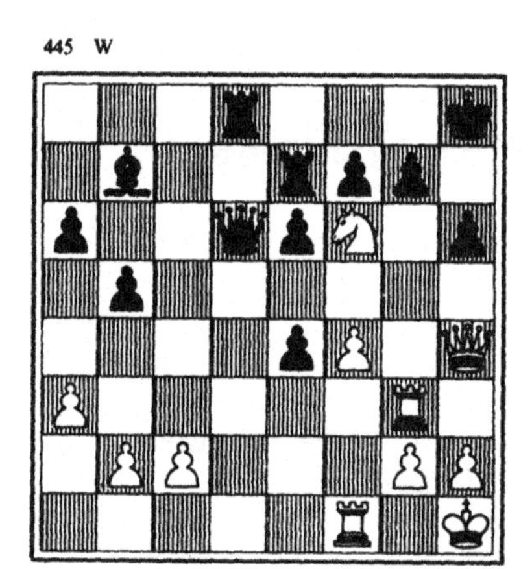

446 B

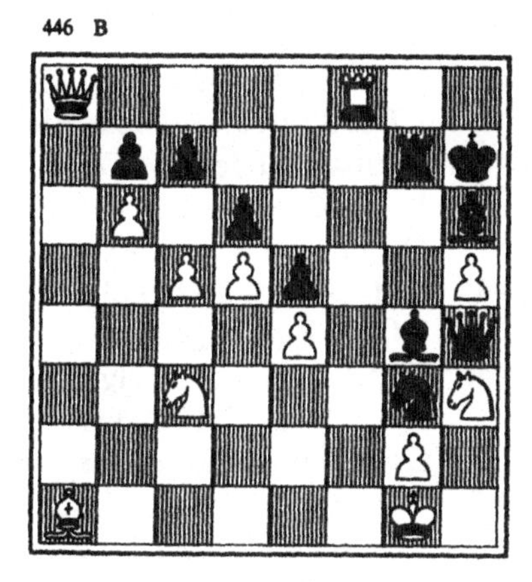

447 W

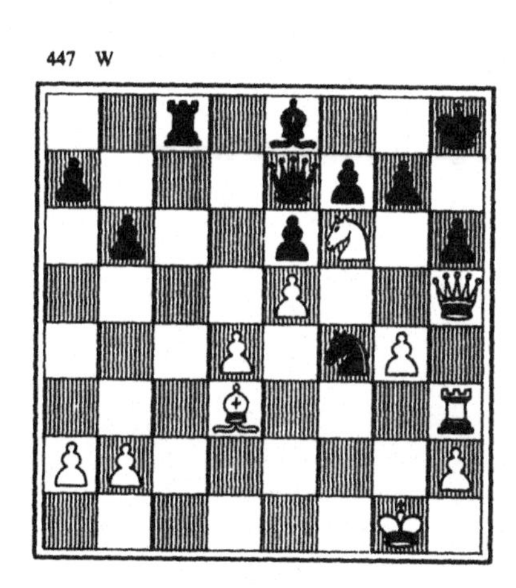

448 W

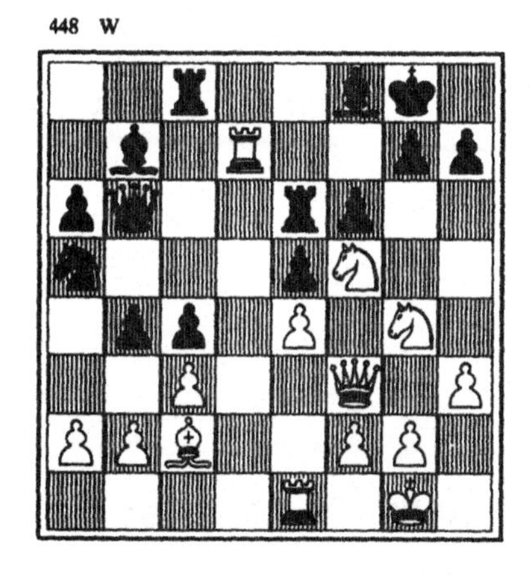

449 B

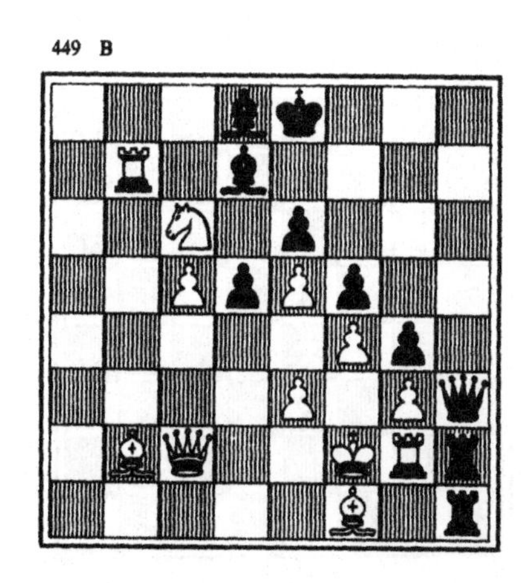

450 B

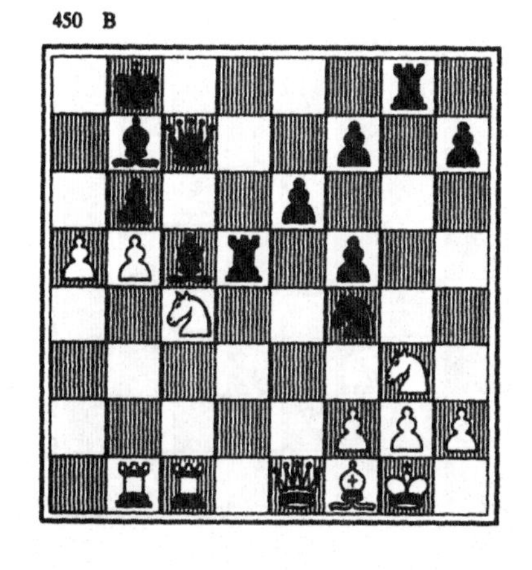

### Solutions to Test 55

443. Doza–Titkos, Hungary, 1961.
1 Re7!! Q×e7 2 Qb2+ Rf6 (or *2 . . . Qg7 3 R×h7+!!*) 3 g×f6 Resigns.
444. Uikman–Andersen, Corr., 1957–8.
1 . . . R×h2+!! 2 K×h2 Rh8+ 3 Kg3 Ne4+ White resigns. If 4 Q×e4, then 4 . . . Q×g5+, or 4 Kf4 Q×g5+ 5 K×e4 Bd5+.
445. Hult–Kolett, Stockholm, 1946.
1 Qg5! Rg8 2 Q×h6+! g×h6 4 R×g8 mate.
446. Radev–Lyangov, Bulgaria, 1967.
1 . . . Be3+ 2 Kh2 Nf1+ 3 Kh1 (if *3 R×f1*, then *3 . . . B×h3*, and wins) 3 . . . Q×h3+!! White resigns (*4 g×h3 Bf3+! 5 R×f3 Rg1* mate).
447. Vinogradov–Fedin, Moscow, 1973.
1 Q×h6+!! g×h6 2 R×h6+ Kg7 3 Rh7+ Kf8 4 Rh8+ Kg7 5 Rg8+ Kh6 6 g5 mate.
448. Muller–Pichler, Dresden, 1972.
1 Ngh6+!! g×h6 (if *1 . . . Kh8*, then *2 Nf7+ Kg8 3 N5h6+ g×h6 4 Qg4+*) 2 Qg4+ Kh8 3 Rg7!! Resigns.
449. Kreculescu–Padevsky, Bucharest, 1950.
1 . . . Q×g3+!! White resigns (*2 K×g3 Bh4* mate).
450. Pitz–Holtz, Copenhagen, 1960.
1 . . . Bh3+! 2 g×h3 R×g3+!! 3 h×g3 Q×g3+ 4 Bg2 Rd1!! White resigns.

### Test 56 Positions 451–458

Conclusion of the theme 'Destructive combinations', Difficulty is no greater than in the two previous tests. Solving time 45 minutes.

451 W

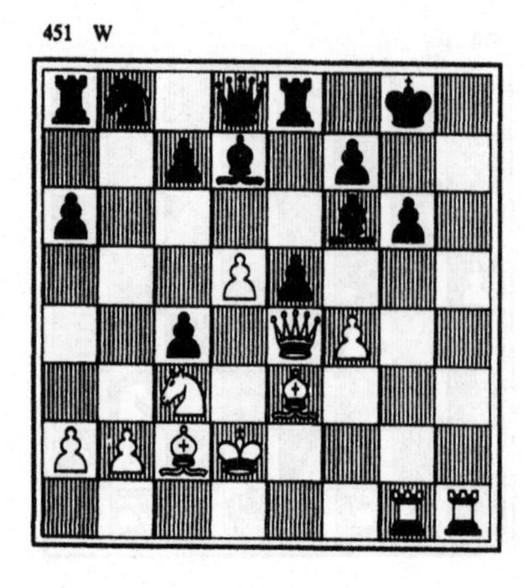

452 W

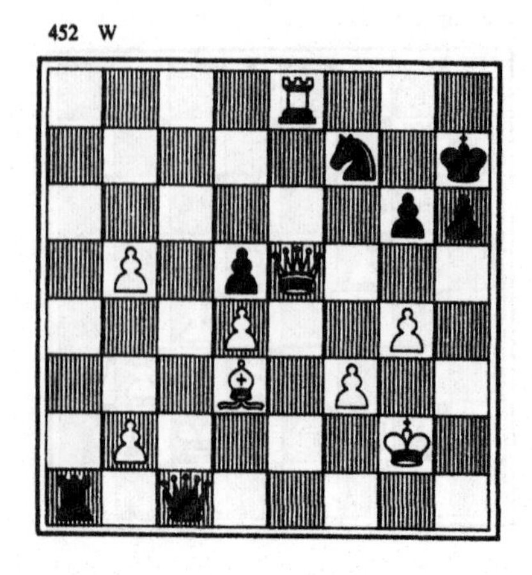

453 W

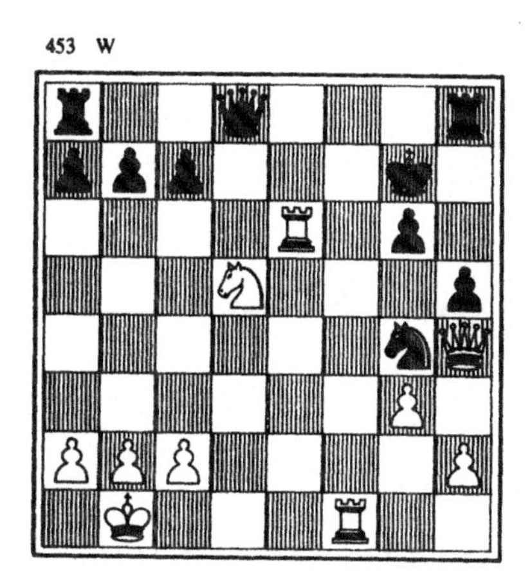

454 W

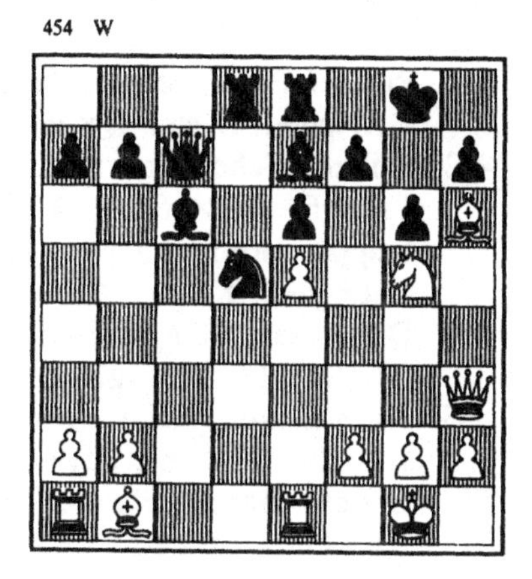

455 W

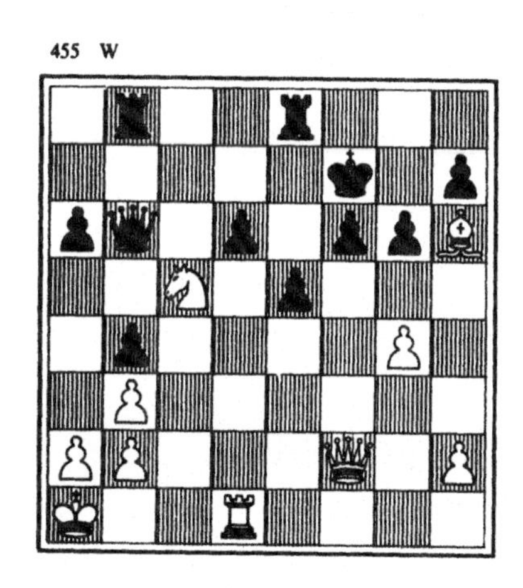

456 W

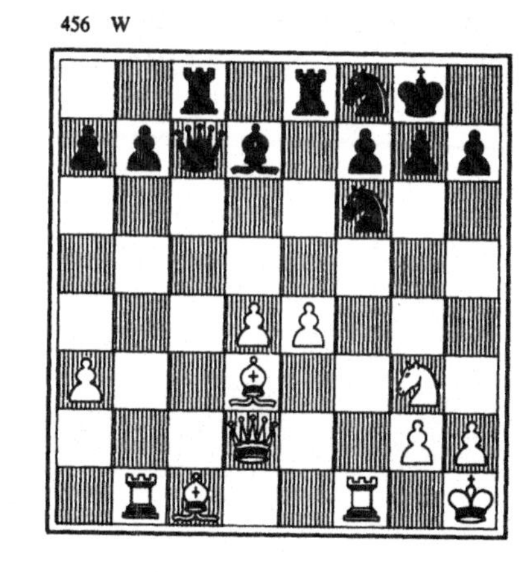

457 B

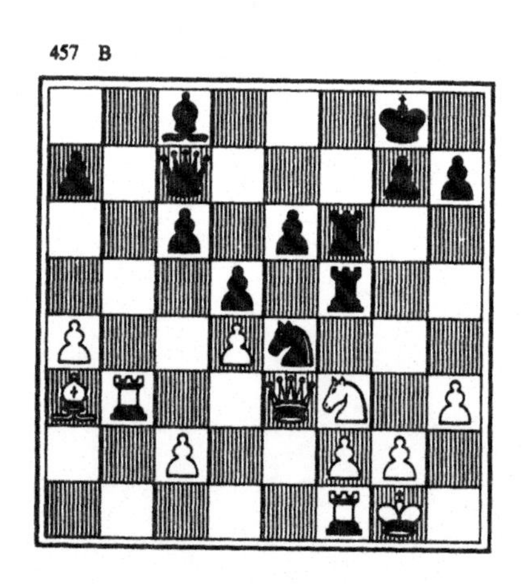

458 B

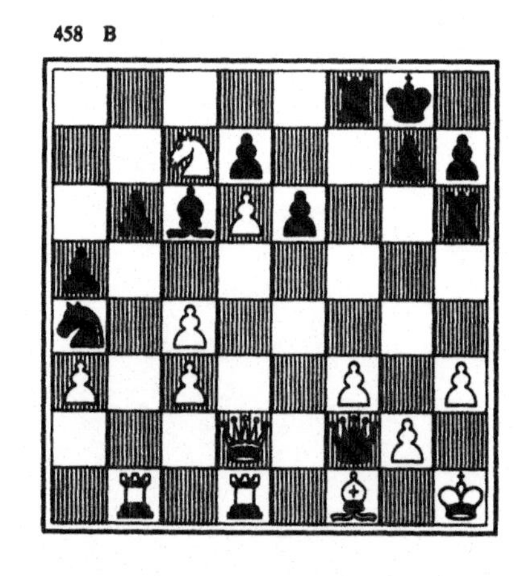

***Solutions to Test 56***

451. Pfeiffer–Blau, Geneva, 1952.
 1 R×g6+!! f×g6 2 Q×g6+ Bg7 3 Rh8+! Resigns.
452. Kolarov–Schonberg, Moscow, 1956.
 1 B×g6+!! K×g6 2 Rg8+ Resigns.
453. Kupper–Norca, Lugano, 1962.
 1 R×g6+!! K×g6 2 Ne7+ Resigns (*2 . . . Kh6 3 Rf6+*, or *2 . . . Kg7 3 Qg5+*).
454. Dely–Glass, Reggio-Emilia, 1960–1.
 1 B×g6!! h×g6 2 Bg7! Resigns.
455. Platz–Lampe, Halle, 1957.
 1 Q×f6+!! K×f6 2 Rf1+ Ke7 3 Bg5 mate.
456. O'Kelly–Barzin, Blankenburg, 1959.
 1 R×f6!! g×f6 2 Nh5 Qc3 3 Qe3 Resigns. There is no defence against 4 Bd2 and 5 Qh6.
457. Kostakiev–Dimitrov, Sofia, 1958.
 1 . . . R×f3!! 2 g×f3 Rg6+ 3 Kh1 Ng3+! White resigns (*4 Kg2 Nf5+*, or *4 f×g3 Q×g3*).
458. Kluger–Szilágyi, Budapest, 1965.
 1 . . . R×f3!! 2 Q×f2 Rf×h3+! 3 Kg1 Rh1 mate.

# Progress Chart

| Test No. | Basic Score (max 40) | Time taken (mins.) | Net Score | Comments |
|---|---|---|---|---|
| 1 | | (45) | | |
| 2 | | (50) | | |
| 3 | | (40) | | |
| 4 | | (50) | | |
| 5 | | (40) | | |
| 6 | | (50) | | |
| 7 | | (40) | | |
| 8 | | (45) | | |
| 9 | | (40) | | |
| 10 | | (50) | | |
| 11 | | (40) | | |
| 12 | | (40) | | |
| 13 | | (35) | | |
| 14 | | (30) | | |
| 15 | | (35) | | |
| 16 | | (35) | | |
| 17 | | (40) | | |
| 18 | | (45) | | |
| 19 | | (40) | | |
| 20 | | (45) | | |
| 21 | | (60) | | |
| 22 | | (45) | | |
| 23 | | (50) | | |
| 24 | | (50) | | |
| 25 | | (45) | | |
| 26 | | (50) | | |
| 27 | | (50) | | |
| | | | | |

| Test No. | Basic Score (max 40) | Time taken (mins.) | Net Score | Comments |
|---|---|---|---|---|
| 28 | | (60) | | |
| 29 | | (40) | | |
| 30 | | (40) | | |
| 31 | | (55) | | |
| 32 | | (45) | | |
| 33 | | (50) | | |
| 34 | | (50) | | |
| 35 | | (45) | | |
| 36 | | (35) | | |
| 37 | | (40) | | |
| 38 | | (50) | | |
| 39 | | (60) | | |
| 40 | | (35) | | |
| 41 | | (45) | | |
| 42 | | (45) | | |
| 43 | | (40) | | |
| 44 | | (40) | | |
| 45 | | (40) | | |
| 46 | | (55) | | |
| 47 | | (50) | | |
| 48 | | (40) | | |
| 49 | | (40) | | |
| 50 | | (40) | | |
| 51 | | (45) | | |
| 52 | | (40) | | |
| 53 | | (50) | | |
| 54 | | (50) | | |
| 55 | | (50) | | |
| 56 | | (45) | | |

# Index of Players